NETAJI IN EUROPE

NETAJI IN EUROPE

Jan Kuhlmann

Translated from the German by Christel Das

RAINLIGHT
RUPA

Published in RAINLIGHT by
Rupa Publications India Pvt. Ltd. 2012
7/16, Ansari Road, Daryaganj
New Delhi 110002

Sales Centres:

Allahabad Bengaluru Chennai
Hyderabad Jaipur Kathmandu
Kolkata Mumbai

ISBN: 978-81-291-2084-7

10 9 8 7 6 5 4 3 2 1

The moral right of the author has been asserted.

Typeset in Aldine401 10.5/13

Printed and bound in India by Repro Knowledgecast Limited, Thane

Contents

Introduction

cℱᴐ

M y enemy's enemy is my friend. This fundamental
conception is repeatedly seen as responsible for the
formation of those alliances in times of war that could
hardly endure under other circumstances. Partners who have nothing
else in common, who perhaps not even have feelings of sympathy
for each other, come to a temporary agreement of mutual benefit in
order to combine forces in the fight against a common enemy. The
collaboration of the Indian national leader Subhas Chandra Bose with
the governments of Germany and Italy during the Second World War
had this character. Bose came to Europe in 1941 to continue from
there his fight for his country's independence from British rule; the
German and Italian governments granted him support because they
expected some benefit from this for their war against Great Britain.

Alliances between powers at war and revolutionary movements
are not uncommon. The best-known example is the one of the
Russian revolutionary Vladimir Ilich Lenin who could leave his Swiss
exile and travel to Russia in order to lead the October revolution to
victory there. The end of the war in the East and the peace treaty
of Brest-Litovsk were the benefits the German Reich gained from
this collaboration. The German government also collaborated with
the Indian national movement during the First World War. They
supported and financed an Indian exile government under Raja
Mahendra Pratap, which wanted to invade India via Afghanistan under
the protection of a German military expedition. Anti-British groups of
Indian expatriates in America were supported with deliveries of arms,
and Indian revolutionaries in exile in Berlin were allowed to engage in
propaganda for the freedom struggle of their people.

The German leadership also cultivated such contacts during the
Second World War. They tried to establish connections in particular

with the Arab world and non-Russian peoples of the Soviet Union. While they cultivated intensive contact with several political leaders of the Arab countries, collaboration with the peoples of Eastern Europe and the Middle East was limited to the formation of volunteer troops that fought against the Red Army with the German armed forces. The Italian government cultivated, especially, the collaboration with politicians in the Islamic regions.

The activities of Bose in Europe between 1941 and 1943 belong in this context. The following work endeavours to give an extensive survey of the India-politics of the Axis Powers, which the collaboration with Bose decidedly influenced. It reconstructs the occurrences that determined and constituted the India-politics of the Axis Powers, mainly based on archival sources and, where these are missing, on the memoirs of direct contemporaries. This should clarify the different motives and driving forces that guided Bose, Adolf Hitler, Benito Mussolini, and the various authorized government officials in the German Foreign Office and the Italian Foreign Ministry.

The term 'India-politics' in this book denotes the decided governmental performance regarding British India. 'Axis Powers' denotes the German Reich, the Kingdom of Italy until the ouster of Mussolini, and the Italian Republic after that. The term derivates from a speech which Mussolini held on 1 September 1936 at the Milan cathedral square. In this speech, he hailed the new alliance between Berlin and Rome as 'an axis for the rotation of all European states possessing the desire for collaboration and peace'[1]. British war propaganda also counted Japan as part of the 'Axis Powers'. English sources of history use this definition occasionally. However, as an axis can only have two ends, the term 'Tripartite Powers' is the only correct one in this case. The transference of the term 'Fascism' to all right-wing national and authoritarian movements creates similar problems. 'Fascism' and 'Fascist' are here only used for the movement which was founded by Mussolini in Italy and represented by the Partito Nazionale Fascista (PNF). For the movement founded by Hitler and represented by the Nationalsozialistische Deutsche Arbeiterpartei, (NSDAP), the terms 'National Socialism' and 'National Socialist' are exclusively used.

Government archives in Germany, Italy, India and Great Britain constitute the main source material consulted for this work. The files of the German Foreign Office in the Political Archive of the German Foreign Office in Bonn and the Federal Archive in Berlin are of particular interest. The India files from the German Secretary of State's office and the files of the Sonderreferat Indien are of special importance here. The Military Archive in Freiburg provides source material regarding the India-activities of the armed forces. Admittedly, only few documents are preserved from the managing practices of the Indian Legion, but the military history section has three portfolios in its collection with records compiled for the archive by veterans of the legion. The Italian Central State Archive keeps informative files of the Italian Ministry for Popular Culture. The Historical Bureau of the General Staff of the Italian Army stores documents of the military's India-activities in its archive. The completely preserved war diary of the Centro Militare India is a significant, though hitherto less noticed, source. The files of the Indian government are available in the National Archives of India in New Delhi. Of these, the police reports of the provincial governments, which inform on the effects of India-propaganda, are important, as are also the Bose and INA documents. Interviews with contemporaries can be looked into at the Nehru Memorial Museum and Library. The British Library in London keeps the files of the India Office, among them reports by the secret service about the India-activities of the Axis Powers. Some papers regarding the Indian Legion and the Wehrmacht's activities in Afghanistan are among the documents of the War Office placed in the London Record Office. One file with a translated excerpt from the legion's war diary had so far been under lock and key and is here scientifically evaluated for the first time.

The utilized files, which were published in the Akten zur deutschen auswärtigen Politik (ADAP), the 'records for German foreign policy', and the Documenti Diplomatici Italiani (DDI), are quoted correspondingly. Joseph Goebbels's diaries are a particularly valuable source. The collection of source material published by Reimund Schnabel in 1968 under the title *Tiger und Schakal* (Tiger and Jackal) is hardly suitable for scientific studies. The volume contains documents from the former Central State Archives of the GDR in facsimile depiction. Besides the fact that the more important sources from the Bonn Archives are missing, the editor has not done any editorial work. Bose's collected works (*Netaji Collected Works*); the edited notes, speeches, writings and instructions by Hitler; and the *Opera Omnia* by Mussolini are valuable for the description of the pre-war period. Tilak R. Sareen published in 1996 a compilation of documents under the title *Subhas Chandra Bose and Nazi Germany* in order to make source material from European archives available to Indian students. The edition serves the purpose well, as it contains not only British but also German and Italian source material. However, the serious student will still have to visit the archives, as the texts are in English translation without the original versions.

The memoirs published by contemporaries after the war occupy an intermediate position between source material and scientific literature. The earliest contribution of this type was *This Europe* by Girija K. Mookerjee, one of Bose's assistants in Germany. It was pulished in German as *Labyrinth Europa*. Nehari G. Ganpuley, another of Bose's assistants in Germany, published a report in Bombay as early as 1959. Ganpuley takes not only his own memories as basis for the report, but also the notes which German officers of the Indian Legion had compiled and which are now kept in the Freiburg military archives. Alexander Werth, at that time deputy director of the Sonderreferat Indian, published a biography of Bose in 1971, *Der Tiger Indiens* (The tiger of India). Lothar Frank, who had met Bose during his first European journey before the war, and some others co-authored the book. Insofar as one can ascertain, Werth's report is in agreement with the statements of the available files and therefore assumed reliable. However, one cannot ignore the author's tendency to absolve Bose from the suspicion of having sympathized with the National Socialists. Werth has also written a report about the India-activities of Adam von Trott zu Solz that is included in the biography published by his widow, the *Lebensbeschreibung*.

The memoirs, which Eugen Rose published in 1979 about his time as interpreter in the Indian Legion, are not very useful. Evidently, the author writes about himself although he uses the name 'Cron', and thus obliterates the dividing line between factual account and fiction. Two valuable Indian contributions are the accounts by Mukund R. Vyas (*Passage Through a Turbulent Era*) and Gurbachan Singh Mangat (*The Tiger Strikes, The Indian National Army*). Vyas was Bose's private secretary during his stay in Germany, and Singh Mangat was one of the first volunteers of the Indian Legion. Both the works appeared only four decades after the occurrences, but all statements are on the whole reliable as the authors relate their own immediate experiences. Bose's escape from India and his stay in Kabul can be essentially reconstructed with Bhagat Ram Talwar's report published in 1976 in New Delhi, *The Talwars of Pathan Land and Subhas Chandra's Great Escape*. Mohammed Iqbal Schedai is supposed to have left behind in Pakistan memoirs in Urdu. Unfortunately, they were not available for this work. The short memories of his comrade-in-arms Sardar Ajit Singh, however, were available in an English language edition (*Buried Alive*). The only memories from the circle of the soldiers of the Centro Militare I are the ones by the Italian instructor Carlo Alberto Rizzi, which appeared in 1986 in Genoa under the title *I guanti bianchi di Warda Ganda* (The white gloves of Warda Ganda)[2].

Rudolf Hartog's monograph on the Indian Legion, *Im Zeichen des Tigers* (The Sign of the Tiger) should be classified as scientific representation and not under memoir literature even though the author was himself member of the troop as an interpreter. His excellent description is based on careful studies of sources, in particular the military historical collection about the legion in the military archives. Since there are hardly any new findings to be added to Hartog's history of the Indian Legion on the basis of the available sources, the treatment of the political aspects has been given priority in the present work over the representation of the legion's history.

So far, historical research has not paid much attention to German India-politics during the Second World War. An Oxford dissertation by Hugh Toye, which was later published in 1962 in an edited version as a biography of Bose (*The Springing Tiger*) has become outdated meanwhile. The same can be said for Gerhard Selter's Leipzig dissertation of 1965, entitled 'Zur Indienpolitik der faschistischen deutschen Regierung während des Zweiten Weltkrieges' (On the India-politics of the fascist German government during the Second World War), for which he could not look into all sources of the Berlin Political Archives. Arvinda Katpitia's dissertation, on the other hand, is an entire treatment of a partial aspect—Bose's negotiations regarding an India-proclamation (Mainz, 1972). Christopher Sykes in his biography of Trott published in 1969 looks at the role the Sonderreferat Indien played for the German opposition. In his standard treatise of 1978 about India in the Second World War,

Joachim Voigt pays special attention to Bose's activities in Germany. Diethelm Weidemann gives a detailed description of Bose's escape to Germany in his essay published in 1995 in the journal *Asien, Afrika, Lateinamerika*.

India in Axis Strategy by Milan Hauner (Stuttgart, 1981; an extended version of his Cambridge dissertation) is by far the most extensive study published on German India-politics up till now. Hauner processes a wealth of German and British files, but not, however, the documents in Italian and Indian archives. Besides India-politics Hauner treats instead, very extensively, the German Afghan-politics, resulting in a monumental size of the publication. The book does not offer the expected understanding of the actual subject, i.e. India's place within the Axis strategy. The author loses himself too often in details and lacks a cognitive structuring of the material. His main thesis, i.e. the Axis Powers had lost the war already in 1942 because they did not succeed in utilizing Asian national liberation movements, allows for an overestimation of the possibilities and leads to an unjust evaluation of German India-politics. Hauner's work cannot be considered a final treatment of the subject for the simple reason that essential sources from the archives in Rome and New Delhi are missing. He gives Italian India-politics a perfunctory treatment so that he does not do justice to the title of his study. A short study on Bose, which Hans-Bernd Zöllner undertook within the framework of a dissertation about German-Burmese relations, does not provide new source material either.

Renzo De Felice was the first historian to concern himself with Italian India-politics. The journal *Storia contemporanea* published in 1987 an essay on India in Mussolini's political strategy. This text appeared in 1988 under the title *Il fascismo e l'Oriente* (Fascism and the Orient) together with contributions by De Felice on Mussolini's Arab- and Zionist-politics. Over and above, this text forms the basis for the corresponding section in the sixth volume, published in 1990, of De Felice's biography of Mussolini comprising eight volumes. There he deals relatively extensively with India-politics. Before that, only Valdo Feretti had thrown light on a partial aspect of Italian India-politics with his study on the ISMEO, the Fascist institute for the Middle and Far East. Gianni Sofri published in 1988 a comprehensive and well-founded study on Gandhi's visit to Rome. Mario Prayer, an Italian

Indologist, has also worked on Italian-Indian relations. His essay on Gandhi and the Indian nationalism in Fascist political journalism appeared in 1988 in *Storia contemporeana*. His study on the reception of Fascism by Bengali intellectuals in the 1920s and 1930s is noteworthy. Marzia Casolari's Pisa dissertation on the connections between Fascism and Indian nationalism, submitted in 1997, has not been published but its manuscript was consulted for this work. Casolari argues in it, that Fascism had a significant influence on certain trends of Indian nationalism, in particular on the forerunners of present-day Hindu nationalism. To prove her point, she compiles, with impressive precision, quotations by Indian politicians and particulars of their biographies to show points of contact with Fascism in their thinking and actions. She succeeds in proving that contacts between Indians and Fascists indeed existed. However, her interpretation that these contacts were decisive for the political development of Indian nationalism, fails to convince.

The present work is the first historical study investigating the India-politics of the Axis Powers, based on all available sources from German, Italian, Indian and British archives. So far, researchers have failed to look at Italian sources together with the German and British ones. The fundamental differences between German and Italian India-politics were consequently overlooked; whereas the present work depicts a triangular relationship between Bose, Germany and Italy, where partly united and partly opposing forces were at work, striving for different objectives. It is the first historical study to show that Hitler and Mussolini, from the very beginning, had different viewpoints regarding India and Indian independence; that both dictators in the 1930s pursued completely different cultural and economic policies towards India; and that these differences also rendered nearly impossible the formation of a common India-politics during the Second World War.

Based on an essentially more solid source foundation as had been hitherto available for research, it was possible to produce now an almost complete documentation of Bose's activities in Europe. Whereas Hauner supports this subject only with German and British files, the present study also utilizes archives in Italy and India. Moreover, Hauner did not have at his disposal volumes 3 to 10 of Bose's collected works published in 1981, and other sources. The same is valid for some memoirs: those of Mangat, Vyas, Rizzi and Ajit Singh were only published in the 1980s. Since Hauner's publication, several scientific monographs have also made a deeper understanding of the subject possible, i.e. Leonard A. Gordon's *Brothers Against The Raj* of 1990, and the already mentioned works of Italian researchers. As the relevant sources and continuing literature had increased considerably in the past two decades, a revision of the subject therefore seemed greatly promising.

The book is divided into two sections. The first deals with the time up to Bose's arrival in Europe, with Bose's development and his relations to Germany and Italy in the 1930s. Hitler's and Mussolini's attitudes towards India and their India-politics up to 1941 are touched upon. It describes the position of India and the Indians in the ideologies of National Socialism and Fascism. This should throw light on the preconditions for the further development of India-politics and its historical background. It will become clear that Hitler and Mussolini were guided by principally different basic perceptions of India and the Indians. The second section deals with the five phases of India-politics that were determined by Bose's changing attitude to the Germans. The first phase consists of negotiations Bose had with the German Foreign Office and the Italian Foreign Ministry, which led to Bose's refusal to perform in the India-centric propaganda of the Axis Powers unless they declared their recognition of India's independence. India-centric propaganda slowly increased in the second phase, albeit hampered by Bose's incognito. India-politics reached its high point in phase three when Bose went public and involved himself actively in the propaganda. However, Bose realized that his work in Europe could have a limited effect only and therefore decided to continue his struggle in Southeast Asia. India-activities continued in the following fourth phase until Bose's departure. However, these were less vigorous. Phase five began after Bose's departure and saw the nearly total collapse of India-politics.

This book is a translation of the main part of a German PhD thesis, which was accepted by Humboldt University, Berlin, and published by Verlag Hans Schiler in 2003. Utilization of relevant Japanese archives would certainly have been desirable. Translations of source editions are unfortunately not available, so one has to visit the archives for studying the files. The expenditure this would have entailed for language studies and research in Japan would have been out of proportion for a dissertation. The same is the case with sources in Russian archives. It was translated into English by Christel Das, retired librarian of Max Mueller Bhavan in Calcutta.

Subhas Chandra Bose

❧

Subhas Chandra Bose was born on 23 January 1987 in Cuttack in the Indian province of Orissa. His family came from Bengal and belonged to the Kshatriya caste. Theirs was a typical middle-class household. His father Janaki Nath was a lawyer by profession. He sent his sons to an Anglo-Indian missionary school run by Baptists. Subhas continued his studies at Ravenshaw Collegiate School where he prepared himself for the Calcutta University admission test. He passed this test in May 1914 as second best with distinction. He became a student of Presidency College, which at that time had the reputation of being a cell for revolutionaries. The college was closed after political disturbances, and Bose could continue his studies in Scottish Church College only in July 1917. There he joined the military training course of the university after he had been rejected by the regular army because of weak eyesight. He passed his final examinations in 1919, again as one of the best.

His father sent him to England in order to prepare for the admission test for the Indian Civil Service. Only a few Indians were admitted into this administrative corps that helped the British rule the subcontinent effectively, and secure a comfortable lifestyle for its members. Bose matriculated from Fitzwilliam Hall that was affiliated to Cambridge University. After less than eight months, he sat for the Indian Civil Service examination and, to his own surprise, ranked fourth. However, to the great displeasure of his father, Bose preferred not to join the civil service. He deliberated for several months before taking this decision. Finally, he realized that he could not reconcile service for the British colonial power, in spite of all the privileges and power this entailed, with his political convictions. Instead, he became a follower of Chittaranjan R. Das who at that time was one of the most influential leaders of the Indian independence movement besides Mohandas Karamchand Gandhi, the 'Mahatma'.

C. R. Das was Calcutta's mayor. At the age of twenty-seven, Bose was appointed director of municipal government by C. R. Das but was soon taken into custody because of his revolutionary activities and deported to Burma. The news of C. R. Das's death reached him in Mandalay prison. After he had been released from prison on the grounds of ill health, Bose returned to Calcutta and became his successor. He soon gained political influence as president of the Bengal Provincial Committee of the Indian National Congress. Within the Congress party Bose belonged to the radical wing that advocated India's quick and complete independence from Great Britain while the moderate wing was prepared to accept a Dominion status. Even though he respected Gandhi very much as a political leader and comrade-in-arms, Bose clashed with him as he did not consider Gandhi's strategy of non-violence suitable means for gaining independence, Swaraj. He commented in his book *The Indian Struggle* on Gandhi's failure to gain Swaraj in one year:

> But Svaraj is still a distant dream. Instead of one, the people have waited for fourteen long years. And they will have to wait many more. With such a purity of character and with such an unprecedented following, why has the Mahatma failed to liberate India? ...He has failed, because the false unity of interests that are inherently opposed is not a source of strength but a source of weakness in political warfare. The future of India rests exclusively with those radical and militant forces that will be able to undergo the sacrifice and suffering necessary for winning freedom. ...Mahatma Gandhi has rendered and will continue to render phenomenal service to his country. But India's salvation will not be achieved under his leadership.[1]

The British arrested Bose many times because of his activities in the struggle for freedom. When he was in the Madras jail, his health had deteriorated so much due to the imprisonment and repeated ill-treatment, that the medical commission recommended to release him on medical grounds. The British government offered him a direct trip to Europe straight from prison at his own expense. Bose left India for Austria on 13 February 1933 for medical treatment.

A SYNTHESIS BETWEEN SOCIALISM AND FASCISM

Principally, Bose was more inclined to socialist ideas in his political thinking without, however, being dogmatic. In the beginning of his political career he envisaged a non-ideological synthesis of socialism and Fascism, as he elaborated in his inaugural address on 27 September 1930 as newly elected mayor of Calcutta. He thereby referred to the programme of his predecessor C. R. Das that he intended to continue: 'I would say that we have here in this policy and programme a synthesis of what modern Europe calls Socialism and Fascism. We have here the justice, the equality, the love, which is the basis of Socialism, and combined with that we have the efficiency and the discipline of Fascism as it stands in Europe.' In *The Indian Struggle* written in 1934, he opposed Gandhi's one-sided partisanship against Fascism:

> Unless we are at the end of the process of evolution or we deny evolution altogether, there is no reason to hold that our choice is restricted to two alternatives. Whether one believes in the Hegelian or in the Bergsonian or any other theory of evolution—in no case need we think that creation is at an end. Considering everything, one is inclined to hold that the next phase in world-history will produce a synthesis between Communism and Fascism. And will it be a surprise if that synthesis is produced in India?[2]

On closer acquaintance with Fascism and National Socialism he distanced himself from this basically positive evaluation. After his election as president for the Congress party in 1938, an Indian journalist requested him to elaborate upon his opinion of Fascism as expressed in his book in an interview. Bose replied that since then his political views had developed further:

> What I really meant was that we in India wanted our national freedom, and having won it, we wanted to move in the direction of Socialism. This is what I meant when I referred to 'a synthesis between Communism and Fascism'. Perhaps the expression I used was not a happy one. But I should like to point out that when I was writing the book, Fascism had not started on its imperialist expedition, and it appeared to me merely an aggressive form of nationalism.[3]

Fascist Italy had shown herself to be an imperialistic power with the invasion of Abyssinia. Bose did not like to be openly interested in Fascism. He now affected a socialistic profile. After the break-up with Gandhi, he and his followers left the Congress party and founded the Forward Bloc. Bose gave this new party a radical socialistic image:

> Forward Bloc will rally all progressive, radical and anti-imperialist elements in the Congress, whether they be Socialists or not. Through this consolidation, the people will equip themselves for the anti-imperialist struggle that will bring India her birthright of liberty. But the attainment of political Independence will not mean the dissolution of the Bloc. It will only mean a new phase in its life and activity. And that phase will undoubtedly be a Socialist one.[4]

The socialistic orientation was not at all incompatible with Bose's politics of seeking collaboration with Germany, Italy and Japan. The Indian political scientist Bankey Bihari Misra analysed: 'In the peculiar colonial situation of the country his leftist views did not go beyond being anti-British. From a socialist point of view it was surprising, though perfectly consistent with the tradition of the Indian revolutionary movement.'[5]

BOSE AND GERMANY IN THE THIRTIES

After Bose had gained renewed strength in Vienna he sought contact with people sympathetic to the Indian freedom struggle or who were in a position to support the same. At first he met politicians and businessmen in Austria, Czechoslovakia and Poland. Later on, he visited nearly all European countries. He studied the national movements of various peoples with particular interest. Particularly Ireland, where he befriended Eamon de Valera, appeared to him to be a model case for India as Ireland had already gained independence from British rule.[6] The developments in Turkey under the leadership of Kemal Atatürk were also of great interest to him, as the experiences gained there could be partly transferred to India. He compared the freedom movements of various countries and formed the conclusion that there was no insurmountable obstacle there. 'The force that has driven other nations to their freedom will also lead us irresistibly to the same goal. The only serious drawback that we have is that we have not yet the right leadership; but that will come before long.'[7]

Bose arrived in Berlin in July 1933. The Foreign Office had earlier requested the German-Indian Association to look after the visitor. Bose also met Alfred Rosenberg, the chief ideologist of the German Nazi movement. The racist did not come to an understanding with the Indian.[8] On the contrary, he managed to annoy Bose so much with his remarks that subsequently Bose wrote a very unfavourable article for a newspaper that caused anxiety to the German office as it found great attention among Indian nationalists.[9]

In July 1933, Bose was received by Ambassador Curt Prüfer, deputy head of Divison III of the German Foreign Office that was also responsible for the British Empire. Bose bemoaned the unfriendly attitude of German politics towards India. Prüfer assured him that though Germany was neutral in the fight between England and India, she nevertheless had great sympathy for the Indians. For the time being, Bose was satisfied with these appeasements and expressed the wish to meet Hitler and Goebbels personally. As per the protocol of the meeting, he states that 'it is of great importance to him to be able to say in private negotiations in India, that he had it from the mouths of responsible German politicians themselves that they are no enemies of India.' Prüfer explained a meeting with Hitler was not possible because of his heavy workload but he would try to arrange a talk with Goebbels.[10] It seems that Bose at that point was thinking already of a German-Indian pact of which he wanted to convince his Indian comrades-in-arm.

On 28 March 1934, Bose went to the Foreign Office to call on Hans-Heinrich Dieckhoff, head of the ministerial department III. He complained about anti-Indian articles in the German press and racist abuses of Indians in public. For a few months it happened that children shouted 'nigger' at Indians and even threw stones at them. This had never happened before. He then mentioned the draft bill of a penal law by the Reich's minister of justice, according to which any relationship between Germans and people belonging to a different race was forbidden. This would mean that Indians also were classified as a sub-race. It would be highly desirable that this bill not be passed. Dieckhoff pacified Bose, asking him not to give too much importance to each and every newspaper article and not to get so upset if children indulged in calling names in the streets. He, on his part, did not get upset either about each foolish publication in the Indian press or each faux pas by Indians against Germans.[11] As a follow-up, Bose submitted, a few days later, a memorandum demanding a stop to the anti-Indian propaganda in the press. The German government had to openly express a favourable opinion about India, and the proposed race bill as well as race education in schools and at universities had to be changed in such a way that Indians were not discriminated against.[12]

Franz Thierfelder, director of the German Academy in Munich, supported Bose's objections. Dieckhoff noted in handwriting under a letter by Thierfelder which stated Bose's objections: 'Much is correct but much is exaggerated.'[13] Bose remained unsatisfied. He later sent a letter to Thierfelder in which he wrote that the racial ideology of the National Socialist government in Germany had spoilt the atmosphere for Indians living in Germany and he hoped that those responsible would endeavour to improve the matter. He wrote: 'I do not demand that you give up your race theory, no matter how many scientific reasons we might offer against it. We only want it to be modified so that it, wittingly or unwittingly, does not provoke any bad opinions about Indians.'[14]

Bose founded the Indian-Central European Association in Vienna on 3 May 1934, together with businessman Otto Faltis. Karl Pesta, a minister retired from active service, was president. The association's aim was the development of various propaganda activities and the establishment of trade connections, but it never made any impact worth its name. The association stopped functioning but was not dissolved, solely out of consideration for Bose. After the annexation of Austria, Faltis approached the Foreign Office in vain with a request for financial support.[15] He even had new prospectuses printed in the middle of 1944 in order to get new members.[16]

In December 1934 Bose had to leave suddenly for India as his father was on his deathbed. But a few weeks later he was again in Europe. In May 1935 he complained in a letter to the Foreign Office about an article in the newspaper *Völkischer Beobachter*, in which Indians were called bastards. Bose guarded his people against this rebuke: 'The fact remains that if there is any country in the world where a systematic attempt has been made to preserve purity of blood not only within the race but also within the caste, that is India.' He mentioned some more examples of anti-Indian propaganda and finally observed: 'From the observations that I have made during the last two years I am driven to the conclusion that the greatest obstacle in the path of Indo-German understanding is being created by the exponents of the new Racial Science.'[17]

In January 1936 Bose had two long discussions with Dieckhoff and Prüfer. None of the talks yielded any result, except that Bose was disappointed in not being allowed to talk personally with the minister.[18] Dieckhoff, who had to listen to the same complaints about the anti-Indian German press and the government's racial prejudice reacted meanwhile with marked irritation as is reflected in the tenor of his reply. He had explained to Bose:

> German politics aimed at an understanding with England, but that did not mean that all problems were slavishly looked at from the English point of view. Of course there was no question of being misused by England against India. If Mr Bose could produce well-founded complaints with regard to remarks in the press or public excesses, etc. against Indians or India, he would certainly have them investigated. But he should not come to him with general, obviously prejudiced complaints.[19]

Bose returned once more to India in April 1936. He was soon arrested. After ten months, however, he was taken to Dalhousie, a hill resort in Punjab, for health reasons. He travelled again to Austria in order to continue his medical treatment. At the end of 1937 he again approached the Foreign Office with a letter, which was handed over to Werner Otto von Hentig by the Indian journalist Habibur Rahman. In the note Bose elaborated the conditions under which a collaboration with Germany might be feasible in his opinion. He demanded nothing less than that Hitler, Hermann Göring and Alfred Rosenberg should tender an apology for negative utterances about India. The race theory ought to be changed and henceforth be based upon the works of an Indian ethnologist. The racial equality of Indians with Germans should thereby be acknowledged by permitting mixed marriages and deleting all discriminatory references against Indians from the German race laws. Bose expected further that the German press publish only friendly articles about India now and that German firms allow practical training to Indian students. In return for these concessions he would permit German propaganda in the Indian press and appeal to Indians to buy German goods. Otherwise, however, he would consider Germany to be an enemy country.[20]

The foreign organization of the NSDAP took note of the letter. It was very astonished at the Indian who confronted the German Reich with such demands. The way Bose formulated his letter was considered to be brusque, all the more so as he was not counted among the influential men in India at that time. Nevertheless, a meeting took place with Hentig and a representative of the NSDAP Auslandsorganization (Foreign Organization).[21] It seems, Bose overestimated his influence when he thought he could induce the leading National Socialists to change their race policy. Hentig, who accepted the note in the Foreign Office, suggested that one should pacify the offended Indian in this matter. The only tangible result of Bose's initiative was that Hentig checked with IG Farben; they did indeed have Indian interns.[22] Bose's talks with Germany's political leaders were disappointing for him. He came face to face with arrogant racism and could not find the support he had hoped for in his fight against British colonial rule in India. Thus he wrote to Thierfelder:

> When I first visited Germany in 1933, I had hopes that the new German nation which had risen to a consciousness of its national strength and self-respect, would instinctively feel a deep sympathy for other nations struggling in the same direction. To-day I regret that I have to return to India with the conviction that the new nationalism of Germany is not only narrow and selfish but arrogant.[23]

However, one should not fail to recognize that during his stay in Europe Bose laid the foundation for his later activities in Germany. He was now known in the Foreign Office and the party, and had been able to make contacts. But first he wanted to go home.

The Congress party elected him as their president in January 1938. Bose returned immediately to Calcutta to take up office. During his term he tried to give the Congress a radical direction aimed at complete independence. He placed himself in opposition to Gandhi but was re-elected against Gandhi's wish. His conflict with the Mahatma, whose moral authority determined Indian politics at that time, led to his resignation in April 1939. His followers formed the

Forward Bloc and had to leave the Congress party along with him.

Despite the barely encouraging experiences with the National Socialists, he continued to come to good terms with the German Reich in India. On 22 December 1938 he invited Oswald Urchs, head of the Landesgruppe responsible for British-India and Ceylon in the foreign organization of the NSDAP, to his home. The meeting lasted several hours. Bose complained again about German racism and the bad press India had in Germany. Urchs tried to relativize these matters. Bose made it clear that he was disappointed about the abolition of all democratic, international and socialistic ideas in Germany and expressed his anxiety about German foreign policy, which was obviously aimed at a closer relationship with England. He finally demanded a friendlier attitude towards India from the German press, and that one of the leading personalities of the Third Reich, if possible the Führer himself, should express a fundamentally friendly opinion about Germany's relationship with India. Bose expressed the desire to meet leading personalities of the Third Reich during his next visit to Germany. He also wanted the status of Indians in Tanganyika of the former German East Africa to be clarified in case the colony should fall back to the Reich. In addition, he suggested, that the collaboration of leading Indians with important Germans should be made easier by arranging for a central office to which Indian politicians could be recommended in case of a visit to Germany.

If these points were clarified to his satisfaction, Bose finally said, the attitude of the Indian press towards Germany would also change. The result would be a better cultural and economic collaboration. Urchs gained the impression, Bose as real politician had concluded from political developments, that Germany was on her way to supremacy in Europe and was the only power that could dare to oppose England. He recommended careful cultivation of the contact to Bose. 'In my opinion we should make use of this opportunity, without any political commitments respectively [*sic*] without disturbing the England politics of the Reich. A friendlier attitude of the Congress though can be of great economic advantage for us in the face of industrial plans under the Congress banner; and we need those desperately.'[24]

As the report of this meeting distinctly shows, Bose had clearly recognized that with the Third Reich a power had risen that could create great difficulties for his opponent, England. As a realistically thinking politician he could not but again and again seek contact with his enemy's enemy. On the other hand, Bose's dislike of Nazi ideology can also be noticed. The form of government of the Third Reich did not correspond with his ideas, and the racial policy hurt his national pride. It must be noted that Bose did not discuss a possible escape to Europe with Urchs. It may be assumed that at that point of time he himself did not consider leaving India. In spite of all his criticism of the Reich's racial policy, Bose, however, did not hide his admiration for Hitler's political success. He carefully observed developments in Europe and the expansion of the Third Reich. After the German armed forces had entered Norway and Denmark, he wrote in a leader of his paper *Forward*: 'Germany may be a fascist or an imperialist, ruthless or cruel, but one cannot help admiring these qualities of hers—how she plans in advance, prepares accordingly, works according to a timetable and strikes with lightning speed. Could not these qualities be utilized for promoting a nobler cause?'[25]

BOSE AND ITALY IN THE THIRTIES

Bose's relationship with the German government was from the very beginning distant and difficult. The Italian Fascists, however, showed interest and cordiality towards him. When Bose reached Venice on 6 March 1933 in a steamship of Lloyd Triestino from India, the local governor had seen to it that the entry into the country, unloading of his luggage and the stay in the city were made as comfortable as possible for him.[26] He did not have to go through the customs and could drive straight to the hotel. The policemen on duty at a checkpoint saluted him. He wrote in a letter to a friend: 'Returning the salute, I began to wonder how strange it was that a man who had been harassed and persecuted by policemen in his own country should be saluted by policemen in a foreign land, where he is a stranger.'[27] The reason for this attentiveness was a recommendation by the Italian consul general in Calcutta, Gino Scarpa. He had read in the newspaper *Liberty* of 22 March 1933 an open letter by Bose to a group of students, written from the vessel *Gange*, praising the comfort of the vessel with the recommendation to travel with Lloyd Triestino rather than with the British shipping line P & O.[28]

In Berlin in August of 1933, Bose visited the Italian ambassador and thanked him for the pleasant reception in Venice. He told the ambassador that he wanted to go to Rome in order to study Fascism, in particular the system of the corporations.[29] In December 1933 Bose travelled again to Italy. He was in Nice when he received an official invitation to Rome to attend the oriental students' congress. Earlier, Bose had made contact in Vienna with Indian students studying there who also attended the congress. Most probably they were behind the invitation.'[30]

Bose took part in the solemn opening ceremony where Mussolini held a speech. 'The speech was a fine one—whatever we might think of the speaker,' he notes. In particular, he liked Mussolini's reference to ancient Rome: it had colonized Europe but the relations with Asia had always been friendly and had been based on collaboration. After the congress, Bose stayed for nearly two more weeks in Rome in order to gain friends for the Indian freedom struggle. He noticed that only a few Romans were interested in India and that the people in general did not know much about the country, but had no prejudices against it either. He termed the Italian government's attitude 'extremely favourable now': 'If such an official attitude had existed in places like Vienna or even Berlin—I am sure that we could have done much useful work there.'[31]

Achille Starace, general secretary of the National Fascist Party, had a similarly good impression of Bose whom he received on 28 December 1933. Bose had attracted the Foreign Ministry's positive attention because he had opposed efforts to turn the congress into a predominantly Muslim affair, and because of his support for the decision to establish the headquarters in Rome. On his wish, the Foreign Ministry arranged an audience for Bose with Mussolini. It had to be kept a secret, though, in consideration for British sentiments.[32]

At 5 p.m. on 6 January 1934, Bose met Mussolini for the first time.[33] Nothing is known about this meeting. It seems Bose abided by the agreement to keep the meeting confidential, as neither in his personal letters nor in his book *The Indian Struggle* does he mention details of his talks with the Duce. In the second supplemented edition he writes only that Mussolini had received him several times between 1933 and 1936.[34]

The newspaper *Giornale d'Italia* published a picture of Bose on the front page, introducing him as mayor of Calcutta and head of the nationalistic youth of India. Bose announced in an interview a new and active phase of the struggle for independence, without compromises. He dissociated himself from Gandhi's methods. He also did not cut down on praise for his host: 'We admire in particular in Fascism the young spirit: the creative enthusiasm.'[35] It seemed the British ambassador, Eric Drummond, felt alarmed by Bose's public appearance and sent a dossier to the secretary of state in the Italian Foreign Ministry, Fulvio Survich, in which he depicted Bose as a communist agitator.[36]

Survich was not particularly impressed when Mussolini granted Bose a second audience several months later when he called at the Foreign Ministry during a renewed visit to Rome.[37] The audience took place on 28 April 1934 at 5.30 p.m. in the Palazzo Venecia.[38] When Bose took a flight from Rome to Calcutta to be at his father's deathbed, he had intended to pay another visit to Mussolini but had to cancel it due to lack of time. He sent the Duce a handwritten letter from the Roman hotel where he was staying. It contained the following sentences:

> I shall never forget the kindness I have received at Your Excellency's hands—nor shall I ever forget the sympathy Your Excellency has shown for my unfortunate country. I carry home with me feelings of profound gratitude towards Your Excellency. I am sure Your Excellency will never forget that India expects much help and guidance from Your Excellency. It may be that Your Excellency is destined to play an important part in the liberation of my unfortunate country, as Your Excellency had already done in the case of Italy.[39]

In January 1935 Bose was once more in Rome and did not neglect to call again on Mussolini. The Duce received him for the third time on 25 January 1935 at 6.30 p.m.[40] Prior to the audience, the Foreign Ministry presented an interesting note to Mussolini. It shows the kind of impression the Italian diplomats had, in the meantime, formed of Bose. The note mentions Bose's 'indirect contribution' at the students' congress in 1933 where he had prevented the congress turning into a predominantly Muslim affair. Then followed an evaluation of his political point of view: Bose was a revolutionary spirit whose ideal would be achieved by a harmonizing of communism and Fascism. He had depicted his ideas in his book *The Indian Struggle*. From communism he borrowed anti-democratic, anti-liberal and anti-parliamentary tendencies, from Fascism the ideas for state-building and economic policies.[41] British and Indian newspapers had reported in September 1934 that one Narain Prasad Arora fom Cawnpore had founded a Fascist party in India and asserted to having the support of Bose. Henceforth, the Italian Foreign Ministry considered Bose a possible leader of an Indian national movement inspired by fascistic ideas.[42]

During his stay in Rome, Bose gave interviews to various Italian newspapers in which he also mentioned his audiences with Mussolini. This induced the British ambassador to write a personal letter to the secretary of state in the Foreign Ministry, pointing out a dossier from the previous year in which he had described Bose as a communist agitator. He requested to pay attention to this warning.[43] However, even this intervention did not stop the Foreign Ministry from continuing to keep contact with Bose.[44] Major Carmelo Umberto Rapicavoli was Bose's contact person.[45] Considering the Abyssinian crisis, the Italians, however, became more careful so as not to provoke the British further: at short notice they dropped the plan to send an Indian student in September 1935 to Bose who at that time was in Karlsbad undergoing treatment.[46] The Italian consul general in Dublin was instructed to keep contact with Bose while he was in Ireland, but to be careful and discreet in doing so.[47]

Bose was guest of honour of the Italian government when he came again to Rome in March 1936 on his return journey to India. The Foreign Ministry paid for his stay in the Grand Hotel.[48] The diplomats knew how to appreciate the fact that due to Bose's influence the tendency of reporting on the war in Abyssinia in the Indian newspaper *Forward*, which was close to Bose, had turned in favour of Italy.[49] On 27 March 1936 at 5.45 p.m., Bose had his fourth audience with Mussolini[50] before he started his voyage on 29 March 1936 from Naples on board the Conte Verde.[51]

Twenty months later, Bose was again in Italy. His KLM plane landed in Naples on 21 November 1937. The Italian authorities committed an embarrassing faux pas: the border police arrested Bose on arrival. His luggage was opened and thoroughly checked. He was of course released at once and a representative of KLM apologized to him, but Bose was annoyed. He complained to Major Rapicavoli and threatened never to come to Italy again and to inform the Indian press about the incident.[52] He continued his journey to Austria by train. He had to undergo the same procedure again at the frontier station Tarvisio. Bose now presumed that the British government had slandered him, and the treatment meted out to him by the border police was a sure sign that the British had gained proximity during his absence.[53]

The British were indeed behind this: the British ambassador's dossier from 1933, describing Bose as communist agitator, had not been taken seriously by the Foreign Ministry but was still lying with the Ministry of the Interior. In October 1936, a Doctor Modrini, of whom nothing else is known, had warned against Bose as a terrorist. Consequently, the Ministry of the Interior had listed Bose's name in February 1937 in the frontier register.[54] However, the Foreign Ministry intervened and his name was at once deleted. Instead, all border police personnel were instructed to treat Bose politely and obligingly on re-entry. Bose was satisfied with an apology by the Foreign Ministry and requested another audience with Mussolini, which had to be kept a secret after the *Corriere della Sera* had printed a photo of his landing in Naples and had mentioned an impending audience with the Duce. Mussolini agreed.[55]

Bose's stay in Italy at the end of January 1938 provided an opportunity for the meeting. He was again a guest of the Italian government on his return journey to India. An apartment in the Albergo Quirinale, a car at his disposal, a train ticket for the journey from Rome to Naples, a flight reservation from Naples onwards, a room in the Albergo Excelsior in Naples—everything was taken care of. The meeting with Mussolini, the fifth, was to his satisfaction. He could also meet the Japanese ambassador in Rome. The date of this meeting is not recorded in the files of the MAE but may be deduced from Bose's letters to Emilie Schenkl.[56] It must have been approximately 19 or 20 January 1938.[57]

After five meetings with Mussolini between 1934 and 1938, Bose was now an old acquaintance of the Duce. Nothing is known of the discussions. The absence of any protocol of these meetings by the

Foreign Ministry indicates that they were more of a social than a political nature. By granting him the audiences, Mussolini showed his appreciation of the Indian politician. He appreciated therewith the role Bose played at the congress of the oriental students and his differentiated stand in the Abyssinian war. Concrete agreements were apparently not made. The personal relationship, however, which was formed with the Duce during this time, proved to be extremely valuable during the war years. The Italians, after all, made his escape from Kabul possible, and it was Mussolini who again and again took Bose's side, against Hitler in the discussions regarding a declaration of the Axis in support of India's independence.

Bose's Escape to Europe

The outbreak of war in Europe changed the situation in India as well. After the British declared war against Germany, Viceroy Lord Linlithgow announced on 3 September 1939, that India too was at war. Bose came to know of this when he delivered a speech in Madras at a gathering of about 200,000 people. Someone handed over a newspaper to him. Bose was thrilled, 'The much expected crisis had at last come. This was India's golden opportunity.'[1] But much to Bose's dismay, other Indian politicians expressed different views. Gandhi announced after a meeting with the viceroy, that India should stand by England at this time of danger. Also Nehru used his influence not to attack the British just then. When on 8 September 1939 the working committee of the Congress met in Wardha, Bose was invited even though he did not belong to this panel. Bose insisted on starting the freedom fight at once and threatened that, if need be, the Forward Bloc would also act on its own. Finally, the politicians decided to offer their collaboration to the British, but only as a free country.[2]

Bose was not at all happy about this decision. According to his assessment, a consequent refusal of any collaboration would have considerably affected British war production in India. By offering the British a compromise, and by delaying a final decision regarding Indian participation in the war, Gandhi and Nehru had indirectly helped the government.[3] While the followers of Gandhi and Nehru showed restraint, Bose started a campaign with the Forward Bloc against collaborating with the colonial masters in the war, and for taking up the struggle for freedom. In October 1939, an anti-imperialist conference took place in Nagpur. The months-long propaganda of the Forward Bloc cumulated finally in March 1940 in a mammoth demonstration in Ramgarh. It was called the All-India Anti-Compromise Conference. The Forward Bloc started a countrywide campaign of civil disobedience in April 1940. Many members were incarcerated.[4]

Bose met Gandhi and tried to persuade him to give a call for passive resistance. 'But the Mahatma was still non-committal and he repeated that, in his view, the country was not prepared for a fight and any attempt to precipitate one would do more harm than good to India,' Bose wrote later in his memoirs. Nevertheless, Gandhi promised to be the first to send Bose a congratulatory telegram should he manage to gain India's freedom in this way. Bose had additional talks with Muhammed Ali Jinnah, the leader of the Muslim League, and Savarkar, the president of the Hindu Mahasabha. According to Bose, Jinnah could not be won over to fight the British, as he was only interested in the formation of a Muslim state, Pakistan. Savarkar did not bother about the international situation but was only concerned about the military training of Hindus in the Indian army.[5]

BOSE'S DECISION TO ESCAPE

After the Second World War, Savarkar wrote that he had advised Bose at meeting on 22 June 1940 to leave the country, to go to Europe, organize an army from Indian prisoners of war there, and with the help of Japan to march into India as soon as Japan had declared war against Great Britain.[6] If one gives credence to this report then Savarkar appears actually to have been a prophet who could foresee the course of history in all detail. Therefore, doubts are appropriate. According to Casolari, there is no contemporary reference of the talk between the two politicians. She does not consider Savarkar's report to be authentic. Savarkar's prestige had suffered in the post-war period as the public connected the Hindu Mahasabha with Gandhi's assassination. She surmises that Savarkar wanted to profit from the newly created myth surrounding Bose by claiming to have been the source of its inspiration.[7]

Before the outbreak of war, Gandhi had already tried, in a personal letter to Hitler, to persuade him to preserve peace. However, the Indian government refused to send the letter.[8] After the attack on Poland, the Mahatma declared that his sympathies were with England and France, the countries that had declared war on Germany. Though Germany's demands towards Poland might be partly justified, Hitler, however, should have let an arbitrary court decide on the issue.[9] He exhorted the viceroy not to make Hitler out to be an absolute demon and told the British that they too were partly responsible for the war, 'I do not believe Herr Hitler to be as bad as he is portrayed. He might even have been a friendly power as he may still be.'[10] He requested the British to use non-violence in their fight against the Axis.[11] He declared India as neutral in this conflict. Neither victory nor destruction of Germany was in the Indian interest.[12] He wrote an open letter to Hitler in December 1940, the publication of which the British naturally foiled. Gandhi writes in the letter: 'We have no doubt about your bravery or your devotion to your fatherland, nor do we believe that you are the monster described by your opponents.' He then criticizes the aggression against Czechoslovakia, Poland and Denmark, explains non-violence to Hitler, and continues, 'We know what the British heel means for us and the non-European races of the world. But we would never wish to end British rule with German aid.' The letter closes with an appeal for peace to Hitler and Mussolini.[13] When Bose violated the assembly ban, they arrested him in 2 June 1940 and threw him into prison. When he was accused of having acted against the Defence of India Act, he knew that he would remain imprisoned until the end of war.[14] He pondered in his prison cell over the political situation. Three points were clear to him:

> Firstly, Britain would lose the war and the British Empire would break up. Secondly, in spite of being in a precarious position, the British would not hand over power to the Indian people and the latter would have to fight for their freedom. Thirdly, India would win her independence if she played her part in the war against Britain and collaborated with those powers that were fighting Britain.[15]

He realized that first he had to get out of prison. He started a 'fast unto death' to force the government to release him. He succeeded and was finally set free after he had fasted for seven days.[16]

Political activities became more and more difficult under war conditions. He was under house detention and constant police surveillance. He would have been imprisoned again had he started political work. Bose now had two options: he could either spend the rest of the war inactive in his house or in prison, thus missing the opportunity to fulfil his life's ambition of realizing India's independence, or he had to leave the country and seek the alliance of foreign powers. The second option had already been under his consideration for a long time.

On 6 November 1939, when Germany was already at war with Great Britain but Italy was still neutral, Bose had contacted the Italian consul in Calcutta. He proposed to him exactly what he was to realize eighteen months later: he wanted to escape abroad, and from there direct the independence movement through broadcasting. He somehow thought he could manage to escape on-board an Italian liner.[17] Rome decided eleven days later not to accept the proposal.[18] It seems the Italians were at this time not prepared to risk a conflict with Great Britain by supporting an Indian freedom fighter, for their policy of 'non-conduct of war' was a rather shaky one. Bose also extended feelers to Japan. In 1940, he sent Lal Shankar Lal, general secretary of the Forward Bloc and his confidant, to Japan. Bose's nephew Dwijen Bose helped Lal obtain a passport under the name of Hiralal Gupta and he travelled on a Japanese vessel to Japan. There he met Rash Behari Bose and talked to government officials. It is not known whether this mission yielded any result.[19]

Finally, he sought the help of the communists. Bhagat Ram Talwar, who later served the German legation in Kabul as contact person under the pseudonym 'Rahmat Khan', reports that sometime in May 1940 two functionaries of the Communist Party of India (CPI), Ram Kishan and Achhar Singh Cheena, came to see him in his native village Ghalla Dher. At that time, Talwar was responsible for helping revolutionaries secretly cross the border.[20] They told him, 'that the party wanted to arrange for the crossing of a very important person of international eminence to the Soviet Union.'[21] The three of them began preparations for Bose's escape. On 1 July 1940, Achhar Singh Cheena met Bose in Calcutta in order to inform him that the venture could take place. He asked the politician why he wanted to leave India. Bose gave the following assessment of the situation: the moderate forces within the Congress had managed to expel him from the leadership. The radical forces could not fight against Gandhi and the British at the same time. However, only an armed rebellion could drive the British out of India. The Second World War had now provided a good opportunity for such a rebellion.[22]

Thereupon Achhar Singh Cheena wanted to know why Bose thought the Soviet Union should give him shelter as his contacts with Germany and Italy were after all well known. Bose replied that he had supported the Soviet Union in their Soviet-Finnish war and therefore they had a positive opinion of him.[23] Nothing came of it though and Bose preferred to continue with his campaign. Ram Krishan and Achhar Singh Cheena at first tried in vain to establish contact with the Soviet embassy in Kabul. After this they tried to enter the Soviet Union themselves. Ram Krishan drowned when they tried to cross the Amu River at the Soviet-Afghanistan border. Achhar Singh Cheena was arrested by the Soviet border police and interrogated in Moscow. Later he writes about his impressions in an interview with Talwar that took place on 19 July 1974 in Amritsar:

> They did not say anything, but my impression was that owing to the international situation prevailing at that time, the Soviet Union was very cautious and did not want to embarrass the British. But the border posts were instructed if he (Bose) comes to give him a safe passage. At the same time, they were feeling that there might be complications if the British, in that case, come to know that Bose is in the Soviet Union.[24]

Diethelm Weidemann argues that the Soviet Union was actually Bose's desired goal. Her geographical position and her reputation as an anti-imperialistic power seemed to make her the ideal allied partner. Already in 1939, Bose had tried to find out if he could expect support from this end but received merely an expression of sympathy. It seems that already since the early 1930s, Moscow had not been favourably inclined towards the Indian communists. There was also the apprehension that Bose might be an agent of the British secret service. Under these circumstances Bose's endeavour to establish contacts was unsuccessful.[25]

Weidemann relies essentially on Talwar's report, which corresponds with the one by Uttam Chand who had published his memoirs as early as in 1946. Bose had stayed with him in Kabul and according to Chand he had told him, 'It has long been my intention to go to Moscow.'[26] Weidemann points out though that the result of his study is of a preliminary nature, as he could not consider the sources kept in the archives of Moscow and Rome.

It may be assumed now that Bose was open as to the choice of his exile, as the documents in the archives of the Italian Foreign Ministry are proof of Bose's request in 1939 to be allowed to stay in Italy. Though his nephews, Sisir Kumar and Asoke, helped him escape, they did not know his destination. While Asoke presumed that his uncle was on his way to the Soviet Union, Sisir was equally sure that he was going to Germany.[27] Presumably it made no difference to Bose whether he would be exiled in the Soviet Union, Italy, Germany or Japan as long as he was able to continue with his political work there. Practical reasons may have played a role towards the end of 1940: the Soviet Union was the only foreign power maintaining a functioning 'Fifth Column' in India, namely the CPI. National Socialists and Fascists had no organized native party members in India, diplomatic representations had been closed since the outbreak of war, and the German and Italian nationals in India who might have been approachable for establishing contacts were kept in internment camps. It was therefore natural for Bose to utilize the structure of the communists for his purpose, i.e. to escape the clutches of the British. He did not hesitate to contact the embassies of Germany and Italy in Kabul soon after having reached there.

BOSE'S DEPARTURE

Bose was released from prison on 5 December 1940 and returned to his Calcutta home on Elgin Road. His relatives noticed with great concern his paleness and tiredness.[28] The hunger strike had impaired his health but that did not stop him from immediately starting his preparations for escape. The secretary of the Forward Bloc in the northwest provinces, Mian Akbar Shah, came to Calcutta personally to inform him that all preparations for his escape had been made. He took the opportunity to purchase clothes suitable as camouflage for Bose in a Muslim shop in Calcutta.[29]

Bose pretended to have gone into seclusion for religious meditation so as to avoid any suspicion his sudden disappearance might create. On the eve of 16 January 1941, Bose dressed in a silken dhoti and sat down for a ritual meal with his family. Only a few of the family members were in the know. He then retired to his room and put on the Muslim garments already laid out there.

Dressed as insurance agent Mohammed Ziauddin he stepped into the car, a German 'Wanderer' of Auto Union, which was parked in front of the house. His nephew Sisir Kumar Bose was waiting in the car and together they drove away in the early hours of 17 January 1941, unnoticed by the police.[30]

At around 8.30 in the morning they reached the house of Sisir Kumar's brother Asoke, in Dhanbad situated about 200 kilometres to the west of Calcutta. Bose rested until the afternoon. Then the two brothers and Asoke's wife drove him to the Gomoh railway station about 50 kilometres away from Dhanbad, where he caught the Delhi-Kalka Mail after midnight.[31] He changed into the Frontier Mail in Delhi and continued his journey on 19 January 1941. He got down in Peshawar and booked a hotel room. Mian Akbar Shah was waiting at the station. He watched Bose's arrival from a distance. He sent Abdul Majid Khan, a lawyer, to the hotel on the following morning to pick up Bose. He was now accommodated in a house belonging to Mian Feroze Shah.[32]

On 21 January 1941, Bose met Bhagat Ram Talwar who was to take him to Kabul. Bose, who could not speak the local language, was now supposed to be Ziauddin, a native deaf and dumb Muslim divine. Bose and Talwar started their journey on the same evening with a local guide. They drove 18 kilometres by car to the British military camp Khajuri Maidan and proceeded from there on foot to a Muslim holy place situated in tribal territory. Partly on foot, partly riding on a mule and finally on the rooftop of a bus, they followed a route south of the Khyber Pass until Jalalabad and from there to Kabul. They proceeded mostly on paths through fields and found shelter with hospitable natives. Bose is reported to have danced for joy after he had finally set foot on Afghan soil. 'What a beautiful country,' he shouted. The surrounding bare hills and withered fields held a special appeal for him: they were free from British rule.[33]

Meanwhile, the Calcutta police were wondering as to the whereabouts of Bose. The intended deception had worked. Two of Bose's acquaintances told the police that they had seen Bose on 25 January 1941 (when he actually had already reached Afghanistan) in his house, sitting on a tiger skin sparsely dressed like a sanyasi. The police had a hunch though: either Bose had really become a sanyasi, or there was some hidden plan behind his disappearance.[34] Only on

26 January 1941, one day before he was in any case supposed to appear in court, his family decided to announce his disappearance. The very next day the news was published in *Anandabazar Patrika* and *Hindusthan Standard*. All-India Radio immediately countered with a canard; the fugitive had been captured near Dhanbad.[35] Gandhi sent a telegram to Bose's brother Sarat Chandra: 'Startling news about Subhas. Please wire truth. Hope all is well.'[36]

Bose's disappearance did not come as a surprise to the police. They could easily understand his situation. The deputy commissioner of police in Calcutta wrote in a memorandum:

> He must have realized that it would be a hopeless proposition to continue the struggle on the same old lines, but he would never, I think, cease to strive his utmost to achieve what has been his life's aim—the complete independence of India. I do not therefore believe that [...] he has renounced the world and become a Sannyasi. He has, as I say, absconded for some definite purpose. He may yet be trying to bring about a mass revolution from within. The other alternative that he is attempting to obtain foreign aid is, however, equally possible.[37]

The commissioner hit the nail on the head with this assessment. Nevertheless, for all that, he did not know to which country Bose had escaped. Still, he presumed Bose had gone to either Japan or the Soviet Union.[38] The police could not know at that time that the wanted fugitive would flee to Germany; Bose himself did not yet know.

BOSE'S STAY IN KABUL

Bose and Talwar reached Kabul on 27 January 1941 at eleven o'clock. They took a room in a simple guest house. One day after their arrival, they tried to contact the Soviet embassy but were not allowed inside. The attempt to establish contact with the embassy via the Soviet trade representatives proved equally futile.[39] The ambassador suspected a British intrigue behind Bose's offer of collaboration, in order to create a conflict between the Soviet Union and Afghanistan, as Bose could be taken across the border only secretly.[40]

He had no option but to search for another host country. The Axis Powers were the only option open to him in this situation. Together with Talwar, he went to the German legation on 1 February 1941.[41] As luck would have it, on the way to the legation they noticed a car stuck in the snow, displaying a Soviet flag. As the person on the back seat appeared to be the Soviet ambassador, Talwar approached him and asked about Bose's name for admission. The ambassador deliberated briefly and drove away without uttering a word.[42]

Bose was luckier in the German legation. Minister Hans Pilger received him. Bose explained his plan of promoting the Indian independence movement from Berlin and requested him to facilitate his journey to Berlin in association with the Soviet embassy. Pilger immediately sent a telegram to Berlin and urgently requested instructions on how to proceed. He also informed his Italian colleagues. He pointed out that Bose was in great danger of being arrested by the Afghans and handed over to the British authorities.[43] For this reason, Bose should not contact the embassy directly as several locals were employed there, but keep in touch through a certain Mr Thomas who was the local representative of Siemens.[44]

It is interesting to note that Pilger writes in the telegram he sent to Berlin only of Bose's wish to come to Berlin. This contradicts Talwar's report, according to which Bose wanted to ask the German minister merely for assistance to establish contact with his Soviet colleague.[45] Presumably, Bose was almost indifferent as to which country would accept him. Talwar, of course, had to be given the impression that he wanted by all means to go to the Soviet Union. After all, he had arranged the escape of this politician on behalf of the Indian communists.

Berlin reacted at once. The Secretary of State Ernst von Weizsäcker immediately ordered a short biography of Bose which was produced on 2 February 1941. The author of this short write-up about the Indian is not known but he was obviously well informed. He was able to sum up the most important details of Bose's life and his position in Indian politics. He also knew Bose's attitude towards Germany, 'Bose has always expected Germany to proclaim a clear political viewpoint with regard to India and has openly shown his disappointment that this has not happened.' Bose himself did not get very flattering remarks, 'Bose is a very vain and pushy character. He engages in opposition for opposition's sake.'[46] Pilger also did not trust the Indian. He warned his colleagues in Berlin that 'certain happenings' may lead to the presumption that perhaps Bose after all did work together with the British. As it happened, an Indian had come to him as Bose's negotiator. He had formed the impression that this man also entertained relations with the British embassy.[47]

Weizsäcker informed the legation in Kabul in spite of this rather unfavourable depiction that Bose could come to Germany if the Soviet Union would issue a transit visa for him. The Germans were evidently very interested in this Indian freedom fighter. Bose's known critical attitude towards National Socialism evidently did not stand in the way. At least since December 1940, preparations were afoot at the Foreign Office for expanding India-specific propaganda. An entry in the diary of Marie 'Missie' Wassiltschikow, who worked as secretary in the Foreign Office during the war years, proves this. She notes on 23 December 1940, after an interview with the scientific assistant in the Foreign Office, Adam von Trott zu Stolz, 'He does many things at the same time, all camouflaged under the official title "Free India".'[48]

At that time, the sections of the political and commercial policy departments in charge of India were also busy with establishing a news service for India. The diplomats had the country's importance as a future export market in view. They decided, at the end of January 1941, to send Carl Rasmuss to Kabul. Rasmuss had been commercial attaché in Calcutta until the outbreak of the war. Stationed in Afghanistan, he was supposed to gather information about the industrial and inner-political situation in India.[49] Bose's sudden appearance must have been extremely convenient for the German diplomats who until then did not have an Indian confidant of calibre. This explains the prompt reaction.

Pilger approached the Soviet ambassador in Kabul who responded with the same cautious attitude he had shown to Bose a few days earlier. Thereupon he sent a telegram to the head office with the suggestion to approach the Soviet government directly through the embassy in Moscow. Meanwhile, the Italian ambassador was also involved in this matter and had informed Rome. He on his part had advised Bose to remain in hiding for the time being.[50]

Bose and Talwar reported to Mr Thomas on 5 February 1941. Thomas was now in a position to let them know that the German government was making preparations for bringing Bose safely to Berlin. Details had not yet been worked out. Bose should report again in three days' time. The two Indians were delighted that the Germans showed more interest than the Russians. However, they were afraid of being discovered by the Afghans if they had to wait much longer.[51]

The Italians also showed interest in Bose. On 7 February 1941, the Italian chargé d'affaires in Berlin enquired from the undersecretary of state for politics, Ernst Woermann, what his government could do for the Indian.[52] Woermann could only tell him that the Reich's foreign minister had not as yet decided how to proceed in this matter. This decision must have been made on 8 February 1941, as on that day Woermann had instructed the ambassador in Moscow, Friedrich Werner Count von der Schulenburg, to tactfully find out whether the Soviet government would be prepared to allow transit to Bose. He should frame the enquiry as personal asylum matter without political background.[53]

Meanwhile, Bose became increasingly impatient. He was afraid of being caught by the Afghan authorities and handed over to the British. Moreover, he had contracted a severe stomach disorder. A policeman or a police informer had already discovered him and demanded continuous bribe so that Bose had to give him even his watch. Bose now remembered his old comrade-in-arms, Uttam Chand, who carried on a wireless business in Kabul. He finally found shelter with him when he felt unsafe in the small hotel.[54] He wrote in a letter via Thomas to the German minister on 18 February 1941, that he would try to reach the Soviet Union on his own. It was not possible for him to continue staying in Kabul. Bose and Talwar had already hired a guide and bought three bus tickets to Khanabad. Thereupon Thomas suggested approaching Pietro Quaroni, the Italian minister.[55] The Foreign Office replied to the Italian offer of assistance, that the Italian ambassador in Moscow might contact Count von der Schulenburg directly and take further instructions as to how to proceed.[56] This was done, and Schulenburg was requested not to get involved.[57] Meanwhile the Italian minister in Kabul tried to find a solution and suggested a journey to Italy via Iran.[58]

Bose met Quaroni on 22 February 1941. He had actually intended to commence his journey north soon after the meeting. The Italian diplomat explained the position of the preparations for his journey to Europe and warned him against travelling alone. He managed to dissuade him from undertaking the bus journey on the following day.

Quaroni cabled to Rome that Bose was extremely impatient.[59] Berlin finally came to know, during these days, what Bose actually wanted to do in Europe. Pilger reported that Bose intended to explain England's position to the Indians through broadcasting from Europe, as people in India did not believe in an English defeat. He was convinced he could influence the Indians and was contemplating a government of a free India after German victory.[60]

On 3 March 1941, Count von der Schulenburg finally cabled to Berlin that the Soviet foreign commissariat had given the information that Bose could receive a transit visa for his journey to Germany.[61] Woermann informed the Italian chargé d'affaires and added, as it were, by way of consolation for the trouble the Italians had taken in vain, that after all, Bose could establish contact with Italy from Berlin.[62]

The Italians continued to work on their Iran plan. They argued that Bose might run into difficulties in the Soviet Union as he had shown himself to be an anti-communist in Calcutta.[63] However, the plan was dropped. Bose left Kabul on 18 March 1941.[64] He travelled on an Italian passport under the name of embassy wireless operator Orlando Mazzotta. The passport photo had been changed after the Afghan authorities had stamped the departure visa on the personal document.[65] Bose took up the identity of an Italian legation employee in order to be able to leave Afghanistan incognito. The fact that he was given an Italian and not a German passport is presumably because Pilger exercised caution. He thought all German diplomats were too well known in Kabul.[66]

It was very important for the German legation in Kabul that the Afghanistan government did not come to know of the undertaking. The travel route should remain a secret even after safe arrival.[67] Bose reached Moscow on 31 March 1941 together with a travel companion, an engineer by the name of Wenger, and two Lufthansa employees. He called on the German ambassador there and continued his journey to Berlin on the same day.[68] Meanwhile, Talwar travelled to Calcutta where he called on Bose's brother Sarat Chandra and his son Sisir Kumar to report on the proceedings. He also handed over a letter in Bengali to the brother as well as two articles entitled 'Message To My Countrymen—From Somewhere in Europe', and 'Forward Bloc—Its Justification'.[69]

The Beginning of India-Politics with Bose's Arrival in Berlin

Bose's arrival in Berlin marked the beginning of German India-politics. To begin with, Bose met the important personalities of the Foreign Office. Even the Reich's foreign minister himself received him. At the start, the collaboration seemed very promising for both sides. Together they drew up plans for a propaganda action called 'British Empire'. The German government was to publicly acknowledge India's independence within this framework. However, the action was cancelled at short notice and the declaration remained unannounced.

BOSE'S FIRST CONTACTS WITH THE FOREIGN OFFICE

On the basis of information received so far, it was quite natural for the German Foreign Office in the Wilhelmstrasse to be under the impression that Bose's intention for having come to Germany was mainly for broadcasting propaganda. Therefore, Hans Queling from the department for radio politics attended to him after high officials from the protocol department had at first welcomed him on his arrival on 2 April 1941. The German government booked him into the noble Hotel Excelsior.[1] Bose could now enjoy some luxury after the fatiguing months in prison and the strenuous escape.

Bose's talks with Woermann on 3 April 1941

Woermann received him on the following day. Bose laid out his plans before the undersecretary of state. First of all, he wanted to form a government in exile and expected the support of the Axis Powers for this. Further, he wanted to fan rebellion in India through corresponding propaganda. Finally, the Axis should march into India with a force of 100,000 men to liberate the country from British rule. He enumerated the composition of the Indian army: 300,000 men only and of these at the most 70,000 Englishmen. The rest of the army would be prepared to desert any time. Woermann listened attentively but made no comments. He advised Bose to first elaborate on his programme in writing and then discuss it with the foreign minister himself. Woermann would have liked to engage Bose at once for German propaganda. His idea was that radio and press should announce Bose's presence in Germany in a grand get-up. Thereafter, the Indian could start with his Hindustani and English broadcasts.[2]

Bose wrote a letter to Emilie Schenkl on the same day and asked her to come to Berlin as his secretary.[3] Bose had met Emilie already in 1934 during his first visit to Europe. According to Bose's nephew Sisir Kumar Bose, they secretly married on 26 December 1937. She was one of the first to know about his presence in Europe. Soon after his arrival in Germany, Bose could also engage the student Mukund Rai Vyas as private secretary. The Gujarati was born in 1918 in Mombasa and grew up in Kenya. He had been studying at the London School of Economics since 1937 and was caught up in the war while studying German in Bonn. Bose had met him during his European sojourn in the 1930s.[4] Vyas narrates how in the evening of 4 April 1941 two sinister-looking men wearing knee boots and long overcoats called at his lodging and took him away without giving his worried landlady any explanation. The men did not take him to jail, though, as his landlady had feared, but took him to the hotel Esplanade. 'As I entered, I stood dazed right at the door. I could not believe my eyes! Right in front of me stood Subhas Chandra Bose! It was a wonder of wonders,' he recalls. He could hardly believe that he stood face to face with the famous politician: 'If anyone else had told me that Subhas Bose was in Germany, I would have treated it as a big joke. But there he was.' Bose now asked Vyas to meet him regularly. He was not allowed to tell his landlady about his experience. In consideration of the poor woman's anxiety about Vyas, Bose gave him a tin of coffee for her. 'This is for your landlady's nerves.'[5]

Bose's memorandum of 9 April 1941

Barely a week after his first meeting with Woermann, Bose presented an elaborate memorandum entitled 'Plan of a Collaboration between the Axis Powers and India'. The basis of this collaboration would be the common goal of destroying Great Britain. He claimed that the Indian people had a very hostile attitude towards the colonial powers and could give materialistic assistance in achieving their downfall. His plan comprised actions in Europe, Afghanistan, the tribal territories between Afghanistan and India, as well as in India herself. He suggested forming a free Indian government in Europe. This government would enter into a treaty with the Axis Powers providing for India's freedom after the war. Free India would reciprocate with 'special advantages' for the Axis Powers. The exile government would then establish legations in as many European states as possible. Thereafter it could incite the Indian people through broadcasting to rebel and send the necessary resources via Afghanistan to India.

A main base would have to be established in Afghanistan, equipped with vehicles and couriers for Europe and India to be connected. Attacks on British military bases could be carried out in the tribal territories. Military experts and a propaganda centre would have to be provided for this purpose. In India, the population would have to be induced through intensive propaganda, particularly through broadcasting, and agents would have to stop cooperating with the British.

Indians should be requested not to join the armed forces, not to pay taxes, soldiers should be persuaded to desert and carry out acts of sabotage. Bose's followers would then incite the population, organize strikes and destroy railway lines, bridges and factories. Individual revolts by civilians in various parts of the country would escalate to a mass revolution. Bose expected the Axis to grant the exile government a loan for financing these actions, to be repaid by independent India after the war. Finally, he suggested sending an expedition of 50,000 soldiers of the Axis Powers to India in order to drive out the British soldiers, at the most numbering 70,000, from the subcontinent.[6]

The demand for diplomatic recognition of a 'Free Indian government' occupies first position already in this first draft of Bose's goals. According to Bose's arguments, establishing Indian legations would convince the Indian people that 'the fact of India's independence has already been acknowledged.' This was already an indication of Bose's desire for an official declaration by the Axis

Powers in support of India's independence, which in the following months would determine his negotiations with Germany and Italy. Woermann accepted the plan with reservations. The formation of an Indian government in exile was out of the question, as this would define the liberation of India as German war aim. The right moment for this had not yet come. To accept Bose as the sole political exponent of India would also not serve any direct political purpose. The followers of Gandhi and Nehru in India would not readily accept this. It was also best not to discuss a military expedition with Bose at this point. Still, he supported a 'generous financial assistance'.[7]

He wanted to engage Bose instead as soon as possible for German propaganda activities. He suggested to the Reich's foreign minister what he had already mentioned to Bose: in the coming week all German newspapers should report Bose's presence in Germany in a grand get-up as front-page news. Bose should then be interviewed by the press and give speeches in Hindustani and English over the radio.[8] Woermann's reaction shows again that the Foreign Office mainly wanted Bose for their broadcasting propaganda. All further plans that might influence German foreign policy were to be ignored. It seems Bose saw through their intentions because he refused to appear in public via radio and newspapers unless an agreement had come about regarding his plan of actions. Bose threatened to go back to Afghanistan and fight in the Indian border territory if an agreement could not be made.[9]

On Woermann's request he presented a few days later a draft for a declaration supporting India's independence. In this he referred to the cultural affinity between India and Germany and deduced from this a deep interest of the Germans in India's fate. The decisive sentence reads: 'Germany therefore recognizes the inalienable right of the Indian people to have full and complete independence.' Skilfully Bose included some of his own ideas regarding a future Indian social order: 'But it is only natural that Germany, in keeping with her own traditions, would like to see in India a united nation, in which every individual is guaranteed food, work, necessities of life and equal opportunities of growth, regardless of religion, class or any other consideration.'[10]

Bose's discussion with Ribbentrop on 29 April 1941

Joachim von Ribbentrop received Bose on 29 April 1941. They talked at great length about world politics and the situation in India. The minister seemed to have read Bose's memorandum carefully. He took the opportunity to get to know the Indian guest and his ideas. At first Ribbentrop asked Bose some questions regarding the situation in India, Gandhi's and the princes' attitudes, the political organization of the Indian nationalistic movement, and the military strength of the British in the country. The minister's question regarding India's attitude towards Germany prompted Bose to complain once again about the National Socialists' racism. Ribbentrop tried to avoid a clear answer by remarking that National Socialism was only for racial purity and not for domination of other races. But Bose did not accept this evasive reply. He declared that it was easy for the British to instill fear of a German rule into Indians. In order to win the Indian masses over to collaborate with the Axis Powers, they would have to first of all acknowledge India's independence through a public proclamation. Bose, who by now had apparently understood that the Germans regarded him more as a promising propaganda figure than an ally to be taken seriously, obviously wanted to make such a proclamation a condition for a collaboration.

The protocol does not record Ribbentrop's reaction. For him it was more important to find out Bose's attitude towards Japan, Afghanistan and Russia. But when Bose did not wish to tie himself down, Ribbentrop reverted to the question as to which possibilities for an Indian resistance he would at all envisage. Ribbentrop tried to make it clear to Bose that the Indians had hardly any chance to drive out the British on their own. Bose should rather consider influencing developments in India through propaganda. Bose disagreed. It was certainly possible for the revolting tribes of the northwest frontier and the civilian population to drive them out. For the first time he suggested deploying the Indian soldiers of the Indian army, held captive in German prisoner-of-war camps, to fight against England. This suggestion set the formation of the Indian Legion through the German Wehrmacht in motion. The minister now explained at great length developments of German-English relations. Ribbentrop finally conceded reluctantly that he would check out any possibilities to harm the British Empire in India. But one should not have any illusions and not proceed in haste. Again he wanted to put Bose off with the prospect of propaganda activities. He now offered him a clandestine radio station so that he could give his inciting broadcasts to the Indian people independently from the official German short-wave transmitters. But Bose refused to be diverted: any propaganda would be effective only in combination with an India-proclamation by the Axis Powers. The meeting ended with the stipulation that Bose's presence in Germany should remain a secret for the time being.[11]

Bose's supplementary memorandum of 3 May 1941

Impressed by the successful German military operations in the Balkan and North Africa, Bose presented a supplementary memorandum after his talks with the Reich's foreign minister. He mentioned in the memorandum that these victories had impressed the people of the Orient very much and had destroyed British prestige. The Axis Powers could make use of this opportunity and win over Indians and Arabs to their side. He repeated his former demand for a proclamation by the Axis Powers in support of India's independence, supplemented with a desire for a corresponding one for the Arabian countries. Furthermore, the time had now come to fan and support rebellion against Great Britain. Bose demanded military assistance for Iraq against England and for the rebellious Afghans who wanted to overthrow their government.

His proposal 'that the Axis Powers do now concentrate on attacking the heart of the British Empire, that is, British rule in India,' shows an amazing boldness. One can hardly assume that Bose seriously expected the leaders of the Axis Powers to act on his proposal and to change their military strategy. But evidently, he did not want to miss any opportunity to stress on India's strategic importance. Bose promised as reward for their engagement in the Orient 'a long chain of friendly pro-German countries' from North Africa to Japan. Though he could have not known about the impending 'Operation Barbarossa', Bose pointed out how important it was for Germany to have the sympathies of the oriental people on her side in case a conflict with the Soviet Union and Turkey became unavoidable.[12]

Woermann, who accepted this supplementary memorandum, felt no doubt that as yet he could not make any political promises to Bose.

Nevertheless, he asked him what official steps he actually expected the German government to take. Bose expressed his opinion very clearly: Germany would have to proclaim an India-declaration. However, he withdrew his demand for an Indian government in exile. He must have understood the impossibility of its realization. During these discussions Woermann wanted to know what Bose thought about Afghanistan gaining access to the sea by annexing Indian territories. Bose was prepared to concede the western part of Baluchistan to the Afghans.[13] The Afghan minister for economics, Abdul Majid Khan, had indicated in June 1940 to the German ambassador in Afghanistan that his country would be prepared to induce the Afghan people in India to rebel against the British if Afghanistan were to gain access to the sea. These plans became topical again as Abdul Khan was in Berlin for medical treatment since February 1941 and had frequent talks with officials of the Foreign Office. Territorial demands on India were also a topic during these discussions.[14] Evidently Woermann wanted to find out whether the Afghan urge for expansion could somewhat be reconciled with Bose's goals.

BROADCASTING PLANS

The Foreign Office did not remain idle while Bose was working on his supplementary memorandum. The section for wireless matters of the department for cultural and educational policy prepared plans on how to enliven German India-propaganda with Bose's help. The head of the section, Legationsrat Gerhard Rühle, presented to the Reich's foreign minister in the beginning of May several detailed drafts for German India-propaganda. The Italians were already ahead: Iqbal Schedai was already broadcasting propaganda programmes via his transmitter Radio Himalaya to India, albeit with dubious success.

Rühle's broadcasting plan

At this time, the German short-wave transmitter was broadcasting daily a half-hourly programme in Hindi. According to Rühle, the Indian people showed great interest in these programmes. Seemingly objective news articles were broadcast which, however, had a distinct anti-British tendency. Bose told Rühle that the German broadcasts enjoyed more credibility in India than the ones from London.[15]

Rühle suggested broadcasting through illegal transmitters as supplement to the official ones. He cited the station Radio Himalaya in Rome from where Schedai sent his broadcasts to India as example. He explained the difference between official and illegal transmissions. With official broadcasts one had to be careful not to interfere too much in Indian internal affairs and thus become discredited, whereas the illegal transmissions could be more outspoken. Bose should mainly appeal to the Indian youth and exhibit a radical, nationalistic Indian attitude. Indian prisoners of war should also be engaged in designing these broadcasts. Rühle elaborated on the intended effect (and gave thereby an exact summary of the aims of German India-politics):

> In this manner it will be achieved that India loses her present importance for British war conduct as material and human reservoir. Over and above, British-Indian troops that could be deployed at African and oriental fronts, would be tied up in India if the broadcasts have the expected effect. Finally, the broadcasts could also be instrumental in increasing the present disturbances in India to an open uprising, thus considerably diminishing British military force in general.[16]

The pirate radio should pretend to broadcast from Indian soil. Transmission was of course possible only through short-wave transmitters in Germany, the occupied territories or friendly countries. Rühle favoured particularly the 100-kilowatt Dutch radio station Huizen that was specially constructed for transmissions to Dutch colonies in India. Transmitting to India was more difficult on medium waves. Other than short-wave transmissions, medium ones could not be received in India. On the other hand, Rühle had found out that about three-fourths of all Indian radio sets could receive only medium and no short waves. So a medium wave transmitter had to be procured. Bose suggested taking a small transportable transmitter into Afghan frontier territory. He explained to Rühle that his agents could take the apparatus from Kabul into the territory if they had one at their disposal.

Transporting secretly a suitable medium-wave transmitter from Germany to Kabul was a problem neither Rühle nor Bose were able to solve at that point. Moreover, Rühle did not have any illusions about the efficacy of the radio propaganda. He confessed at the end of the report: 'Starting a rebellion in India solely with broadcasts might well be impossible considering the small number of listeners.' Nevertheless, German propaganda for India received an enormous impetus in the time to come.

Schedai's Radio Himalaya

Meanwhile, the Italians had not been idle either. Shortly after they had joined the war they thought of using a radio transmitter for seditious propaganda directed at the Indian army. It took some time to realize these plans. Iqbal Schedai was now broadcasting with Radio Himalaya since 14 February 1941.[17]

Schedai was the most important Indian man of confidence the Italian government had during the Second World War. He was born in 1892 in Sialkot, Punjab. In February 1915 he joined a group of young men who tried to initiate an uprising in the Northwest Frontier Province. He was imprisoned by the British in 1918 in Sialkot. In May 1920 he escaped to Kabul. Later he was in Tashkent and in Moscow, before he came to Italy in October 1923. He tried to get a permission to return to India, but the British wouldn't let him return. Since 1928 he lived in Marseille, later in Paris. Then he was the European representative of the Ghadr Party. According to the British police, he was the liaison person to the Soviet Union.[18] A handwritten and undated curriculum vitae, apparently self-written, states that during his time in Italy he assisted merchants of Milano who wanted to export goods to India. He claims to have met Arnaldo Mussolini, the Duce's brother. He also claims to have introduced Nehru to leading Fascists.[19] The Fascist Party, however, wishing to avoid any diplomatic problems with Britain, refused to cooperate with the Ghadr Party.[20]

Schedai worked for the Italian Foreign Ministry as an informant in France and Switzerland. The Foreign Ministry regarded his reports on British activities as useful and reliable. When Italy entered the war, he was invited to Italy in 1940. Schedai moved to Rome, but he remained idle for the following months. Like in Germany, the Italian propaganda work for India only started when Subhas Chandra Bose appeared surprisingly.[21]

On Radio Himalaya, Schedai told his listeners that he was transmitting from Indian soil or close by. The Indian police, however, found out through careful listening that the actual location had to be Rome. The broadcasts did attract attention in India but were not much liked because of their offending and indecent style. A police report notes: 'It abuses all Indian leaders except communists and revolutionaries.'[22] Even the Italians noticed this with displeasure. A few weeks after having started with these broadcasts, Schedai had to justify himself for his aggressive style.[23]

Schedai was offended. In the beginning of April he threatened to stop broadcasting as the Italian radio association FIAR allegedly did not cooperate.[24] He did continue but his revolutionary appeals were not effective. The criminal police in Pune reported that people refrained from listening because of the bad reception. 'Others who managed to tune in were disgusted with the filthy language used and deprecated the false and anti-British propaganda.' Police stations from other provinces wrote similar reports. Schedai could win over some faithful listeners only in Assam and Hyderabad.[25]

The working plan of the Italian Foreign Office

While Bose negotiated with German diplomats in Berlin, experts of India in the Italian Foreign Ministry had not been idle either. They drafted a detailed plan of action for propaganda in India in April 1941 entitled 'Schema di lavoro per l'India'.[26] The drafting of the plan was caused by a remark made by Leopold Amery, the British secretary of state for India, that India had to send ten to twenty million soldiers to the front. The authors warned it was imperative to eliminate India as a British supply base and thus bring about the fall of the British Empire. However, Bose's arrival in Europe may have been the actual background for the growing interest in the Indian freedom movement. Schedai's influence no doubt also played a role.

The working plan was divided into actions in the political and the political-revolutionary areas. Radio broadcasts in the political field were supposed to incite the Indian population to labour revolts, sabotage and terrorism, and guide them in these activities so that war production would be impeded. A nationalistic-revolutionary Indian committee was to be founded in Italy with the objective of forming a nationalistic-revolutionary Indian government after the troops of the Axis Powers had reached the Levant.

The political-revolutionary part of the plan envisaged an intensified collaboration with the rebellious tribes at the Indian northwest frontier. For this purpose the rebels were to be supplied with arms and equipment. Some military technicians were to assist the Fakir of Ipi in manufacturing weapons, equipment and ammunition and to teach him maintenance and handling of the same. In addition, all Indian prisoners of war in North Africa were to be transported to Italy so that soldiers suitable for political, technical and military training could be selected from their numbers. These could then be brought to the rebellious tribes in the Indian northwest frontier—if possible by submarine or plane—for working there as political agents or technical trainers. In case a sufficient number of Indians were willing, an Indian troop could be formed and used for action at the front against the Indian army.

Propaganda pamphlets in Indian languages were to be dropped over units of the Indian army in North Africa, appealing to the soldiers to desert or go over to the other side. The authors of the plan also thought it would be possible to supply arms to India with submarines, speedboats, or planes after the troops of the Axis Powers had advanced to the Red Sea and the coasts of the Indian Ocean. Indian revolutionaries could use these arms to start a violent uprising. The military was supposed to finance these actions. Accordingly, a military person, Colonel Giovanni Tavazzani, was to be entrusted with the realization of the working plan. Tavazzani had been interested in India for a long time. He had also kept in touch with Indian nationalists in Italy and so the Italian Foreign Ministry considered him to be an expert on India.

The Foreign Ministry was not the only authority to dwell on the subject. The Ministereo della Cultura Popolare, the Italian propaganda ministry, evolved a plan for establishing a propaganda centre for India in Afghanistan in the guise of Missione Archeologica. They were supposed to print publications and smuggle them into India. The project failed though due to lack of funds. Nevertheless, a large number of propaganda cards, brochures and pamphlets were printed with editions of up to 150,000 pieces. This material was to be taken into India via the embassy in Kabul.[27]

The experts on India in the Italian Foreign Ministry now felt that they had to counteract a diversification of India-specific propaganda. On 2 May 1941, section II of the Overseas Divison in charge of matters relating to India, sent a circular to the War Ministry, the

Admiralty and Air Ministry, as well as to the ministries for Italian, African and Popular Culture. The circular states that cooperation with Indian revolutionaries in Rome was the sole responsibility of this department and that India-specific propaganda would be under centralized control of the Foreign Ministry.[28]

It seemed though that at that stage only the concerned experts were interested in India. The authors of the action plan tried their best to convince their superiors of the importance of the propaganda for India by pointing out that the other Axis partner would be in a position to take all credit for the expected success, but apparently to no avail.[29] In those days Mussolini was not interested in India. He was surprised when Ribbentrop at a meeting with the Duce and Ciano on 14 May 1941 in Venice, mentioned Bose's presence in Germany.[30] Actually, Mussolini should really have been aware of the Indian's escape; after all, his ambassador in Kabul had kept him constantly informed.

The group of Indian revolutionaries in Rome on which the action plan was based consisted of three persons, namely Schedai and two of his compatriots from Punjab: Ajit Singh and Labh Singh—according to the British, two of the most important men of the Ghadr Party. The real name of Labh Singh, born around 1886, was actually Rattan Singh. He lived in Paris during the 1930s and was the leader of the European section of the Ghadr Party. He had the reputation of being a fierce anti-Fascist and an admirer of the Soviet Union. He tried in August 1939 to return to India via East Africa but was not allowed to enter, and so ended up in Marseille. The French banished him to a small coastal place where Schedai and Ajit Singh visited him after the French capitulation. They persuaded him to go with them to Rome in spite of his hatred for Fascism. The Ministry for Popular Culture used him for intercepting radio transmissions in Hindustani. He died in 1943 in Rome.[31]

The Indians were very particular to be considered revolutionaries in exile and not agents of the Italian government. In order to document this status, Schedai informed the Italian Foreign Ministry on 7 May 1942, that a branch of Azad Hind (Free India) Republican Party had been formed in Italy offering collaboration with the Italian government in the fight against England. Ajit Singh was president of the party, Schedai general secretary.[32]

PLANS FOR SEDITIOUS ACTIONS IN INDIA'S NORTHWEST

The Axis Powers had already tried inciting rebellion against the British in India's northwest before Bose's appearance. They thought in this manner British troops could be permanently tied down in India. The Italians managed already in 1940 to establish first contacts with the rebellious tribes. Besides that, the Axis diplomats tried gaining influence with Bose's followers through Talwar and his people after Bose's departure.

Contacts with the Fakir of Ipi

Hazi Mirza Ali, known as the Fakir of Ipi, was the leader of the mountainous tribes of Waziristan in the Indian-Afghanistan frontier region. A representative of the Fakir of Ipi came to the Italian embassy in Kabul in September 1940 and requested support in their fight against the common enemy.[33] Quaroni suggested financial aid in his report to his ministry. The Fakir would at least be in a position to start disturbances in the frontier province and thus keep the British occupied.[34] Rome accepted the proposal.[35] Afghani agents handed over to the Fakir a larger amount of money in February 1941; half of it came from the Italian, the other half from the German embassy. The Fakir agreed to collaborate with the Axis Powers provided they gave him generous financial support.[36]

First Lieutenant Dietrich Witzel started work in Kabul in May 1941 as intelligence agent of the Wehrmacht's secret service. He reported that with the help of some money one could incite rebellion in the northwest frontier at any time. It was not even necessary to supply arms and ammunition. He proposed training Bose's followers in sabotage and suggested to start preparations for large-scale sabotage activities connected with rebellion at the northwest frontier.[37] Witzel wanted to accompany the Italian councillor of the legation, Enrico Anzilotti, on a journey to the Fakir. Quaroni, however, rejected the proposal. After a brief dispute the Germans relented and the Italian proceeded alone in June 1941. After Anzilotti's return, Quaroni concluded on the basis of his report that the Fakir would not be in a position to start general rebellion at the frontier. His influence was limited and the number of his followers not large enough. Besides, they could only fight under the protection of the mountains and did not have sufficient weapons. It was also not possible to supply them with rifles as the passage through the Soviet Union was now closed. For these reasons Quaroni thought it best to support the Fakir with money only and nothing else, as long as the Axis Powers had not reached Iran.[38] The Germans were more optimistic. As the Italians did not wish to cooperate, they tried on their own to establish contact with the Fakir.

Talwar the double agent

Meanwhile Rasmuss had arrived in Kabul to start his work as secret agent of the Foreign Office. On 6 May 1941 he had a meeting with Quaroni, Quaroni's wife, Anzilotti and Talwar in Paghman, a spa situated 40 kilometres away from Kabul. Talwar had just returned from Calcutta. He had brought two comrades from India along, Sodhi Harmindar Singh and Santimoy Ganguly who wanted to undergo training in Afghanistan in underground combat. Axis diplomats and freedom fighters got to know each other without, however, agreeing on a common mode of action. Talwar explained that he would be prepared for joint activities only after corresponding instructions from Bose.[39]

Rasmuss and Quaroni did not know that, following Talwar's instructions, Sodhi continued trying to establish contact with the Soviet embassy. They were communists and had guided Bose to the border only because they presumed he would go to Moscow. They had no problem keeping contact with the Axis Powers as well, as long as they thought of the Soviet Union and the German Reich as allies owing to the 'Hitler-Stalin Pact'. However, they were faced with a severe loyalty conflict after the German attack on the Soviet Union. Should they continue to be on Bose's side and collaborate with the German and the Italians or should they now consider him to be a traitor?

Talwar met Sarat Chandra Bose in Calcutta who asked him to stay in touch with the embassies of the Axis in Kabul so that they could pass on his messages. Back in Kabul, Talwar received a message from Bose via the Italian embassy. Bose asked Talwar, in collaboration with the Axis Powers, to continue organizing an anti-British movement in the tribal regions. Sodhi meanwhile had managed, in a drastic manner, to get in touch with the Soviet embassy in Kabul: 'He had just gate-crashed into the Soviet embassy and now contacts had been established.'[40] From then onwards Talwar played a double role: he took money from the Axis Powers and as agreed handed it over to the

Indian revolutionaries. At the same time he kept the Soviet diplomats informed of his activities.[41] He mentioned to a comrade-in-arms that he intended only to exploit the Germans: 'They were helping us to build an organization here which they thought would be useful to them to defeat the British when the time came. But that time might not come for them at all. But this organization of ours would certainly be immensely useful when time came for us to drive away the British.'[42]

OPERATING WITH PRISONERS OF WAR

Many Indians serving in the British army were taken in German captivity in the wake of military successes of the German Africa Corps. The first interrogations of Indian officers showed that some of them were definitely prepared to work together with the Germans. They cited as reasons condescending treatment and poor provisions by their English superiors. The Information Divison of the German Foreign Office saw at once the opportunity to make use of the Indian soldiers' dissatisfaction.[43]

Gurbachan Singh Mangat reports that British comrades had subjected the Indian prisoners of war in the Italian camps to discrimination. Thus the Indians had been unfairly treated in the distribution of food supply: 'The discriminatory attitude of the British undermined whatever of the Indian loyalty to the crown was left by those days.' Captain Sher Jang Panwar complained about this to the Italian camp superiors. The Italians reacted at once and turned the tables. Now the British had to clean the Indians' latrines. The Indian viceroy's commissioned officers (VCOs) had been put on a par with the British king's commissioned officers (KCOs).[44] As a result, one of the VCOs is said to have sent a petition to Mussolini offering to fight on the side of the Axis Powers against the British until these had been driven out of India.[45] Bose came to know on 14 April 1942, that of the 40,000 Allied soldiers taken captive in North Africa, 15,000 were Indians, and that some of those had bitterly complained about the unfair treatment meted out to them by their British officers. German and Italian officers were immediately instructed to treat the Indians with utmost consideration.[46]

On 16 May 1941, twenty-seven members of the Third Indian Motor Brigade, who had been selected after interrogations by German officers, were moved from the prisoner-of-war camp Barce near Benghazi, to Catania in Sicily. Alexander Werth, scientific assistant in the Information Division of the German Foreign Office, and Kirpa Ram Dhawan, a close associate of Bose hailing from northwest India like most of the prisoners of war, were there waiting for them. They questioned them intensively about their political inclinations. After that, the prisoners of war travelled on to Germany. Twenty men were brought to camp Annaberg, which was to be the central camp for all Indian prisoners of war. They were supposed to assist the camp authorities to learn about Indian food habits and other peculiarities. The remaining seven Indians were shifted to the Schlieffenufer barracks in Berlin.[47] The Germans needed their language skills. Some of them received training in telecommunication in the Foreign Office; others worked for the radio.[48]

The Italians were keeping guard over the prisoners of war as the Italian commando supremo was in supreme command of all troops of the Axis Powers in North Africa. They too did not want to miss the opportunity of using the Indians for their political aims. The Italian Foreign Ministry had prepared a 'Schema di lavore per l'India' in 1941 in which they provided for selecting soldiers from the prisoners suitable for political, technical and military training. These were then to be moved to the rebellious tribes at the Indian northwest frontier for operating as political agents or technical instructors. If a sufficient number of Indians were willing to cooperate, an Indian troop was to be formed to counter the Indian army or maybe for an invasion of India. Colonel Giovanni Tavazzani was put in charge of working with the Indian prisoners.[4950] Schedai was included in these operations. He was to act as Indian confidant. Schedai met Tavazzani on 26 April 1941. He was at once prepared to take up political propaganda among the Indian soldiers. He urged the officials of the Foreign Ministry, who took part in the discussion, to allow him to meet the prisoners of war, but they still had some reservations.[51]

THE ACTION 'BRITISH EMPIRE'

It seemed for a short while that Bose's wish for a declaration of India by the Axis Powers would be fulfilled. Woermann informed the heads of the departments that Hitler had sanctioned such a declaration. It was to be published within eight to ten days but the minister wanted to meet Bose once more before that. Bose and the experts of the German Foreign Office were to work out the text of the declaration together. In addition, everything was to be prepared in the matter of propaganda. They even considered arranging for a medium-wave transmitter in the Indian frontier region.[52] The head of the Foreign Office was in charge of propaganda action against the British Empire. Ribbentrop discussed the action with Ciano and Mussolini during their meeting in Venice on 13 May 1941. The protocol of the meeting notes that the Duce had agreed, without further discussion, that Italy together with Germany would 'stand up for the liberation of all peoples under British oppression'.[53]

The declaration on India to be proclaimed together with Italy was to start a large-scale action under the name 'British Empire'. It was further planned that faked enquiries at the press conference would provide an opportunity to the Foreign Office to recognize also the independence of Ireland and the South African Union. A repetition of the already proclaimed declaration of independence for the Arab countries was to be the high point of the action.[54] The 'Proclamation for a liberated India' had already been drafted. It was the abbreviated translation of a draft by Bose. It contained the sentence that Germany and Italy recognize 'solemnly the irrevocable right of the Indian people of complete and unlimited independence'. Based on Bose's draft, the proclamation further mentioned the exploitation of India through British imperialism, the right of Indians to chose their constitution, and the unity of the Indian nation. The German revisers added a reference to the Indian soldiers who 'have to shed their blood on the battlefields in Europe, Asia and Africa...'

The last sentence of Bose's draft underwent a small but significant change. While Bose had written: 'Germany [...] waits for the day when independent India will have her own national government, Germany will gladly recognize that government and establish friendly relations with it,' the German draft read: 'Germany and Italy [...] await the day when an independent India will have her own national representation.' The Germans did not want to give the promise to Bose of recognizing an independent India.[55]

Bose prepared a 'Detailed Plan of Work' which saw the opening of a 'Free India Centre' in Berlin with branches in other states as core pieces. This centre was to be the 'brain of the Indian revolution'. The liberation of India from colonial rule was to be directed and supported through propaganda from there. In order to achieve this, he wanted to engage radio, press, and a weekly publication with editions in German, Italian, French and Spanish. In addition, the plan contained a series of suggestions on how to further the revolution in India. Bose proposed now the building of a landing place in the tribal territory so that weapons and equipment could be brought into this region. A training centre for Indian officers should also be established there. He urged the formation of a 'Free Indian Legion' that should fight against Great Britain and later be sent to India.[56]

The Foreign Office found Bose's plans well suited to their plans. Ribbentrop was prepared to be generous in his support for the Indian. He granted the proud sum of one million Reichsmark for his work.[57] Bose's illegal transmission was supposed to start at the same time. Rühle now suggested installing a short-wave transmitter in Afghanistan so that Bose could broadcast from there.[58] The radio division and the Reichspost deliberated together how they could load the transmitter onto a lorry and send it like this to Afghanistan.[59] In spite of the detailed planning, the action 'British Empire' never took place. Trott called Bose in the third week of May and explained that there would be a small delay. The Indian was surprised: 'The speed with which the Führer had acted earlier, appeared to be out of step with this new attitude.'[60] The delay turned finally into a refusal.

On 23 June 1941, Woermann met representatives of the Italian Ministry for Popular Culture who happened to be in Berlin accompanying their minister Alessandro Pavaloni. Among other topics he also wanted to discuss India-politics. They readily came to an agreement: the Indian independence movement was to be supported without any interference in Indian internal politics and without giving any concrete statement about the future status of India.[61] Thus the declaration of India was already ignored during this conference. The Italians accepted without further argument the cancellation of the action, even though it had been discussed with Mussolini only a few days before. Woermann informed Bose on 24 May 1941 about Ribbentrop's decision that a declaration on India would not be proclaimed for the time being. However, preparations should be made for establishing the 'Free India Centre'. Bose had no option but to agree to the delay.[62]

It is not clear from the sources why the German Foreign Office first planned the large-scale propaganda action with considerable expenditures, only to cancel it again at short notice. Arvinda Katpitia presumes the reason to be a connection with the flight of Rudolf Hess to England on 10 May 1941: Hess had intended to offer Great Britain a 'peace settlement'. A declaration on India would have been inconvenient at that time.[63] Andreas Hillgruber also writes: 'There seems to be a connection when viewed upon axiomatically with Hitler's foreign policy in mind.'[64]

Milan Hauner offers the following interpretation: the German government lost interest in the Orient after Rashid Ali al-Gailani's coup d'état in Iraq had failed and the followers of King Faisal II with the help of British troops had the upper hand again. Rashid Ali al-Gailani had been favourably inclined towards the Axis Powers. Instead the Soviet Union now occupied centre place in Hitler's plans.[65] This interpretation is also supported by the fact that later on Ribbentrop mentioned to Bose the failure in Iraq as reason for the repeated refusal to proclaim a declaration on India.[66]

The department of the Foreign Office—for matters concerning India—seemed to look upon the plan of a declaration on India as delayed only and not as cancelled. They even planned to proclaim an Indian government in exile. Bose was to be 'President', Dhawan 'Prime Minister'. This plan never materialized even though Dhawan had already started to look for 'ministers' among the Berlin Indians.[67]

BOSE'S JOURNEY TO ITALY FROM MAY TO JULY 1941

Just before the cancellation of the propaganda action against the British Empire, Bose had received an invitation by the Italian government which he readily accepted.[68] Woermann was in favour of this journey to Rome.[69] Ribbentrop though had reservations. He demanded a report from Woermann about the way Bose had been treated while in Germany. In particular he wanted to know which person attended to Bose constantly, what financial means he had at his disposal, and whether he had been allotted a house in the meantime.[70] It seems he was worried that Bose would prefer to work with the Italians after the disappointment of the cancelled declaration on India. Woermann tried to reassure the minister that Bose's Italian journey had been planned from the very beginning. The Indian did not plan to stay longer than a fortnight in Rome. He intended to work together with the Germans also in the future. In order to motivate Bose, Woermann suggested an audience with the Führer.[71] Ribbentrop, however, remained cautious. He requested Woermann to prevent the journey. Yet he did not want to rule out the prospect of a meeting with Hitler.[72]

Bose travelled to Rome in spite of the minister's reservations. He arrived there on 29 May 1941 together with his secretary and companion Emilie Schenkl.[73] The Italian embassy in Berlin had been informed about the position of German India-politics and had also received a copy of a draft of the proposed declaration on India. Ribbentrop expressed the opinion that basically he agreed with the draft's contents but considered the formulation too inaccurate. The text was under revision. The Italians did not yet learn that the Führer had already prevented the declaration's publication.[74] The German embassy in Rome was instructed to keep a check on the Indian and to see to it that he returned to Germany as soon as possible.[75] Woermann also gave the reason for this: 'We are decidedly interested that Bose who had worked with us confidentially should not be persuaded to move the centre of his activities over there.'[76]

So the German Foreign Office was still very much interested in continuing to work with Bose. The diplomats must also have noticed Bose's dissatisfaction with the hitherto existing collaboration.[77] When Bose had not reported to the German embassy even after having been in Rome for eight days, Ambassador Otto Christian Prince von Bismarck Anlass thought it necessary to send a telegram to Berlin. On the occasion of his first reception by the Italian foreign minister Ciano on 6 June 1941, the responsible official experts drew Bose's attention to the German embassy's desire for contacting him.[78]

Bose responded and called on Bismarck on 11 June 1941. Bismarck requested him to return to Berlin soon. Bose declared he was not under the impression of being urgently needed in Berlin but clarified that he had no intention of moving the centre of his activities to Italy.[79][80] He promised to return to Germany shortly. Berlin was satisfied with this information. The embassy in Rome was now instructed not to bother Bose any more about a definite date of departure. Woermann received a letter from Bose giving his date of arrival in Berlin as 22 June 1941.[81] The departure was delayed, though, as Ciano wanted to meet Bose once more.[82] This meeting took place on 26 June 1941.[83]

Bose's meeting with Ciano

During the first meeting with Ciano on 6 June 1941, Bose did not deviate from the point of view he had expressed to the Germans as well. He did no longer press for a government in exile but stressed the importance of a declaration on India by the Axis Powers. He aired his views on propaganda activities, acts of sabotage and the formation of the Indian Legion, and talked about establishing a 'revolutionary committee' in Berlin or Rome as substitute for a government in exile.[84]

Ciano knew that Bose's proposals had been accepted in Berlin with great reservations. He too did not entertain great expectations by supporting Bose. He did not take him quite seriously. Besides, he did not quite know what to do with Bose.[85] He received him thus with cold diplomatic politeness.[86] It is therefore not surprising that Ciano readily agreed to the German politics with regard to India in the absence of any ideas of his own. The Italian foreign minister met his German counterpart in Venice on 15 June 1941 when they also discussed Bose. Ribbentrop explained that he wanted to support Bose's anti-British propaganda but considered a declaration in support of India's independence too premature. So far the Führer had not received Bose. However, the Indian wanted to stay in touch with the German Foreign Office.[87]

Ciano allowed himself to be influenced by his German counterpart's opinion. During the second meeting on 26 June 1941 he informed Bose that he was in agreement with the Reich's government in considering it more purposeful to postpone the declaration on India for some time. Bose was deeply disappointed and declared that under these circumstances he could not engage in any activities without compromising himself before the Italian public. The Palazzo Chigi now held the opinion that it would be best to let Bose wait in a neutral country until one could make use of him again.[88] Woermann though called this proposal misguided.[89]

Bose and Schedai

It is also possible that Ciano was influenced by Schedai in his reserved behaviour towards Bose. Bose had several meetings with Schedai and his followers during his stay in Rome. Schedai pulled his fellow countryman to pieces in his reports to the Foreign Ministry: 'We absolutely refuse to cooperate with him and he has not gained our confidence,' he let them know. Two days before Bose's meeting with the foreign minister, Schedai questioned in a letter Bose's importance as political leader and warned against cooperating with him:

> He has no organization of his own in India which is really a revolutionary one. [...] I have told you that all parties in India are against Mr Bose and especially the All-India National Congress which expelled him from its ranks for three years. It is a pity that none has faith in him. He has some followers in Bengal but most of the Bengalis are against him. [...] If he can be of some use at present he must be used but I would request you to be very careful.[90]

It is not surprising that Ciano did not take Bose seriously as he had read this letter before the meeting. Actually Schedai must have been well informed about Bose's real political importance. However, personal rivalry made him refuse any cooperation with him and induced him to run him down before higher authorities. Schedai had worked hard at achieving the position as preferential Indian confidant with the Italian government. And now Bose arrived and might make him take a back seat. Bose was immediately received personally by the foreign minister while Schedai waited in vain for such honour.

Bose returned to Berlin on 8 July 1941. He had not managed to achieve concrete agreements with the Italian government. A cooperation with his fellow countrymen had also not been realized. Anyhow, he had left a strong impression on the Foreign Ministry's staff: 'He is without doubt a strong personality of the first order whose work will be useful for us,' the Foreign Ministry informed the German embassy.[91] The three Indian revolutionaries quarrelled because of Bose: Labh Singh saw in Bose the man of the hour and preferred to accept his leadership. Ajit Singh on the other hand took Schedai's side and took up his hostile attitude towards Bose. The disagreements resulted in a break-up that lasted until the end. Neither Ajit Singh nor Schedai went to Labh Singh's funeral in 1943.[92]

BOSE AND THE OPERATION BARBAROSSA

Bose came to know of the German attack on the Soviet Union while in Rome. With the beginning of 'Unternehmen Barbarossa' on 22 July 1941, Bose's overland connection with India was cut off. His plans of bringing men and material via the Soviet Union to Afghanistan and India could not materialize any more. In his detailed plan of work Bose had still written: 'A German-Soviet agreement on the question of India would be exceedingly desirable.'[93] Now such an agreement was out of question. The changed circumstances dimmed his hope of being able to realize his revolutionary plans at all. He was not very keen to return to Berlin. He wrote to Woermann: 'The public reaction in my country to the new situation in the East is unfavourable towards your government.' However, he let himself be persuaded finally to return to Germany.[94]

After his return Bose went to call on Woermann on 17 June 1941. He explained to the undersecretary of state the difficulties arising for him from the German-Soviet war. The Soviet Union had always been for the Indian an anti-imperialistic power. The Hitler-Stalin pact of 1938 had made it possible for the Indian intelligence to look upon Germany also as a friendly power. Now public opinion was more on the side of the Soviet Union. It was now easy for the British to claim Germany to be a dangerous imperialistic power also for India. Thereupon Woermann promised him the declaration on India at a 'suitable point of time'.[95]

This suitable point of time, however, was still elusive. In the coming weeks Bose limited his activities to drawing up general plans and routine contacts with the representatives of the Foreign Office. For the time being Bose decided not to contact Indians living in Germany because of the uncertainty in the wake of the German-Soviet war. In the succeeding weeks he kept himself more or less isolated and without any activities in his new residence in the Charlottenburg Sophienstrasse. His private secretary, Vyas, was the only fellow countryman he met regularly.[96]

The Progress of India-Politics during Bose's Incognito

‿◈‿

Bose refused at first to participate in the Third Reich's India-politics without the official declaration in support of India's independence. Thus he stayed for several months incognito in Germany. He continued to call himself Orlando Mazzotta, the name he had originally assumed as disguise only for his journey from Afghanistan to Europe, until he decided at the end of the year to revert to his own name because of the developments in East Asia. Meanwhile, the India-politics of the Axis Powers progressed considerably in spite of restrictions due to Bose's disguise.

THE 'SONDERREFERAT INDIEN'

During Bose's stay in Rome, the Information Division of the German Foreign Office had formed a special working group dealing with India, the 'Arbeitskreis Indien'. As a reaction to Bose's memorandum, together with the Indian and in constant consultation with the political department, they began hunting for experts to assist them in their India-specific propaganda. The working group grew into the 'Sonderreferat Indien' (SRI), the Special Department India.[1] Besides others, Ludwig Alsdorf and Franz-Josef Furtwängler were some of the experts to work for the SRI. Alsdorf taught Indology at the Münster University and had published a handbook on India[2] that was very popular at that time. Furtwängler was a former trade union official and had written several books on India. The Foreign Office employed the writer Giselher Wirsing as German language teacher for Bose who lived secluded in his hotel room for the initial months of his stay in Germany. Bose grasped the language very fast, and he could give his public speeches later on in German.[3]

The Sonderreferat and the German opposition

The scientific assistant Adam von Trott zu Solz was in charge of the Sonderreferat. Trott had studied as a Rhodes scholarship holder in Oxford after completing his law studies. After the beginning of the war he was asked by the Foreign Office to go on a study tour to North America and East Asia.[4] After this he worked in the information divison. There he was put in charge of the special sections on America and East Asia. His critical attitude towards National Socialism is well known. He belonged to the Kreisauer Kreis and was part of the group responsible for the assault on Hitler on 20 July 1944. Carl Friedrich Gördeles's shadow government had provided for him the post of secretary of state in the Foreign Office because of his good contacts with the Anglo-Saxon world. Trott was executed in Berlin a few weeks after the failed coup d'état.

Trott had already worked on an India project since the end of 1940.[5] After Bose's arrival in Germany, Trott was asked on Woermann's recommendation to attend to Bose. Woermann wrote: 'Trott has the necessary initiative, he speaks excellent English and would be eminently suited for Bose, particularly from the psychological point of view.'[6] The India-section was in various ways important for Trott's oppositional activities. It was possible for him to undertake various travels abroad to neutral and occupied countries where he could have contact with like-minded people.[7] The Indian fight for independence fitted well into his political concept. Had the coup d'état against Hitler succeeded, the new government would have had to enter immediately into negotiations with the war opponents in order to end the war as soon as possible. Each weakening of England's position would have meant a strengthening of the German position in negotiation. Trott did not view British rule over India sympathetically even though he had made many English friends during his time in Oxford. He shared with his English friends the notion that England's imperialism was as detestable as the Nazi regime. The struggle for India's freedom became Trott's niche where he could serve the German government without having to compromise his convictions.[8]

Trott did not confide in the Indians with whom he worked. But they sensed that actually they were for him just the means for another aim. Vyas criticized later that Trott had not been able to hide a hostile attitude towards Bose and that he had actually not desired India's freedom: 'He never expressed it plainly, but behind the diplomatic expressions he frequently used, lurked the suggestion that the best India could aspire for was a gradual transition towards a 'distant goal' of dominium status in the British Empire.' In spite of all differences Trott had been always cordial and never malicious and had always kept all agreements.[9]

The Kreisauer Kreis was not unanimous in their attitude towards British colonial rule. Helmuth James Count von Moltke, whose mother was English, had a definite England-friendly attitude. For him the Empire was the model of a world organization and he regretted the independence endeavours of its members.[10] He had an argument with Furtwängler about the future status of India. While Furtwängler stood for the independence of the subcontinent, Moltke would at most concede dominion status.[11]

The position of the Sonderreferat in the Foreign Office

The Sonderreferat India was separated from the information department and placed directly under SS-Gruppenführer (lieutenant general) Wilhelm Keppler who held an unusual position in the Foreign Office as secretary of state for special duty. Keppler had discontinued studying mechanical engineering and had been working as a businessman in the chemical industry. He joined the NSDAP in 1927, and as Hitler's economical advisor had established contacts with industrial magnates and bankers. In 1938 he held the temporary post as Reich's commissioner and then the Reich's representative for Austria. He was also in charge of the head office for the NSDAP's economic organization and president of the Reich's office for soil research. As secretary of state for special utilization, he worked mainly in special diplomatic missions. Thus he organized together with Arthur Seiss-Inquart the annexation of Austria; made preparations for establishing the Protectorate of Bohemia, Moravia and independent Slovakia; was instrumental in founding the Croatian Ustascha-State; and was actively involved in the occupation of Hungary. Keppler was considered one of the exponents of the SS in foreign policy and thought of himself more as being an SS leader than a diplomat.[12]

Ribbentrop put Bose under Keppler's care in June 1941 and

transferred the overall direction of the propaganda for India to him as well. The political approach with the Indian, however, remained in the hands of Secretary of State Ernst von Weizsäcker.[13] Thus India-politics continued to be the responsibility of the political department while the related propaganda received the status of a special mission. The Reich's foreign minister's decision of putting Keppler in charge of propaganda is proof of the great importance he gave to this mission. Bose's private secretary Vyas writes in his memoirs that Hitler had personally put Bose under Keppler's care in order to be able to intervene directly in India-politics and to raise the value of Bose's position: 'This established a direct link between him [Hitler] and Subhas Bose, as would be the case between the head of a state and the German Chancellor. It removed the danger of the lesser bureaucrats of the German Foreign Ministry treating the Indian affairs as merely a departmental affair.'[14]

The political attitudes of Trott and Keppler, the two personalities responsible for Bose, could not have been more different at that time: On the one hand, a man of the resistance movement and conspirator; a deserving party member and SS general on the other. In spite of their ideological differences it seemed Trott and Keppler worked together amiably. Thus Keppler used his influence when Trott was to be promoted to the civil service and later on to the position of councillor of a legation.[15]

The objectives of the Sonderreferat

The special fund of one million Reichsmark which Ribbentrop had granted so generously for India-related activities and which was to have been used for the action planned for May 1941, the action 'Britisches Weltreich' or 'British Empire', was still available and was now under the administration of the Sonderreferat India. The money was to be used for the objectives defined as follows:

1. Publication in Germany of valuable propaganda material about India,
2. Compilation of political and economic news for the various departments in the Foreign Office,
3. Producing manuscripts for radio propaganda,
4. Establishing an information service with confidants in Asia,

5. Preparing a list of all Indians and experts on India in Germany and in friendly or occupied countries and looking after them,
6. Financial support for Bose and his followers in India,
7. Training of Indian prisoners of war for propaganda work and for forming the Indian Legion,
8. Looking after and directing the 'Zentrale Freies Indien' (Free India Centre) and the Indian colonies in Germany and abroad, and
9. Harmonizing and cooperating with the personalities responsible for Italian India-politics.[16]

The series of writings on India were published quite early. Some of the first titles to be checked by Franziska Kruse, reader for the information divison, were 'India's Economy' by Hermann Luft and 'Men and Powers in the India of Today' by Bose's private secretary Mukund R. Vyas,[17] followed by 'What is India?' by Hermann Beythan, a handbook with the Indian Professor Kodavooru Anantarama Bhatta as co-author, and 'Monuments of Indian Art' by Wilhelm Kruse. Bhatta's book 'India in the British Empire' was a depiction of Indian history. 'The Social Question in India' by Beythan dealt with the subontinent's social history. Alsdorf's contribution about 'German-Indian Spiritual Relations' and 'The Islam in India' by Abid Hasan rounded off the series comprising eight volumes, published in Heidelberg by Kurt Vowinckel under the title 'India in Monographs'. The SRI was to publish a series on the 'supply of a lucid source of foreign affairs information for all German government departments dealing with India.'[18]

After this they tried contacting nationalist Indian groups in neutral countries.[19] An official circular was sent to the German representatives in Ankara, Buenos Aires, Rio de Janeiro, Washington, Lisbon, Mexico, New York, Chicago, San Francisco and Dublin with the instruction to 'establish contacts with more active national-Indian elements in an unobtrusive manner'. These endeavours, however, hardly yielded any results. The German embassy in Washington though did manage to distribute propaganda pamphlets through the India League of America, thanks to Consul General Karl Kapp, who had once been posted in Bombay as consul. Sudhindra Bose, lecturer at the University of Iowa, agreed to publish a manuscript of the SRI under his name.[20] However, when the American press reported on 11 November 1941 that Bose was either in Berlin or in Rome, it was feared that all publications referring to him would be considered as German propaganda only.[21]

The department of 'Reichsführer SS and Head of the German Police' sent a list with 148 Indians registered in the Reich.[22] This list, however, contained many names of persons who had already left Germany long ago.[23] It was finally possible though to find qualified persons from the Indian colony of the Reich for cooperating with the Foreign Office. As a curiosity this list contains also some Indians classified as 'Volksdeutsche', i.e. ethnic Germans abroad. This 'ethnic German' Indians were evidently children of German mothers and Indian fathers. As per law valid at that time the wife of a foreign husband obtained the husband's nationality and her children their father's.

Trott made contact with Carl Rudolf Rasmuss, commercial attaché in Kabul. Rasmuss was to obtain information about India for the information department. Thereupon the SRI received most of the information from India via Afghanistan.[24] Bhagat Ram Talwar, who had assisted Bose in his escape, was a confidant of the German embassy in Kabul and worked now for the Germans under the code name Rahmat Khan. The German embassy was in a permanent dangerous situation as the governments of Great Britain and the Soviet Union had considerable influence in Afghanistan. The Afghan government finally yielded to the pressure of the Allied Powers and expelled all German and Italian nationals with the exception of the diplomatic corps.[25] The embassy continued to function but Trott thought it expedient to find alternative means of obtaining news from India, all the more so as they never managed to achieve regular courier service or a reliable wireless connection via the frontier territory to Bose's followers in India.[26] The embassy in Bangkok was instructed to establish a courier service to Calcutta.[27] Ambassador Georg Thomas located a Bengali who had Thai nationality. This gentleman agreed to receive Bose's confidants as his personal visitors. A regular courier service could not be established though as the British kept strict guard over the border to Burma and Malaya.[28] Trott also thought of a connection via neutral Portugal and her Indian colony Goa.[29]

In the event of a possible closure of the German embassy in Kabul, they had the following plan under consideration: a wireless operator from the embassy was to be hidden in the Afghan mountains with a transmitter and a wireless connection maintained from there.[30] However, the embassy in Kabul was active until the end of the war and supplied an abundance of information about India to Berlin. The fortnightly 'Indienberichte' (reports from India) published by the SRI for the other departments of the Foreign Office were based on these informative reports. The 'Indiennachrichten' (news from India) were regularly compiled from press and agency announcements and distributed in editors' offices of German newspapers on broadsheets decorated with the Indian national colours saffron, white and green.

Ribbentrop attached great importance to the fact that his ministry should remain the principal German governmental department for India-politics. When the foreign minister of the Reich came to know that his rival Alfred Rosenberg, Reichsminister for the occupied territories in the East and head of the foreign affairs department of the NSDAP, had managed to get Hitler interested through a presentation about British rule in India, he on his part wanted to make a presentation to the Führer on the same subject. He ordered his staff to work out a paper of about thirty to forty pages, highlighting 'British artfulness in *divide et impera*.'[31] Ribbentrop formed a working committee with Ambassador Karl Maria Count Podewils-Duernitz and Consul General Kapp, two diplomats who had been posted in India before the war, as members. The expertise of the SRI was to be represented by Alsdorf.[32] Ten days later a paper of fifty pages was ready, entitled 'Basis, Construction, and Methods of British Rule in India.'[33] Ribbentrop could proudly present this to his Führer. It is not known whether Hitler had at all taken the trouble to read this voluminous memorandum. Later on he recommended presenting Alsdorf's book on India to Rosenberg, which he had read himself.[34]

THE 'ZENTRALE FREIES INDIEN'

One of the tasks of the SRI was the formation of the 'Zentrale Freies Indien' (ZFI), the Free India Centre. While only German experts worked in the SRI, the ZFI was to be managed by Indians only. At first the ZFI was to function as the 'unofficial collecting point for all Indian national endeavours under Bose's leadership.' On Ribbentrop's instruction, the ZFI was to function in public after the German government had published its declaration on India. The centre's activities were to be constantly monitored by the Sonderreferat and it was to serve as its 'mouthpiece'.[35] Bose suggested the founding of the Zentrale for the first time in his 'Detailed plan of work' of 20 May 1941. Initially it was to serve as 'core piece' of the propaganda action 'Britisches Weltreich'.[36] In spite of the action's cancellation the foundation was to take place.[37]

Initially the ZFI was to function in Berlin, but 'by establishing the head office in Switzerland a neutral image was to be created.'[38] The embassy in Bern, however, had reservations about this endeavour. Swiss officials did not take kindly to establishments engaged in propaganda against one of the parties at war. They might disrupt the functioning of an India-centre in Switzerland or even stop it completely. Thereupon the plan of moving the Zentrale into a neutral country was dropped altogether. Woermann called all representatives of the departments engaged in India-politics for a meeting.[39]

The objectives of the ZFI

At the meeting, the undersecretary of state presented a detailed organization plan regulating construction and functioning of the ZFI. There were to be nine sections. A general department was to be responsible for the administration; a press department was to obtain Indian newspapers, survey the news services of various countries, distribute a news service for the German press and friendly countries, and publish a weekly journal in German and several foreign languages. Similarly, the radio department was to survey radio stations, pass on their news through a press service, and prepare transmissions for their own transmitter 'Freies Indien' (Free India).[40]

The organization plan shows clearly that the ZFI was to be used mainly for propaganda purposes. In the same way the Foreign Office wanted to use Indian nationalists for their own propaganda activities. This was certainly in keeping with Bose's ideas about the functioning of the Zentrale. His plan for a Free India Centre also provided for using the same mainly for anti-British propaganda. Bose even wanted to let the Zentrale engage in 'subtle propaganda in favour of the Axis Powers'.There was, however, one difference between Bose's plans and those of the Foreign Office: Bose wanted to extend the Zentrale to be the 'brain of India revolution', an objective not considered in

Woermann's draft.[41] This shows once more the basic problem of Bose's collaboration with the German government officials: the Indian wanted solely to serve the freedom struggle in his own country from Germany, while the Foreign Office wanted to use him as a propaganda figure. Bose was able to carry his ideas through when finally the Free India Centre started functioning. Keppler's 'Working plan for India propaganda' drafted in autumn 1942 mentioned explicitly that planning for the new construction of India 'was part of the objectives of the Zentrale. German government departments were even supposed to support these activities.[42]

A commission of representatives of the Foreign Office, the Home Office and the Ministry for Propaganda sat together with Bose to discuss preparations for organizing the ZFI. They were very surprised when Bose demanded for the Zentrale the status of a legation of a free country, complete freedom in organizing radio propaganda and financial independence. The government officials did not want to make concessions and resorted instead to threats in order to force Bose into submission. The Indian risked causing a stir and informed his negotiation partners: 'I have not come to Europe to live an idle, luxurious exile. I know your secret service is efficient. But so is the British CID. in India, and I have risked my life to escape them. I shall not mind trying to go elsewhere if my mission requires it.'[43] The officials of the German government were not used to such speeches from foreign allies and collaborators. But Bose carried his point. Keppler intervened and requested Consul General Kapp, who knew Bose from Calcutta, to come to an agreement with the Indian. Essentially Bose carried his ideas through: the Free India Centre became an independent establishment under his direction with financial autonomy, enjoyed diplomatic immunity, and was allowed to freely shape radio transmissions.[44]

Bose's search for assistants

Bose needed to find suitable staff before the Zentrale could start functioning. The SRI helped by locating known Indian personalities. The medical practitioner Kirpa Ram Dhawan, born in 1895 in the Northwest Frontier Province, became the first staff member. He had come to Europe in 1921, studied medicine in Berlin, and had been actively involved in the Hindustan Association.[45] Later on he worked at the Charité. He was the Foreign Office's confidant for Indian matters.[46] He was introduced in this capacity to Bose soon after his arrival. Emilie Schenkl and Mukund Rai Vyas were next in line.

N. Gopal Swami from Madras became another close associate. He was born in 1911 in Kalanivasal in the district of Tanjore and had come to Germany for studying at the Technical University in Charlottenburg. He met Bose in Berlin and also kept contact with Nambiar. In August 1935 he participated in the Oriental Students' Congress in Rome. In December 1938 he was one of the leaders at a meeting of the Asians in Berlin at the German Oriental Association and was the main speaker in January 1939 at a rally of the Indian Students' Association on the occasion of the Indian Independence Day.[47] He worked for Siemens after his final examinations as certified engineer, in order to gain some professional expertise before returning to India. He kept his position after the outbreak of war and only had to report to the police once a week. Initially he refused any request from the Foreign Office for assisting in propaganda transmissions. Government officials introduced him to Bose in mid-August. Swami resigned from his job and started working for Bose.[48]

Abid Hasan, born in 1911 in Hyderabad in the Deccan, was a friend and fellow student of Swami. He had been imprisoned in Bombay for six months for having participated in Gandhi's non-cooperation movement in 1931 and emigrated to Germany after that. Like Swami, he was also involved in the Indian Students' Association and is said to have published government-friendly press articles in Germany. He wrote an article for the German armed forces entitled 'Islam in India—India in World Islam'.[49]

The journalist Arathil Candeth Narayan Nambiar , born in 1896 in Tellicharry in south India, was carrying on an Indian information bureau in Berlin since 1929 as representative of the Congress party. The bureau was closed by the Gestapo in 1933 and Nambiar was expelled. He stayed at first in Prague where he worked as correspondent for Indian newspapers and engaged himself actively for India's independence. He met Bose several times and helped him with the founding of the Indian Students' Association and the Indo-Technical Association. Nehru visited Nambiar in Prague and engaged him as Europe correspondent for the Lucknow paper *The National Herald*. Nambiar went to Paris after the Germans marched into Prague.

There he continued working for the Indian papers *The Hindu, Amrita Bazar Patrika, Bombay Chronicle* and *The National Herald*. After the Germans marched into Paris, he fled to the unoccupied zone in the south of France. The British police had him registered as '100 per cent anti-Nazi'.[50] Initially it was difficult for the German embassy in Paris to locate him.[51] It was not easy to persuade him to cooperate because of his bad experiences with the National Socialists. Bose had to go personally to Paris in August 1941. Werth and the Indian Iqbal Schedai, who was working for the Italians, accompanied him. Nambiar finally agreed to go to Berlin with Bose. In Paris Bose had the opportunity to meet the president of the Cabinet Council of the État Français, Pierre Laval. Laval was favourably inclined towards the Indian independence movement, even as the administrations of the French colonies in India had subordinated themselves under Charles de Gaulles's government in exile.[52]

Nahar Govind Ganpuley, born in Pune in 1895, was engaged as a businessman in Germany since 1922. He represented German firms during his travels to India. He represented an electrical undertaking from Bombay and Lahore in Germany since August 1939. Habibur Rahman was born in Delhi in 1901 and enrolled as a mechanical engineering student in Berlin in 1923. He married a German in 1933 and like Ganpuley was involved in the Indian Students' Association. He worked with Bose since 1934 as a journalist and correspondent for Indian newspapers. He accompanied Hitler on his journey to Italy in 1938 and reported on the Reichstag. After the outbreak of the war, he wrote articles about India for leading German newspapers such as the *Frankfurter Allgemeine Zeitung* and the *Deutsche Allgemeine Zeitung*.[53] Kodavooru Anantarama Bhatta, son of a Hindu priest, was born in 1908 near Madras. He came to Germany in 1931 for studying medicine but changed his mind and taught Sanskrit instead at the universities in Tübingen and Berlin.[54]

Girija Kanta Mookerjee was born in East Bengal in 1905. He came to London in 1931 and studied for some time at the School of Oriental Studies but was expelled because of political activities. He managed to get away on his journey back and returned to London. Supported by Gandhi's friend Charles F. Andrews, he published in 1937 the book *The Rise and Growth of the National Indian Congress*. He was holding the post of a Sanskrit lecturer at the Prague University since October

1937. He met Nambiar in Prague. After the German troops marched in, he fled to Paris where he managed to survive as correspondent of *Hindustan Times*. After the French capitulation, the Wehrmacht interned him as a British subject.[55] He was soon released though and told that 'the German Reich does not consider Indians as enemies'.[56] Free again, he was twice visited by Nambiar and he accepted the latter's invitation to come to Berlin 'because I had visions of a heated room and a warm bed as I was sure that these would be available in the stronghold of Europe's rulers.'[57]

Dattatraya Ramnath Keni, born around 1915, hailed from the Portuguese colony of Goa. He went to Berlin in 1937 and received a diploma in electrical technology from the Technical University. Like Swami and Hasan, he too was involved in the activities of the Indian Students' Association. He was in India at the outbreak of the war but returned in March 1940 on an Italian liner.[58] Ambika Charan Majumdar, born in 1905 in Bengal, had come to Berlin in 1936 as leader of a group of singers and dancers who had won a gold medal in supporting programmes of the Olympic Games. He had toured Germany with the group in 1938. He studied music in Königsberg on a scholarship until 1939. Bose knew his family in Calcutta and convinced him to join the ZFI. Majumdar initiated the cultural programme 'Namaste India' in the short-wave service of the Reichsrundfunkgesellschaft, the official broadcasting corporation of the Reich, from April 1942 onwards.[59]

Khurshed Burjorji Mama, a Parsee, was born in Surat in 1914. After his finals at the Bombay University, he worked at the local branch of the AEG. They sent him to Berlin for training in September 1938. Ali Mohammed Sultan was born in 1905 in Hyderabad in the Deccan. In early 1931 he went to England and later to Berlin for studying botanical science. The outbreak of war surprised him when he was about to return to India. He was married to a German. Braja Lal Mukherji, born in 1912 in Midnapore (Bengal) came to Germany in 1937 to study textile dye methods. He worked in several firms of the paint industry.[60]

Lekh Raj Ahuja, born in 1916 in Bannu in the Northwest Frontier Province, studied medicine in Indore in the Central Province and came to Vienna for further studies in 1938. Saidudin Swallhay, born in 1917 in Meerut (United Provinces), had studied agriculture in Aligarh before he came to London in 1931 for further studies on a scholarship by the Indian government. He received a scholarship in 1936 for his doctorate in agriculture at the Berlin University.[61] He presented a dissertation in 1943 on the subject 'The New Development of the Dairy Market in England and Wales as well as a Short Comparative Depiction of the Dairy Business Position in India'.[62]

Pappu Balkrishna Sarma was born in 1910 in Puthur, Madras Presidency. After studying natural sciences in London, he came to Berlin in 1933 for practical training in a sugar factory. He worked for one year in a pharmaceutical factory in Barcelona, fled then from the civil war and started studying in Vienna for his doctorate in chemistry and physics.[63] His father could not send him any money after the outbreak of war and he received a stipend for studying at the Berlin University.[64]

The number of assistants increased rapidly. A list compiled in March 1942 showed thirteen Indians working for Bose. Eight were active in radio propaganda only. Three German female secretaries were also employed, as well as the Orientalist Freda Kretschmar as librarian, and the scientific assistant Kurt Assmann as liaison officer to the Sonderreferat Indien.[65] With this, Bose was supported by a staff of men hailing from various regions of India and belonging to various religions, all between twenty-four and forty-seven years of age. Nearly all of them had academic training and had been living in Germany for several years. Many were active in the Indian Students' Association. Some Indians living in Germany kept completely away from politics during the entire war, like Gopal Mamdapurkar, who studied medicine in Berlin during the war.[66] Besides Dhawan, Vyas, Swami, Hasan and Nambiar, no one knew of Bose's stay in Berlin. Bose was very particular about keeping this a secret. The meetings with his confidants amounted almost to a conspiracy.

Solemn inauguration and selection of symbolism

Sarma remembered later that he did read about Bose's escape in the newspapers and that he also had heard rumours about his stay in Germany, but could not see any rhyme or reason in it when one day he received a telephone call from the Foreign Office: 'I remember exactly, it was the 8th of January 1942, all of us received telephone calls from the Foreign Office asking us to come to tea at the Hotel Kaiserhof in

Berlin. We all went there, and when I came into the lobby, I saw Netaji Subhas Bose.'[67]

Mookerjee remembered having received quite a shock when he received the information that he would soon meet Bose. He was a guest at a celebration in honour of Bose's birthday on 25 January 1942 and met there some of his compatriots and future fellow travellers. He describes impressively how the politician charmed his guests: 'How different Subhas was from our other Indian leaders! Everyone sensed his greatness but no one was overawed; he was completely natural and won over the hearts of even those compatriots who did not share his convictions.'[68]

Many Indians had reservations about working with Bose. They had suffered bad experiences with the National Socialists and found it very difficult to work with them. Mookerjee reports that Bose's repeatedly mentioned argument that 'England's enemy is my friend' convinced the freedom-loving Indians. He is said to have observed that the freedom struggle remained an entirely Indian matter even though the Germans supported it. In this connection it was irrelevant what the Germans did in Europe.[69]

The Free India Centre, 'Azad Hind Sangh' in Hindustani, was solemnly inaugurated on 2 November 1941 after the Foreign Office had arranged a function for it in the Tiergarten (Lichtensteiner Allee 2a), the part of Berlin where the diplomats stayed. The staff of the ZFI enjoyed the same status as the members of foreign diplomatic missions. Bose had so far lived in various hotels and moved now to a representative villa in Charlottenburg (Sophienstrasse 6-7).[70] The Centre was financed by the Foreign Office as loan to be repaid by the government of an independent India after the war. Bose had suggested this procedure in his memorandum of 9 April 1941. As a matter of fact, the Japanese government handed over half a million yen to the German ambassador in Tokyo in 1944, a sum Bose had collected from East Asian expatriate Indians as head of the 'Provisional Government of Free India' which the Japanese supported.[71]

In spite of the diplomatic status, the Germans kept the Centre and Bose under constant surveillance. Bose knew that his telephone conversations were intercepted and conversed therefore in Hindi or Bengali with his assistants. He found out that his personal belongings were repeatedly checked and that his domestic staff spied on him.

Therefore he could discuss important matters in the garden only. He suffered very much because of this mistrust but was prepared to carry on in spite of these unpleasant circumstances.[72]

Four resolutions concerning Indian national symbolism were decided upon during the first meeting at the inauguration on 2 November 1941. As various religious communities in India use different forms of salutation, it was necessary to create a common salutation stressing national unity that should be used by all Indians. The salutation Jai Hind, meaning 'Victory to India', was selected as substitute for Namaste or Ram Ram of the Hindus and the Salam Aleikum of the Muslims. The title given to Subhas Chandra Bose was even more influenced by the German example. German government officials addressed him as 'Excellency'. His friends chose another title for him. As Gandhi was called the Mahatma, Bose became now Netaji, a combination of the Hindustani word for leader and the suffix 'ji' expressing reverence.[73]

The poem 'Jana Gana Mana' by the Indian Nobel laureate Rabindranath Tagore was declared the national anthem in preference to 'Vande Mataram' used by the Congress party. Independent India agreed with this decision and declared Tagore's song as the official national anthem.[74]

Another decision concerned the national language of India. Many different languages are spoken on the subcontinent. The official language of British India was of course English which had replaced Persian used by the Mughals. The nationalists desired to introduce a language of Indian origin as the official language. At that time Hindustani was the most-spoken language in South Asia, and it enjoys this status even today. Hindustani is the lingua franca of north India and encompasses Urdu as well as Hindi. Urdu contains many elements of Persian and Arabic. It is written in a version of the Arabic script called Nastaliq. The Persian and Arabic parts have been replaced with Sanskrit elements in Hindi. Hindi uses the Devanagari script of Sanskrit. Muslims speak mostly Urdu; Hindus mostly Hindi. Bose wanted to introduce a Hindustani using the Latin script in order to overcome these differences, thus creating a common national language for all Indians.[75] Independent India later introduced Hindi as the national language. Urdu became the national language of Pakistan. Nowadays the Indian armed forces use a simplified Hindi written in Latin script.

The saffron-white-green tricolor of the Congress party was chosen as the national flag. However, a springing tiger replaced the spinning wheel in the centre of the Congress flag signifying Gandhi's principle of non-violence. This flag was envisaged as the battle flag and was to be replaced with a more suitable symbol after obtaining independence.[76] It was hoisted over the compound of the FZI during each function.[77] Later on it became the banner for the troops of the Indian Legion.

RADIO AZAD HIND

Soon the ZFI staff members were mainly busy with preparing the daily radio transmissions which the Indians could transmit on their own and independently of the Indian programmes of the German short-wave transmitter. Plans for a secret Indian transmitter had already been initiated soon after Bose's arrival. The realization of these plans was delayed, however, as Bose and the Foreign Office could not agree on a common concept for India-related activities. Bose did not want to address the public unless the Axis Powers guaranteed Indian independence. On the other hand, he could also not sit idle for months on end. Therefore, he made an application towards the end of the year to be allowed to start the transmissions the prospect of which had been held out to him on his arrival. Ribbentrop and Joseph Goebbels, Reichsminister for mass education and propaganda, gave their consent.[78] The Foreign Office defined the guidelines in a working agreement between the two offices from 22 October 1941; the production and transmission of the programmes were, however, the responsibility of the Ministry for Propaganda.[79]

This ministry decided in agreement with the Foreign Office that Bose be allowed to transmit for thirty minutes daily.[80] Censorship was to be the common responsibility of the representatives of the Foreign Office, the Ministry for Propaganda and the German Radio Corporation. In order not to offend Bose's sensibilities, censorship was to be carried out 'with utmost care so that Mr B. on no account might notice it.'[81] This censorship must have been done very discreetly if indeed it was done at all. Vyas, who was in charge of radio transmissions in the ZFI, relates in 1982 that Bose could ward off any attempt by German government officials to influence the shaping of the programmes and that the transmissions were never censored.[82]

The first transmission of Radio Azad Hind (Radio Free India) went on air on 6 January 1942. Bose could transmit his programmes every day from 5 p.m. to 5.30 p.m. via the Czech radio station Podiebrad.[83] Radio Azad Hind belonged to the group of Concordia transmissions, then existing besides the official German short-wave programmes. Outwardly, they were engaged in a completely independent propaganda directed at nations or groups that might be dissatisfied with the British government. The British Broadcasting Station and various radio stations aimed at separatist Scots and Welshmen, a station called Workers' Challenge and a programme for pacifists by the name of 'Christian Peace Movement' were some of them.[84] These stations were feared by the British authorities. The Ministry for Propaganda intercepted a transmission by Radio Daventry on 13 March 1942, warning its listeners thus:

> One of the methods used by the Germans in order to spread doubt, terror, worries and disturbance, and which they use in particular for undermining trust in the government, are the fraudulent transmissions pretending to originate in the country chosen for harassment. The Germans are now busy in broadcasting transmissions stating to be the voice of free India, the voice of free Egypt, and even the voices of Australia and New Zealand.[85]

The programme of Radio Azad Hind was composed of news, commentaries, interviews and the so-called talks on political, cultural or humourous themes. The speakers were all Indians. The programmes were designed not to betray any German influence outwardly. For this reason, 'a certain independence in commenting on European problems was permissible,' even though the broadcasts were aimed at 'educating the Indian listener in the German and anti-British sense.' Any interference in internal Indian political controversies was to be avoided. Therefore, Bose was to refrain from attacking any of his political opponents in the Congress party.[86]

Bose accepted these restrictions with poor grace. But already during the first talks, the SRI staff member Furtwängler showed him the limitations of his possibilities: 'You may not even dream of opposing under the protectorate of Hitler the revered aged Mahatma to whom India owes thanks for everything.'[87] Initially, all broadcasts were in Hindustani, soon to be followed by programmes in Pashto, Bengali, Persian, Telugu, Marathi, Kannada, Gujarati and English with Indian accent. Four hours were alloted for these broadcasts daily.[88] Bose was responsible for shaping the programme of the secret radio station and he could extensively air his own political positions, but Bose's part in these was kept a secret for the listeners. Bose refused to have his name mentioned in connection with Radio Azad Hind as long as the demanded declaration on India was pending.[89]

Pappu Balkrishna Sarma, one of Bose's assistants, reminisces in 1971 about the working of the production department: 'At the beginning we all used to meet practically every day in our office and discuss what sort of programmes we should broadcast and how we should set about it. Netaji and also Mr Nambiar used to give us guidelines and indicate as well the main points to be included in the talks that we had to write.' In addition, the Indians met twice or thrice a week in the evenings in the office for night-long discussions. Bose was the integrating personality of the group: 'Netaji also had a marvellous capacity for making us sink our differences and work as a united team.'[90]

OPERATION TIGER

Besides the Foreign Office and the Ministry for Propaganda, the German armed forces were also actively involved in India-related activities. The Military Intelligence of the OKW had already been engaged since the end of March 1942 in preparing for 'Operation Tiger'. A direct contact with the Fakir of Ipi was to be established for this. In addition, the agent of intelligence in Kabul was working on plans for preparing the German advance into India through the formation of a 'fifth Column'. Disguised as a commission for studying leprosy, soldiers of the training regiment Brandenburg under the command of the well-known leprosy research worker Lance Corporal Manfred Oberdoerffer, were supposed to establish contact with the Fakir of Ipi and use this opportunity to demolish some important war objects in India.[91] The Italian embassy had established contact with the Fakir in February 1941. Legationsrat Anzilotti had even called on him personally. However, because Quaroni did not want any German to accompany him to the Fakir and as he also felt that a strengthening of the contact would not serve much purpose, the Germans now wanted to establish relations on their own.

'Operation Tiger' was a failure. Oberdoerffer and his companion, intelligence agent Fred Brandt, chanced upon an Afghan sentry who, without much ado, opened fire. Oberdoerffer was shot, Brandt slightly wounded.[92] He was captured and interrogated by an English captain of the Indian news service and then released. Back in Berlin, Brandt said that Anzilotti had not met the Fakir at all. The German embassy in Kabul, Brandt reported, was of the opinion that the Italian had kept the money meant for the Fakir and shared it with the ambassador's wife, if not with the ambassador himself.[93]

According to a report by the British embassy in Kabul, the incident happened like this: the two Germans had applied for admission to travel outside Kabul. The permission was not granted. In spite of this they left the city, together with some locals, in the night from 18-19 July 1941 and proceeded towards the south. Near Pul-i-Alam they chanced upon a police or military sentry who had been posted there especially for them. The group tried to escape and Oberdoerffer drew his gun. The sentry opened fire. Oberdoerffer was shot in the abdomen and died when he was taken back to Kabul. He was buried on 20 July 1941. Brandt was slightly wounded and taken to a hospital. He was interrogated but did not reveal anything.[94] Money, documents and maps which the agents had carried were handed over to the German colony through the Turkish embassy. They kept the arms though. According to rumours, one of the Afghan agents had betrayed the operation to the government. It seems the local companions had quarrelled about the distribution of the reward. One of them had felt cheated and informed the government officials.[95]

The Afghan government was annoyed about this incident and requested the Germans to abstain from such actions in future. They served no purpose and would only give the British an excuse for increased political pressure.[96] The Foreign Office was not exactly thrilled about it either. Woermann made it known to the ambassador: 'It has been determined that the intelligence in Afghanistan is not to carry out any undertakings without the prior permission of the Foreign Office, and this will not be granted until further notice.'[97] Ribbentrop instructed the ambassador to see to it that all Germans kept a low profile in Afghanistan so as not to give Great Britain and the Soviet Union any reason to exert pressure on the Afghan government for severing relations with Germany.[98]

The embassy expected the Allied forces to invade the country. In that case the diplomats had decided to surrender. Legation officer Witzel and radio operator Doh, however, were to hide in the mountains and continue working under the protection of Afghans who were friendly with the Axis Powers. The Germans had secretly rented a house near Kabul for this purpose and kept a transmitter, provisions, clothing and money there in case it would be needed.[99] Kabul sent a message a few months later: 'Made direct contact with the Fakir of Ipi and received a letter from him. Intend establishing a relay independent from the Italians.'[100] A British secret service report mentions that two German agents had been with the Fakir in Gorwelcht from 25 February to 21 March 1942.[101] On 30 May 1942, Rasmuss reported the arrival in Kabul of the first direct messenger from the Fakir with a letter. However, these contacts with the freedom-loving hill tribes never achieved any military or political significance.

SCHEDAI AND ITALIAN INDIA-POLITICS

Iqbal Schedai in Rome tried very hard to keep his influence on the Axis Powers' India-politics. He was afraid that with Bose's help the Germans would now take over while the disinterested Italians would readily fall in line with German India-politics. Soon after Bose's return to Berlin, Schedai wrote a letter to Lanza d'Ajeta with the proposal to send a mission to Berlin, headed by the deputy head of the overseas department, Adolfo Alessandrini, for discussing a common policy concerning India, Persia and Afghanistan. Italy should not keep out of this, he warned. Italy should form an Italian-German committee instead. The Italians should not relinquish their competence in Near East politics so easily: 'I can assure you that no one can beat us in this work. We can do wonders if you are ready to handle the work on proper lines,' he promised the Italians.[102]

Bose would have preferred if Schedai had stayed in Berlin so that he could have him under better control. Soon after Bose's return to Berlin, Keppler wrote a letter to the German embassy in Rome stating that Bose would like Schedai to come to Berlin 'for detailed discussions concerning problems in India-propaganda' and requesting him to stay in Germany.[103] Schedai followed up on an invitation by Woermann and stayed for two weeks in Berlin. He was disappointed as neither Ribbentrop nor Woermann nor Keppler received him, even though the Italian embassy had asked the minister to grant an audience to Schedai.[104] As Ciano had granted an audience to Bose, the Italians thought it appropriate if Ribbentrop would do the same favour to their Indian. Still, the Germans arranged a trip to Paris for him. The German ambassador organized a lunch for him on 25 August 1941 with Pierre Laval, the future minister of the Cabinet Council of the État Français.[105]

It was Trott who had been assigned to look after Schedai. Trott lent a patient ear to him and his proposals: he would be prepared to collaborate if, firstly, the German government would proclaim an India-specific declaration together with the Axis states, and secondly, if his Italians assistants were allowed to come with him to Berlin. Of course Trott could not make any promises but told him to first start working in Berlin. His conditions would then be met. Schedai refused to be part of the German activities related to India under Bose's direction. He did not want to give up his Italian backing and demanded therefore the founding of an Italo-Germano-Indian Committee.[106] Bose refused to oblige. Schedai also met the Near East expert Hentig who was to be nominated as ambassador to Kabul. This posting could not be effected though because of British objections.[107] Neither Hentig nor Wuester could manage enticing the Indian away from Italy.[108] Keppler and the speaker, Legationsrat Wilhelm Melcher, head of the Orient section of the political department, also had talks with Schedai, but to no avail.[109] Thereupon, Consul General Walther Wuester, head of the information department, met Schedai in Rome and assured him that a German-Italian committee would be founded,[110] but Schedai did not shift to Germany in spite of this assurance. However, he readily accepted the governmental support from Germany for his activities in Italy. The information department sent him radio manuscripts and a cheque for ten thousand lire.[111] On Schedai's request, the German Hindustani radio programme referred to Radio Himalaya, his own radio programme.[112] Bose on his part showed his irritation as the Germans supported another Indian besides him. Trott, however, considered it important that the two rival revolutionaries should follow a uniform line of action.[113]

Nonetheless, the Italians stuck to Schedai. On 4 October 1941, the Italian Foreign Office announced officially that Count Ciano had ordered the opening of a special department, 'where under the direction of the Indian Schedai all official, semi-official and private endeavours connected with the Indian freedom movement should be combined.'[114] This department functioned under the name of Ufficio India. The Italian asserted, however, that this office should remain as small and unobtrusive as possible.[115] They found it difficult to recruit suitable Indians for their Indian propaganda. Besides the three Ghadr revolutionaries Schedai, Ajit Singh and Labh Singh, the Ministry for Popular Culture managed to find only two other Indians in Italy: a Mrs Sita Devi[116] and a Mr Rayas Ul Hasan. But both refused point-blank to work with the ministry. After much trying, the officials could locate only one Indian with some knowledge of Hindustani. This Mr Santa Maria, however, did not have enough command over the language for broadcasting.[117]

The Italian Ufficio India was to counterbalance the ZFI. Initially, it was supposed to be completely under Italian direction with Schedai as assistant. Only in the event that the Germans acknowledged Bose as officially representing India, would the Italians concede the same status to their Schedai.[118] Like this, the Italian Foreign Ministry made their India-politics dependent on one of the Axis partners. They did not want to lag behind in case the Germans advanced their India-politics. Schedai had to keep himself ready for this purpose, but until then, however, he was to be kept in his place. The Italian India-politics differed from the German one in as much as the Italians concentrated on the Muslim inhabitants of the subcontinent. This line of thinking was in direct contrast to Bose's political ideas. He desired the Indian nation's unity. Bose was therefore for the Italians not a very desirable partner. Schedai as Muslim was better suited for their concept.[119]

During his visit to Rome in October 1941, Trott noticed with concern that the Italians treated the Indian question as part of their Near East politics. Schedai belonged to the Islamic wing of the independence movement and liked to work together with Islamic nationalists of other countries. In spite of this, Trott formed the impression that 'being treated according to expectation he would work with us in a loyal manner.'[120] Schedai offered to come to Berlin every month for one week for broadcasting, but then Bose would have to restrict himself to writing radio speeches only. Furthermore, he wanted the orientalist and SRI assistant Freda Kretschmar to work for him, ostensibly because of her language skills.[121]

Wuester, Trott and Werth had a meeting with Schedai and representatives of the Italian Foreign Ministry on 8 December 1941 in order to collate their India-politics. A compromise was arrived at: In future any propagandistic and political promotion of the Pakistan-movement, encouraging a separation of an Islamic state from India, was to be omitted.[122] On the other hand, no explicit opinion should be expressed against Pakistan either so as not to annoy the Indian Muslims. The German diplomats now knew how to get on with the self-willed Schedai. The Indian, who had stayed in the luxury hotel Adlon during his stay in Berlin, thanked the head of the information department: 'I personally must thank Herr Wuester who did everything to make my stay in Berlin comfortable.' His opinion about the German activities related to India also changed accordingly: 'The German authorities are very sincere and keen to help us, the Indians.'[123] Nevertheless, after that Schedai attracted the Foreign Office's attention again and again unpleasantly as he did not keep to the agreement by engaging in propaganda for Pakistan, calling Bose's Forward Bloc 'contaminated with communistic ideas',[124] attacking Bose personally in his broadcasts,[125] and violating the valid language regulations with aggressive attacks against Gandhi and Nehru.[126]

THE QUESTION OF A PROCLAMATION ON INDIA BY THE AXIS

While the Foreign Office and the German armed forces were abler to constantly improve their India-related activities with Bose's help, Bose himself never tired of demanding again and again from the German government a guarantee on the declaration for India's independence. Also after he had returned from Rome, Bose remained firm in his resolve not to be part of German India-politics unless such a declaration was published. During his first meeting with Woermann on 17 July 1941 after his return from Rome, Bose was told that such a proclamation for a free India was provided for but a suitable date had not been fixed. 'Mr Bose became quite excited here,'

Woermann recorded after the meeting. The Indian had insisted on the proclamation as early as possible as the British were busy planning reforms in India that would get public opinion on their side. Also the war with the Soviet Union had damaged Germany's image very badly in India; Germany was now viewed as an imperialistic power.

Bose explained to Woermann that the question of the declaration was of prime importance for him. Without this declaration he was not interested in founding the Free India Centre.[127] Ribbentrop did not at all share his opinion. When Keppler presented him a few days later a paper with his ideas about India-specific propaganda, the minister returned it with the request to present the same again a fortnight later. He thought it advisable, first of all to observe the political development in the Near East.[128]

The foreign minister's disinterest left a propagandistic vacuum which the Allied tried to fill. On 14 August 1941, the British prime minister, Winston Churchill, and Franklin D. Roosevelt, the president of the USA, at that time still a neutral power, together proclaimed the 'Atlantic Charta', in which both states acknowledged that all nations had the right for self-determination. The image of the United States as an ideal democratic state enhanced the propagandistic value of the Charta. A proclamation by Great Britain alone would not have achieved the same effect. Bose realized the new situation at once.[129] He wrote a warning letter to Ribbentrop on the day of the Charta's proclamation and asked Woermann to forward the same. The Indians, themselves deserving freedom fighters, had become influenced by the Soviet-British-American propaganda machinery, persuading them to believe that the Germans wanted to rule the world. The Americans who desired an agreement between Gandhi and the British government, would gain more and more influence in India's internal politics.

> There is still time to save the situation in India, but if there is further delay in issuing the declaration regarding Indian Independence, I am afraid it will become extremely difficult for us to win over the Indian people to the side of the Axis. Once the majority of the Indian people go over definitely to the Soviet-British-American side, the declaration will no longer have any value for India. Further, if there is no declaration regarding

Indian Independence, the nearer the German armies move towards India, the more hostile will the Indian people become towards Germany. The march of the German troops towards the East will be regarded as the approach, not of a friend, but of an enemy.[130]

Woermann saw that the conditions in India urgently required the publishing of the India-declaration in India. He wrote to Ribbentrop that it 'could provide a weapon to the nationalistic forces against Gandhi's growing preparedness for compromise by yielding to British-American influence.' However, the problem could not be seen solely from this point of view. One would have to wait for a 'general politically suitable starting point,' for instance a British advance into Iran.[131]

Ribbentrop replied only after he had received Hitler's decision. Hitler favoured Woermann's opinion: the declaration on India had to be proclaimed but should be postponed to a later date. He was afraid that such a declaration given at this point of time would provide an excuse for the British to march into Afghanistan. However, it is also possible that he still hoped to come to an agreement with England. Hitler mentioned to a small circle gathered at his headquarters that he did not consider the Indians capable of governing themselves: 'India would perish if the British were driven out.'[132] Probably Hitler came to this judgment as a matter of course because of his racial worldview and feared that he would be ridiculed if he supported India's independence in all seriousness. The Reich's foreign minister sent a note to Bose, letting him know that he was still very interested in his plans but would have to postpone the proclamation for some time 'until our operations in the East will start having a larger effect on the position in the Near East and South Asia.' Only then could he prevent a possible British countermeasure of occupying Afghanistan.

Actually, the time for a proclamation on India would have been just right as Churchill declared before the Lower House that the Atlantic Charta did not apply to India, and thus destroyed all hopes its publication had kindled there.[133] The date proposed by Woermann also passed unutilized. British and Soviet troops occupied Iran on 25 August 1941. It would have been a suitable occasion for the declaration but the opportunity was not utilized even though

Secretary of State Weizsäcker had proposed an 'immediate action programme' to the minister. A declaration in support of independence for India and the Arab countries was part of this programme. The, secretary of state argued: 'It will be difficult to again find such a plausible occasion.'[134]

Meanwhile Bose had left Berlin and gone into retreat to his favourite health resort Bad Gastein. Trott called on him there and delivered the foreign minister's decision. Bose was bitterly disappointed and wrote a cool, almost sarcastic letter to Woermann: 'I need hardly add that though we have not yet what we have been fondly expecting, I am profoundly grateful to you for the help and support you have always given to our cause.'[135]

Nevertheless, the top of the Foreign Office deliberated seriously at that time to shift attention to India after the expected fall of the Soviet Union, should the British not be prepared for negotiations until then. Weizsäcker noted down on 31 September 1941: 'The collapse of Russia will have a weakening of England in its wake. We would be a threat to India then. If necessary, we form with Mr Bose an Indian self-government, which we have avoided so far as we did not want to prevent England completely making a conciliatory move.'[136] This note shows also why the German government hesitated so much with proclaiming support for India's independence struggle: coming to terms with England was still possible. For the time being, Keppler as well as Woermann considered shelving the declaration on India, and the expansion of India-specific propaganda a better move.[137]

Bose's position became more and more difficult in the following months. On 10 November 1941, the Indian radio network broadcast an official announcement by the British government, according to which Bose stayed in Berlin or Rome preparing, together with the Axis Powers, for the invasion of India. Two days later, the Indian Independence League cabled a solidarity declaration to Bose from Japan, the content of which was made public by Radio Tokyo.[138] Keppler thereupon prepared a note for Ribbentrop, urging him to grant an audience to Bose now, as there was the dangerous possibility that the British propaganda might depict Bose as 'Quisling'.[139] He considered it extremely important now to provide Bose and his followers with 'suitable notifications' as arguments for counteracting the expected propaganda.[140]

Finally, Bose had managed to convince Keppler in the matter of the declaration. What else could 'suitable notifications' mean than the declaration demanded for months? However, Woermann stuck to his position that the time was not yet ripe for the proclamation. That Bose's collaboration with the Axis Powers had been made known was no reason to embark on propagandistic activities, as he made clear in a 'note to the Führer' on 6 November 1941. He saw the British announcement as a sign that Bose's stay alone was sufficient to alarm the British. He did call the declaration the 'starting point of our India-politics', but wanted to postpone the actual proclamation to a date as remote as possible. The declaration was to be announced only when it was 'clearly obvious that England was in no way prepared for peace negotiations after the final collapse of Russia.'[141] Woermann firmly believed that an understanding with England was possible. An expanded propaganda in favour of India's independence, and therewith the dissolution of the British Empire, would have been counterproductive for peace negotiations. Woermann envisaged the possibility of support for Indian independence only in case the desired of object could not be achieved.[142] Ribbentrop nevertheless knew that he could not put off Bose indefinitely without annoying him. The Foreign Office considered a meeting between Bose and Hitler now appropriate, particularly as the Grand Mufti of Jerusalem as representative of the Arabic freedom movement had already been received by the Führer.[143] But first he himself had a discussion with Bose on 29 November 1941.

Bose pointed out to Ribbentrop during the talks that British propaganda tried to brand him as a traitor. He showed English newspaper cuttings to prove his point. They had to react to these attacks as otherwise his followers would desert him. Ribbentrop tried to pacify him. The fall of the British Empire was unavoidable. He then explained why he could not yet agree to a public declaration on Indian independence. German politics was not in favour of declarations that did not have any powerful backing. The failures of the German Near East politics showed that it might even be dangerous to proclaim something one could not carry through.

Bose would have to be patient until German troops had crossed the Caucasus. He could then form an all-Indian committee in Tiflis, that could, in a grand style, have a propagandistic effect on

India. Propaganda alone would never achieve India's independence. England's 'nimbus' would first have to be destroyed by military force. Bose did not at all agree with these arguments. He declared that the Arab experiences could not be transferred to India. India was situated much farther away from Germany, English propaganda was much more effective there. Hitler's remarks in *Mein Kampf* could be made the most of by the British if the Führer did not declare his actual intentions soon. Ribbentrop asked him for suggestions for carrying out German propaganda on India. Bose suggested a secret radio station. He himself would be in charge of the programmes but would remain incognito. He also requested to be granted an audience with Hitler to give him the opportunity for presenting his ideas.[144]

After the meeting, Ribbentrop gave Keppler a questionnaire regarding India-related activities, which was returned to him on 3 December 1941, duly filled in. On the question as to whether a strengthening of propaganda on India made sense, Keppler declared that because of the extra propagandistic strength of the British, this was to be recommended only after further military advance. However, he suggested to allow Bose to broadcast 'already here and there illegal transmissions' through a secret radio station. It should be properly worded : 'Germany views these endeavours with sympathy.'

He wanted to announce Bose's stay in Germany and his contacts with government officials through the press. In this way, 'Bose would become again a focal point of the Indian press and be assured of a good resonance for his later public appearance.' Keppler pointed out that Bose was 'very unhappy' about the non-appearance of an official proclamation on India. As he was after all a very important politician he considered an audience with Hitler appropriate.[145] Keppler agreed with Ribbentrop and Woermann, who considered a large-scale propaganda campaign against British rule in India premature. He nevertheless saw Bose's point of view and understood his position. Therefore he considered a public sympathy announcement for the Indian independence movement appropriate. This was not the guarantee declaration as demanded by Bose but nevertheless more than Ribbentrop and Woermann were willing to concede.

The Height of India-Politics after Bose's Intervention

⌘

German troops did not cross the Caucasus. On the contrary, German advances already came to a halt before Moscow in December 1941. On the other hand, a new adversary now threatened British rule in India. The Pacific War started on 7 December 1941 with a surprise attack on Pearl Harbour by the Japanese armed forces. They also started a simultaneous offensive in Southeast Asia. Within a few weeks they succeeded in occupying the Philippines, Hong Kong and Singapore. The Japanese government aimed at the establishment of a 'Great East Asian Prosperity Sphere' under Japanese leadership.[1] India's inclusion as part of 'Great East Asia' had not been clearly defined. India was situated at the margin of the planned Great Empire. It could become part of it, but an inclusion was not necessarily a must. A fight for the subcontinent was an enormous risk for Japan but also held the promise of a colossal gain. So the Japanese decided to attack India for the time being through propaganda only and not with military action.[2]

The happenings in the East Asian theatre of war naturally caught Bose's special attention. He soon realized that Japanese propaganda for India and the Indian expatriates in Southeast Asia could also influence developments in India. Groups of Indian expatriates sought his leadership. In order to be able to influence happenings at the other end of the world, he had no option but to finally intervene actively in Germany's India propaganda. His speeches that were broadcast via short-wave band to Asia created a great stir among Indians. Germany's India-politics reached its peak after Bose's intervention. Since December 1941, India-politics was no longer the sole prerogative of the Axis. Now the Japanese as well were to play a decisive role.

JAPAN ESTABLISHING CONTACT WITH THE AXIS POWERS

Even prior to the attack on Pearl Harbour, Japanese diplomacy had already put out feelers towards the Axis regarding a possible collaboration in their India propaganda. Schedai, who on 22 November 1941 had asked the Japanese counsellor in Rome, Yoshiro Ando, for assistance,[3] now received an encouraging reply, which he immediately forwarded to the German embassy. It stated that Japan intended to further the Indian freedom movement by collaborating with the same and that they would be prepared to issue a declaration of support for Indian independence immediately after eruption of war between Japan and Great Britain.[4] The German ambassador in Tokyo also sent a cable stating that the Japanese in that case would 'take up anti-British propaganda in order to shake British rule.'[5] The Japanese embassy in Tokyo let it be known that Japan was definitely interested to be part of the German-Italian collaboration in India-politics.[6]

On the strength of this, Woermann let the Japanese know that Germany did not consider it desirable for Japan to play a lone hand in the matter of India propaganda. It would be greatly appreciated, if a possible declaration of support for Indian independence would be first agreed upon with the Axis.[7] The Japanese Foreign Office claimed that Ando's remarks to Schedai had been of a 'private' nature and explained that Japan intended to study the Indian question. The German government would be contacted in due time.[8] The Germans were in no hurry either. The representatives of the SRI ascertained in a discussion with the Italian partners that a declaration regarding Indian independence would be issued only when the military position would make it possible that this promise could be carried through. But in order to be prepared in case the Japanese advanced further towards India, preparations for starting liberation 'propaganda at a moment's notice' should now be made.[9] Keppler had already requested the German embassy in Shanghai in November to freeze India propaganda, mentioning a 'total action at a later date'.[10] German radio propaganda was kept on hold at that time. A report from the propaganda ministry stated:

> As an opinion of the Reich's government on the Indian question is still awaited, our propaganda to India has to be restricted to a depiction of Germany in her battle for freedom

under the leadership of Adolf Hitler as an inspiring example for the oppressed Indians, and apart from that to denounce English oppressive methods. Japanese success announcements are deliberately being given prominence since war activities commenced in the Pacific region. So far, intervention in Indian domestic problems has not taken place, this depends on the opinion expressed by the Reich's government which is to be expected within a reasonable space of time.[11]

To be on the safe side, Woermann took out the old draft from May of that year and presented it once more to the Reich's foreign minister. But the propaganda action as proposed by Woermann, which also included a reception of Bose by Hitler besides the issuing of the declaration, did not find the minister's consent.[12]

Bose in Berlin observed the Japanese advance with great attention and he could not remain inactive in this situation. He paid a visit to Woermann on 17 December 1941 and pointed out the new situation to him. The fact that Japan had already reached Burmese soil made the declaration of support for Indian independence even more urgent. He now wanted to discuss this also with the Japanese ambassador. The German diplomats had already held negotiations with the Japanese regarding the India question. Woermann now informed Bose that it had been agreed upon to inform each other prior to issuing a declaration regarding Indian independence. On the following day, Bose paid a visit to the Japanese ambassador Hiroshi Hoshima and put his request forward. The ambassador explained to him that he gave great importance to the question of a joint declaration on India by Germany, Italy and Japan, and intended to discuss this matter soon with the German foreign minister.[13]

At the same time, the German ambassador reported from Bangkok that the nationally minded Indian expatriates had established there a branch of the Indian Independence League under the leadership of Rash Behari Bose, an Indian domiciled in Japan. They wanted to achieve Indian independence with the help of Japanese troops. The committee founded in Bangkok now decided to request Subhas Chandra Bose to take over the leadership, as apparently he was considered more suitable than his namesake in Tokyo.[14]

Keppler considered it 'politically absolutely expedient' to gather the nationally-minded Indian forces under Bose's leadership. He again proposed a reception by the Führer. Bose should then formally accept the leadership of the Indian expatriates in East Asia. He expected a 'significant backlash for the effectiveness of Indian troops under British command' from this development, 'that could decisively influence the position of English rule in India itself.'

Bose and Schedai had an opportunity at the end of November 1941 to explain the urgency of a declaration on India to representatives of the Foreign Office and the Italian Foreign Ministry. They repeated the well-known arguments and received the well-known replies. They stressed in particular that a joint declaration of the Tripartite Powers would be a hindrance to Japan considering the inclusion of the subcontinent into their envisaged 'Great Empire'.

But German and Italian diplomats anyway understood clearly that Japan's appearance on the Eastern theatre of war had changed the situation. Only, the Germans could not act as long as Hitler stuck to his refusal, and the Italians did not want to quarrel with their allies over this matter. Still, Allessandrini remarked at the end of the discussion, that the Axis should not completely keep out of India politics and thus leave all advantages to the British. So it was agreed for the time being to continue with moderate India propaganda and wait and see how the Japanese would act.[15]

GERMANY, ITALY, JAPAN, AND THE DECLARATION ON INDIA

Japan's advance let Hitler reconsider his attitude regarding the declaration on India. It seemed that he now thought the time ripe for stoking British difficulties in Southeast Asia with a propaganda offensive, because Ribbentrop declared after a meeting with Hitler that large-scale propaganda action could be expected soon.[16] He entered a corresponding agreement with Japan's ambassador Oshima.[17] However, this action did not include an actual declaration; it provided though for a proclamation of the Tripartite Powers in support of independence for the Arab countries.[18]

Ribbentrop talked with Oshima on 2 January 1942. The foreign minister informed the ambassador that now Germany desired the issue of a declaration regarding Indian and Arabian independence as a starting signal for an active India-cum Arabia propaganda.[19] The ambassador met Hitler the following day. He explained to him that a joint declaration of support for Indian independence would be extremely important in order to assist Japanese troops in destroying Britain's strong points in India and thus gain access to the Persian Gulf. Hitler did not agree to the declaration and told the ambassador that the Japanese should rather restrict themselves to safeguarding the Southeast Asian territory, as otherwise England could shift her central basis to Australia and New Zealand and from there pose a threat to Japan. A little later, he abruptly took up the India question again: 'If England loses India then a world will collapse. England gained her entire wealth from India.'[20] Though Hitler—according to the records—had neither explicitly spoken for nor against the declaration, Oshima must have formed the impression that he would be favourably inclined towards it. In any case, he sent a cable to Tokyo soon after his visit to the Führer's headquarters, asking to insist on the declaration but received no reply.[21]

A few days later, Woermann presented a new draft for a declaration regarding Indian independence to be proclaimed on 26 January, the day when in 1930 the Indian National Congress had decided on the manifesto for India's independence. The text was a stylistic redrafting of the earlier text drafted on 19 May 1941. The sentence stating that in the future constitution neither religion nor class should be taken into consideration was deleted. Presumably this was done so that Indian Muslims should not have any cause for misunderstanding. Woermann suggested checking this new draft with Bose and then presenting it to the Italians and Japanese in order to issue it jointly and simultaneously with a corresponding declaration for the Arab countries. Prior to the declaration, it would also be pointed out to France and Portugal that it referred to British India only and not to French and Portuguese colonies in India. The spatial demarcation of the proclamation had also not yet been agreed upon with Japan. Neither Ceylon nor Burma, where Japan had special strategic interests, was mentioned in the draft.[22]

The Italians also wanted to take part in the action and sent a corresponding cable to Tokyo. The Japanese, however, rejected a joint declaration, giving the reason that the Axis Powers at present were not very much liked in India. Particularly, Indian Muslims had nothing at all against British rule in India. Therefore, a declaration without the backing of military power would be ineffective. The right time for the declaration would come only when military operations had advanced further. Oshima, who still awaited an official answer from Tokyo, came to know of this refusal only indirectly, namely from the Japanese ambassador in Rome. He did not give up, though, and sent another cable to his ministry, but withour any success.[23] Finally, he had to report to Ribbentrop that the Japanese government did not consider the time suitable for a declaration.[24]

Most probably the Japanese had realized the real motivation of the European allies, namely, to keep Japan's expansionist operation within limits. This was a bad bargain from Japan's point of view: why should the Axis partners be allowed to interfere in their India-politics just for the purpose of gaining a rather dubious propaganda effect?

It was easier for the three partners to come to an agreement regarding the Arabian declaration.[25] Mohammed Ali al-Husaini, the Grand Mufti of Jerusalem, had already urgently demanded the declaration October 1941, and he also presented a draft.[26] The Germans, however, preferred to wait for issuing the declaration until the right time for it had been agreed upon.[27] Woermann explained to the Italian ambassador Dino Alfieri, that as long as the Japanese did not agree to a joint declaration, the German government would not be prepared to proclaim an Arabian one.[28]

It stands to reason though whether the Japanese would have agreed to a declaration regarding Indian independence, if it had been issued at all. It was Hitler who still had the last word in German foreign policy, and as much as ever he did not seem to be convinced that a commitment for an independent India was necessary. Hitler's thinking and politics in 1942 were also still governed by the desire for a settlement with England after a victory over the Soviet Union.

He explained the reasons for his expectations to the small gathering in the Führerhauptquartier: 'The Empire stands and falls with India. India cannot be reconquered any more.'[29] And: 'There is no Englishman who does not constantly think of India now. If they had a choice to leave the continent to Germany and keep India instead, 99 out of 100 Englishmen would choose India. India has also become some sort of a symbol for the English: the fundament of their world rule.'[30] It seems Hitler was afraid to lose a bargaining point for possible negotiations with the British if he committed himself to a declaration on Indian independence. Besides, he doubted the ability of Indians for self-government:

There have been bloody revolts in India. The difficulty is: how is one going to bring the princes with the Brahmins, the Hindus and all the other castes and ethnic groups in one line? There have always been revolutions in India. Gandhi tried it in a different way. All Indians want to be free from British rule. Some would like to achieve this with Bolshevism, others with us, and again others in the very old Indian manner. The aim is the same with all of them. They do not waste a thought on the chaotic conditions that will prevail when the British go, all they want is freedom.[31]

The German-Japanese military convention

At the same time, Germany and Japan negotiated the settlement of a military convention. The Japanese had proposed to define 70 degree East longitude as the demarcation line of the two partners' operational zones. According to this, the entire area of India towards the East of the mouth of the Indus would come under Japanese domain; the Arabian area, however, would fall to Germany. The German military leadership had reservations about such a distribution. They quite rightly feared that the actual meaning of the distribution of the operational area was a demarcation of the political spheres of interest. The convention was signed on 18 January 1941 by Germany, Japan and Italy, though Germany still had reservations about it.[32]

By presenting a declaration on Indian independence during the negotiations, the German side had actually violated the sphere of interest demanded by Japan. Possibly, one wanted to show in this manner that the 70 degrees east longitude would be accepted as a purely operative borderline only and not a political one. As a countermove, the Germans offered the Japanese participation in issuing the Arabian declaration. The German government had no intention to be pushed completely out of India-politics in such a way. Ribbentrop had meanwhile decided that Bose should accept the offer by the Bangkok Indian expatriates of taking over the leadership of their organization. Bose also agreed to this.[33] Apparently, Bose was supposed to assist in influencing happenings in East Asia.

However, Woermann had second thoughts after having experienced Japanese sensibilities in this matter. He now suggested to the Reich's foreign minister to ask the Japanese for their opinion before undertaking this step.[34] Ribbentrop decided therefore, that Bose should wait for some time before accepting the Bangkok offer. Meanwhile, German diplomacy tried to dispel Japan's reservations about a joint venture into India propaganda.[35]

The Japanese did not like any interference into their India-politics, the Italians wanted to keep charge of the Arabian politics, and the Germans would have preferred to have the last word in both matters. Ribbentrop now had the idea to form a Tripartite Power Commission for Indian and Arabian politics. The seat of the commission should be Berlin and it should consist of a representative each from the Foreign Office as well as the Italian and Japanese embassies.[36] This commission was supposed to coordinate the propaganda of the three powers, whereby these could continue to pursue their own activities.[37] The Foreign Office obviously intended to make their own seat the centre of the entire combined Indian and Arabian politics. Naturally the Italians did not like this at all: they raised the objection that such a commission was superfluous. So far, propaganda coordination had functioned quite well through direct contact with the responsible department of the participating ministries. If at all, two commissions should be formed, one for India and one for the Arab countries. This Arabian commission should naturally have its seat in Rome, as after all Italy had priority interests in this region.[38]

Now the Japanese took the initiative. On 27 January 1942, the Japanese embassy presented a diplomatic note to the Wilhelmstrasse stating that Japan was now willing to participate in anti-British demoralizing work The Japanese government would agree to issue a joint declaration regarding liberation not only of Indian, but of all 'peoples under British yoke.'[39] The Foreign Office tried through propaganda to enter the Japanese sphere of interest; the Japanese countered with the request to now have the secured right to have a worldwide say in anti-British propaganda. However, collaboration should only become concrete after the Japanese military position in Asia had reached such a stage that anti-British propaganda might be profitable to them. The time would be ripe only after operations in Burma had advanced further.[40]

The intelligence service arranged a talk with the Japanese military attaché Colonel Bin Yamamoto, and at the end of January, Bose had the opportunity to present his views to him. He envisaged a Japanese attack on India. Such an offensive would have to be carefully prepared through well thought-out propaganda measures. The Indian people would have to be given detailed information about the intentions of the invaders as otherwise they would side with the British. Bose received the same replies from the Japanese colonel as he was used to get from the Germans: of course some propaganda measures would be taken up. But one had to wait for the right time for an official declaration in support of Indian independence.[41] Yamamoto explained during another discussion a few days later that an attack on India would be only one of several possibilities open to the Japanese forces after capturing the Malacca peninsula. An advance towards Australia would not be very likely; an operation against the Soviet air force in East Asia was more likely to be on the cards. Just in case Japan opted for the Indian operation, he asked Bose to explain how his organization could be used as 'fifth column' for the Japanese advance.[42]

The Italian advance

So far, the Italians had hardly bothered about India-politics and had readily accepted German ideas, but their attitude changed with the advance of Japanese troops in Asia. The Germans were eager to agree with Japan on a joint propaganda on India. The Japanese, however, considered India to be part of their sphere of interest. They wanted to concede the right of involvement in this propaganda to their European allies only if they, on their part, would in return concede the same to Japan in the Arabian propaganda. This demand had to have a startling effect on Italy: the Arab countries belonged to Mussolini's territory.

Mussolini's war aim was the hegemony of Italy in the Mediterranean territory. The annexation of Albania, the marching into Egypt and the invasion of Greece were steps taken towards this goal. In order to drive out the British from the Levant and Egypt, he now wanted to make use of the Arabian peoples' aspirations for independence. Mussolini intended to take up the role of a protector of young nations under Italian supremacy. Of course, this could work out only if the Italian dictator could pose alone as guarantor of Arabian freedom. Any influence of the allies could therefore become a dangerously disturbing factor. On the other hand, he needed their cooperation in order to achieve his aim.[43]

Hence, the sudden Italian eagerness to push for the declaration of support for Indian independence is to be attributed to the fact, that they viewed the same solely as an appendix to a similar declaration for Arabian countries, where they hoped to establish their influence. They now wanted to demonstrate their right in these regions with a suggestion for a joint Indian and Arabian declaration, which, however, was not accepted by the Foreign Office as they refused to take any action in this regard without Japanese participation.[44] The Japanese now on their part did not think the time favourable for such a step. The Japanese ambassador in Berlin, Oshima, told his Italian counterpart Alfieri that one ought to wait until such a declaration could be combined with a military advance.[45] It did not help either, that on 4 February 1942 the German, Italian and Japanese ambassadors in Kabul jointly demanded a declaration on Indian independence by the Tripartite Powers as a suitable moment had arrived now with the advance of the Japanese troops.[46] Also Schedai's detailed draft for a Japanese declaration on India did not seem to make an impression either.[47]

While the Foreign Office waited for a final answer from Japan in the matter of the India-declaration, they came to know that Japan had already started a lively propaganda on India within the territory under their power. The embassy in Bangkok reported Japan's close collaboration with the Indian Independence League. The league was in favour of gaining India's independence with the help of Japanese troops and was being paid and directed by Japanese military authorities. Besides that, there existed an Indian National Council that was indeed an independent organization, but was also now collaborating with the Japanese. The council hoped to gain India's liberation through a revolution. In addition, the Japanese were engaged in very successful demoralization propaganda for Indian troops in the British army, which had already induced many Indian soldiers to desert to the other side.[48]

Now that the Japanese had started a lively propaganda in Southeast Asia, the Japanese ambassador in Berlin told his Italian counterpart, that the Japanese government wanted to keep the India-related propaganda in check and would like it, if the Axis Powers would do likewise with their Arabian propaganda.[49] In the debate about the demarcation of interest spheres, the Japanese now were more and more conspicuous in their endeavour to make both questions a joint venture.

THE FIRST ACTION ON INDIA

India-politics became again a subject of priority interest through the conquest of the British Far East bastion of Singapore on 15 February 1942, in which the Indian National Army, consisting of deserted Indian soldiers, had also taken part. The Japanese prime minister, Hideki Tojo, in a speech in parliament, demanded the end of British rule in India, without however explicitly mentioning independence for the country.[50]

The time had come for Bose to give up his reticence and to become actively involved in propaganda on India. He now wanted to turn to the Indian people with an express opinion. He explained the motivation for this decision in a letter to Woermann. It was to be expected after Tojo's speech that the British would instigate known Indian politicians, such as Nehru, to make a statement against the Japanese. In order to influence public opinion in his country in the opposite direction, he would now have to openly declare his willingness to collaborate with England's enemies.[51] A guarantee of Indian independence by the Axis Powers was now no more a condition for him. It had obviously become clear to him that insistence on this declaration did not further his aim.

The Foreign Office accepted his views readily. They feared that the visit to India in February 1942 by Chiang Kai-shek, who wanted to win the Congress party's firm support for the allied conduct of war,[52] would bring about an agreement between the Indian National Congress and the British, and that had to be avoided. Ribbentrop, therefore, thought it better that Bose should now actively intervene in the propaganda on India. He trusted the Indian in that 'he would effectively oppose English-friendly tendencies in India. Bose should therefore be allowed to express his opinions by broadcasting and through the press.'[53] Japan's assistance was required as the range of the German media was limited. The allies in the Far East were contacted again in order to win them over for a joint action. The question of a joint declaration on India came up again in this connection. Ribbentrop now wanted the same issued as soon as possible but desired Japan's and Italy's collaboration.[54]

In order to achieve this, the Reich's foreign minister had a new draft pepared for the declaration. This draft differed considerably from the one that waited to be published since May 1941 in the files of the Foreign Office. The central statement, namely that the right of independence and free choice of her future political system would be recognized, remained, and was put under the catchy heading 'India to the Indians'. For the remaining part, the text was composed in such a way as to motivate the Indians to refuse to take part in British war efforts. Thus it read:

> England is the common enemy of the Indian people and the peoples of the Tripartite Powers. The Tripartite Powers have always had friendly feelings for the Indian people, and the close cultural and economic relations they had with India have contributed further to strengthen these feelings. In spite of that, the Indian people are being forced by a foreign British government to consider themselves at war with Germany, Italy and Japan and to sacrifice wealth and blood for keeping the power of their oppressors intact.[55]

The Japanese government expressed their willingness to broadcast Bose's speeches via their media but hinted that in other respects they were somewhat critical of Bose. They did not yet give their consent for a joint declaration[56] whereas the Italians favoured Bose's India-specific propaganda without reservations.[57]

Ribbentrop now gave detailed orders for the first large-scale action of the Foreign Office concerning India. The action should aim at 'eliminating India as English war factor'. 'No speculations as regards framing of constitutional and international law of the Indian future should be entertained' thereby. Rather, the Indians should be made convinced that now they had to involve themselves against the British for their freedom. Attacks against Gandhi and Nehru should be avoided as well as violation of 'possible Japanese sensibilities'. The action should commence with Bose expressing his opinion through Radio Azad Hind. After this, the German and allied radio networks and the press should take it up and give it great prominence. Bose's presence in Germany should still be kept a secret. As a follow-up the media would occasionally report on India until it would finally be the right time for the declaration on India. This was the opportunity for the Tripartite Powers to play the role of liberators of suppressed peoples.[58]

Of course, the articles appearing in the German press were not meant for Indian consumption. Besides influencing the Indians, the action served yet another purpose namely, justifying the war with England to the local population. A committee of the press department met almost daily since January in the Foreign Office to deal exclusively with press propaganda about India and the Arab countries.[59] The press department of the Foreign Office published a series of 'standard theses' as guidelines which had to be followed by German newspapers in their reports on India. These stressed the criminal character of the British rule in India as opposed to Germany's friendly attitude towards the country and were supposed to create the impression that the Germans were not alone in their fight against the British Empire. Their central points were the following:

- Rich, distinguished India is being ruined by England.
- English promises are nothing but lies.
- The historic hour for India's liberation has come.
- Any service for England as soldier or in the armament industry is a betrayal of the Indian people.
- England created artificial differences within the Indian population in order to be able to rule over India.
- Freedom and bread are the alternatives of exploitation through the British.[60]

Simultaneously, the German press received the order not to mention Bose's whereabouts, not to reflect on India's political or legal future, to avoid any indication as to the position of the Axis Powers towards Indian independence, and to omit any polemic regarding Gandhi and Nehru.[61] The Italian minister for popular culture, Alessandro Pavolini, thought it important to request the journalists not to depict the India-related action as a Japanese initiative but as joint action of the three allies. After all, even Rome had a circle of national-minded Indians.[62]

The action on India took off according to plan. Goebbels noted in his diary that now the propaganda battle for India had commenced: 'For a long time we practised here restraint for the simple reason, that matters in India had not advanced sufficiently, and one should not start shooting until the enemy is within reach.'[63] For the first time after his flight, Bose spoke to the Indian people on 28 February on Radio

Azad Hind. He stressed in his speech that British imperialism was the eternal enemy of India and he warned his countrymen against any compromise with the English:

> Standing at one of the crossroads of history, I solemnly declare on behalf of all freedom-loving Indians in India and abroad that we shall continue to fight British imperialism till India is once again the mistress of her own destiny. During this struggle and in the reconstruction that will follow, we shall heartily cooperate with all those who will help us in overthrowing the common enemy. I am confident that in this sacred struggle, the vast majority of the Indian people will be with us.[64]

The proclamation had the desired effect. The fortnightly reports sent by the provincial governments to the home department of the Indian government reflected the prevailing mood. The Government of Bihar reported: 'There is now a very great danger of the people getting demoralized and the broadcasts from Germany and Japan help to aggravate the panic. [...] This influence is drawn from the prominence which has been given by the German radio to the speech of Mr Subhas Bose.'[65] 'Axis propaganda has again been responsible for a number of wild rumours,' reported the Northwest Frontier Province.[66] The Government of Punjab thought it advisable to take actions against 22,000 owners of radio sets who were suspected to spread fifth columnist's rumours from the broadcast of the Axis Powers.[67] A staff member of the BBC, during these months on tour in India, reported being upset that the enemy broadcasts and All-India Radio were now much more favoured by Indian listeners than the BBC: 'The usual question when an Indian buys a wireless set, I was told by big dealers in Bombay, is "Can I hear Germany and Japan on this?"'[68]

Even though Bose had not yet mentioned his whereabouts, people assessed particularly in Bengal, his native province, that the Germans and the Japanese supported him.[69] Some Indians were indifferent to the powers behind Bose. A district manager from the United Provinces (UP) expressed surprise: 'There have been anti-Japanese and anti-Axis speeches accompanied by shouts for Subhas Chandra Bose. The fact is that they do not know where they stand or whither they are going. The Forward Bloc seems to be trying to take advantage of this confusion.'[70] What the colonial official did not understand was that in the war, Indian nationalists neither sided with the Axis nor with the Allied forces. They supported their leader in the fight for a free India and abhorred each and any imperialistic power.

All-India Radio felt motivated to remark on India's relationship with Germany without, however, actually mentioning Bose himself. Radio Azad Hind could be clearly and strongly heard in Thailand as well so that the enthusiastic Indian expatriates were able to savour each and every word.[71] The Indian National Council in Bangkok printed Bose's text in nine languages as pamphlets for distribution to the Indian population in Southeast Asia. The Japanese radio network repeated Bose's broadcast several times.[72] The German and the international press received the content of Bose's speech on 28 February 1942 through a notification from the German news agency.[73] Bose's speech was prominently published in Germany and all occupied and allied countries.[74]

When the text of the speech was read out to a mass congregation of Indians in Bangkok and created great enthusiasm there, the question came up again whether Bose should become the leader of the Indian expatriates in Thailand.[75] The Japanese were not very comfortable with this idea. They had broadcast Bose's speech in Southeast Asia, albeit on a small scale, only because Germany insisted on it. It was mainly the Indian National Council that desired Bose's leadership.[76] In this way they wanted to secure their independence from Japanese military authorities. Keppler therefore instructed the German embassy in Bangkok to see to it that any discussion regarding the leadership be avoided for the time being.[77] While sympathy for Bose was desired, anti-Japanese tendencies were not.[78]

Ribbentrop was nonetheless thrilled with the successful outcome of the action. He gave instructions that Bose should now prepare for broadcasting to India a light satirical commentary at least daily, and a longer talk twice a week, and read out the text himself. Bose should be allowed to work with his people as freely as possible. It was now his task to win over the Indian people for freedom.[79] Goebbels noted the success as well: 'Bose's statement has made a great impression on public opinion. The Indian crisis can no longer be ignored.'[80] And: 'Bose's manifesto for instigating the Indian people to rebellion has now achieved sensational importance. The British admit already that India is seriously threatened, and they now see their entire East Asian position wavering.'[81] He concluded: 'Therefore, we have to activate our India-propaganda, which is being done good and proper now.'[82]

On 12 March 1942 Bose transmitted again a second statement. He drew his listeners' attention to the Japanese victory. Burma had been liberated, whereas India was drawn by the British into a war that was not their own. One should not believe Churchill's offer of granting dominion status to India after the war. The British Empire would crumble down; the future was with the Tripartite Powers, the friends of India. He concluded his speech with pathos:

> Let us therefore rejoice that under the simultaneous blows of the Tripartite Powers the British Empire—our eternal foe—is fast crumbling down. Let us rejoice over the rapid and victorious advance of the Japanese forces in the Far East. Let us rejoice that the old order, which was set up at Versailles, is crashing before our eyes. And let us rejoice over the coming dawn, which will bring for India freedom and justice, happiness and prosperity.[83]

On Ribbentrop's suggestion, daily transmission time was extended to one hour and repeated in the early hours of the morning.[84] The declaration was immediately taken up by the German short-wave transmitter and then also spread further by the Italian programmes for India and East Asia transmitters. The circulation of the declaration in Germany and Europe was also taken care of. Bose's proclamation was broadcast by Germany's inland services and an additional fifteen services in occupied and allied countries.[85]

On Ribbentrop's instructions, Bose's second text was given even more prominence than the first one in the German daily press.[86] The press department was able to fill a new file under the title 'Latest appeal by Bose' with newspaper cuttings of articles on Bose's appeals published in the following days.[87] The army's general staff, however, reported that a demoralizing effect of the propaganda on Indian soldiers in the British army could not be established.[88]

The public proclamation of a declaration in support of India's freedom struggle envisaged as the high point of the entire action was still missing. The Italians already demanded this urgently in order to avoid that the Japanese played a lone hand in it.[89] The Japanese ambassador in Berlin, Oshima, considered the moment also favourable but insisted on a simultaneous publication of a declaration regarding the Arab countries.[90] The Germans were in no hurry about this. Goebbels wrote in his diary: 'We do everything to pour oil into the fire without anyone being able to establish our authorship.'[91] Obviously one was already satisfied with the course the action had taken so far and did not expect additional advantages from a public participation by the Reich's government. Hitler finally declared his refusal to have a declaration regarding Indian independence issued. He explained to Himmler that he considered independence of the country not only inopportune but in addition also unfair towards the British: 'I agree here with the opinion of the British Tories: if I subjugate a country only in order to grant it freedom again—why all this? Those who have shed blood also have the right to rule. Indian freedom would not even last for twenty years. [...] England exploited India, but English rule has also benefited the country.'[92]

THE CRIPPS MISSION

Not only the Tripartite Powers, but also the British had their difficulties with a declaration regarding India. So far, the British had not thought it necessary to make any concessions to India, but now Japanese advances forced them to take pains in getting Indian political leaders to cooperate.

The British War Cabinet formed a committee for drafting a declaration regarding India. This provided for the formation of an Indian Union as the established aim of British politics, which as a dominion of the Commonwealth would have the right to withdraw from the same. The question whether the provinces or princely states should have the right not to join the Union remained unsolved. The recognition of this 'local option' would have made the formation of a separate Muslim state Pakistan possible. The viceroy of India, Lord Linlithgow, declared his resignation in case a declaration with such a clause was publicly issued.[93]

In this situation, Sir Stafford Cripps, known for his socialist ideas and for being an opponent of Churchill, offered to fly to India in order to discuss in the name of the War Cabinet the declaration regarding India with the leaders of the Indian parties. Actually he had very little scope for negotiations. He could only make an offer, which could either be accepted or rejected. Cripps arrived in New Delhi on 23

March 1942.[94] The Cripps Mission provided a new starting point for the Axis propaganda. Ribbentrop asked Bose to publish an open letter to Cripps in order to induce the Indians to ignore the compromise offer. This became a dilemma for Adam von Trott. Cripps was his personal friend since their common Oxford days. It bothered him that as expert advisor for Indian matters he had to do his utmost to spoil his good friend's chances of succeeding in his mission.[95]

Maybe it was due to his influence that Bose initially refused to write the required letter. Trott conveyed to his superiors that in Bose's opinion it was the tactic of uncompromising nationalists to ignore Cripps as far as possible. The Indian would rather write a letter to his mother, explaining to her the reasons for his flight and use this opportunity to ask all Indian mothers to shoulder the burden of the struggle for freedom. He wanted to make an offer of public alliance to the Japanese prime minister, Tojo, in lieu of the declaration regarding India's independence, which had not been issued as yet.[96]

Ribbentrop considered a speech to Tojo also a good idea. It might dispel Japan's mistrust and also remove the journalistic rivalry between the Bose in Berlin and the other Bose in Tokyo. However, he set great value on it that Bose should also mention Germany and Italy as helpers in the freedom struggle, and that only the Japanese press would report on this, not the German one. Meanwhile, he also thought it opportune for Bose to meet Hitler and that his presence in Germany be made public.[97] However, Goebbels disagreed. He did not yet want Bose's whereabouts to be known so as not to undermine his credibility in India.[98]

Finally, however, Bose had to write the open letter. In addition, he had to show his text prior to broadcasting to the Reich's foreign minister, as he might want to make some changes. The approved version finally read as follows:

> Since 1939, British politicians and the British propaganda machinery told us continuously that India was being threatened by the Axis, and now one even tells us India is threatened by the enemy's invasion. Is this not pure hypocrisy? India has no enemies outside her borders. India's only enemy is British imperialism and the only attack India has to fight is the ever-lasting attack of British imperialism. The British government

declared India against her will to be engaged in warfare, and in addition since then has forcibly exploited India's forces for English war-aims.[99]

Bose read the text programmed in Radio Azad Hind on 27 March 1942. It was distributed on the same day by the German news agency, which claimed to have recorded it directly from the secret transmitter.[100] Actually, the press agency had indeed received the text through the press department of the Foreign Office, but the public was not supposed to know this, as Bose was still incognito. The letter was published in the German morning editions of 28 March 1942.[101] Radio Azad Hind was again allotted additional transmission time. In order to make this feasible, transmission time for attending to the troops of the armed forces had to be curtailed.[102]

The propaganda ministry instructed the press in their daily statement to depict the Cripps mission as an attempt to draw on the Indian population as canon fodder.[103] The journalists were told to keep the subject topical. Derogatory remarks about India made by Churchill in 1929, 1931 and 1937 were compiled and the editors were asked to quote these in their commentaries. The German news agency distributed a longer report of the general mood prevailing in India, dwelling on the difficult economic situation in India, food shortage in Ceylon, and the loss of British prestige in India.[104] In these days, India was the main subject in the German press. But the newspaper editors behaved rather clumsily at times. Thus the diplomatic agent Braun von Stumm had to request press representatives to be careful with caricatures regarding India: 'Scantily dressed Indian ladies and naked Indians, depicted as being typical, will after all hardly please the numerous Indians living here.'[105]

The Foreign Ministry in Rome instructed the Italian press to be somewhat reserved with Bose as a person, so as not to make him appear an agent of the Axis. The Italian Foreign Ministry was not sure how the Indians would react to Bose's appeal. After all, he had been away from India for more than a year now and quite possibly had lost touch with Indian politics. The official Italian radio network for India should therefore restrict itself to transmitting his appeal, and describe him briefly as former Congress president. The secret transmittor Radio Himalaya, however, should further add supporting comments.

The local press was instructed to simply publish the appeal without any commentaries.[106] The minister for popular culture, Pavolini, admonished the journalists not to underrate Italy's role in this action, and to point out that each member of the Tripartite Powers supported Bose equally.[107]

British propaganda countered Bose's activity with the announcement that Bose had lost his life in a plane crash in Japan. This canard, however, achieved the certainly most unintended effect that the Indians showed their solidarity with Bose: Gandhi sent a telegram expressing his sympathy to Bose's mother.[108] The Congress party in UP organized hartals and meetings to condole his death.[109] Goebbels commented: 'The English tactic is very transparent, one tries to create confusion in the Indian national-minded circles in order to fish in troubled waters. The English are cunning colonial politicians.'[110] The démenti over the German short-wave transmitter caused a sensation in India so that even All-India Radio had to confess to the canard.[111]

The British started worrying about the impression Bose's propaganda might have on the American public. The secretary of state for India, Leopold Amery, feared that the allies might get the impression that England had lost her grip on India. Already more and more press comments demanded immediate independence for India. 'The fear of a breakdown of Indian morale is being worked to death by the American press as an argument for the grant of Indian independence without delay,' Amery warned the viceroy of India. The Associated Press had reported that Bose had the maximum number of followers exactly in the regions from where the Indian army recruited most of their soldiers, namely Punjab, Maharashtra and the Northwest Frontier Province.[112] The viceroy declared this to be absolute rubbish and tried his best to downplay the effect of Bose's broadcasts. They had created rather more curiosity than interest outside Bengal. Some Indians even had denied that it had been Bose's voice they had heard, as they felt ashamed to see that such an eminent political leader had joined the enemy camp.[113]

Cripps came to know upon arrival in India that German radio propaganda had tried to wreck his mission. Full of apprehension, he sent a telegram to the British Broadcasting Corporation that had so far paid little attention to the German propaganda. In response, the writer George Orwell, who at that time worked with the British radio on the editorial staff in charge of India, produced a series of special programmes in support of the Cripps Mission.[114]

Berlin observed with great attention Cripps's negotiations with the Indian politicians. It was expected that his endeavour would come to naught when it became clear that Gandhi and the majority of the Congress would not accept his proposals. In case this happened, Keppler expected the tensions between England and India to have a deteriorating effect on the country's military performance. He suggested issuing a declaration on Indian independence by the Axis henceforth in order to consolidate Gandhi's position and thus contribute to the failure of the negotiations. As he knew meanwhile that Hitler did not think much of such a proclamation, he suggested deleting from the text the statement of explicit recognition of India's independence. He also presented a new draft with an explicit reference to the Cripps Mission. This draft said that the Indian people now had to face the decision of destiny—whether they would take their fate into their own hands or whether they wanted to be seized by the terrors of war in accordance with England's will.[115]

German propaganda did not tire of depicting Cripps's endeavour as an attempt to betray the Indian people. It was highlighted that Cripps did not promise true independence to India but only a limited autonomy under British sovereignty that was to be realized only after the war. A daily statement to the press read: 'This clumsy manoeuvre is […] most unequivocally to be compared to Wilson's betrayal of Germany and England's betrayal of the Arabs and to be dismissed with utmost severity.'[116] However, one carefully desisted from predicting a failure of the negotiations, as it was not after all certain how the Indian spokesmen would finally decide.[117]

While Berlin could still not decide about speaking directly to the Indian public, Tojo addressed a declaration to the Indian people on 6 April 1941. At the same time it was officially announced that Japanese armed forces had now started an attack on Ceylon. Tojo asked the Indians not to be led astray by British promises but to seize the opportunity to get rid of foreign rule. However, the speech did not mention the Axis as joint partners in war.[118]

After three weeks, Cripps had to finally admit failure. Gandhi compared the British government's offer presented by Cripps to 'a post-dated cheque on a bank that was failing' and advised the Englishman to take the next flight home if he had nothing better to offer. Cripps followed Gandhi's advice and left India in the beginning of April.[119] The German propaganda was officially instructed to depict the failure of the negotiations as personal defeat for Churchill and Roosevelt: India would not allow herself to be drawn into England's war as it did not believe in its victorious outcome.[120]

The mission left a bitter taste with the Indians. The political leaders were embittered, as the British were absolutely unwilling to make even a small concession. Even though many of them still sympathized with the British and their allies in the war, they now considered it unbearable how they were treated by the colonial masters in their own country: 'The time had come, they felt, for a final assault on imperialism.'[121] The failure to arrive at a compromise clearly showed that the public supporters of independence in India had gained the upper hand over those who had still been prepared to arrive at an understanding with the colonial masters.

Bose's propaganda had played a traceable part in this shift of strength. Gandhi wrote in his journal *Harijan* that he would consider the Axis, were they to come to India, as enemies and not as liberators, and that he considered Bose's method of collaborating with England's enemies as wrong, but he nevertheless praised his readiness to make sacrifices and his patriotism. 'The old difference of opinion between us persists. This does not mean that I doubt his sacrifice or his patriotism. But my appreciation of his patriotism and sacrifice cannot blind me to the fact that he is misguided and that his way can never lead to India's deliverance.'[122] Even though he rejected Bose's way, as it would lead astray, he nevertheless respected him as an honest patriot. Maulana Abul Kalam Azad who was at that time president of the Congress party, wrote in his autobiography that Gandhi had been greatly impressed by Bose's escape to Germany and also by his stand on Cripps's offer:

> Many of his remarks convinced me that he admired the courage and resourcefulness Bose had displayed which unconsciously coloured his view about the whole war situation. This admiration was also one of the factors, which clouded the discussions during the Cripps mission to India. [...] Cripps, however, complained to me that he had not expected a man like Gandhi to speak in such glowing terms about Subhas Bose.[123]

While Azad and Nehru had been prepared to accept Cripps's proposals, Gandhi rejected them from the beginning. The majority of the Congress Working Committee followed his example so that the Congress party's negative stand was decided upon.[124] If Azad's version is correct, and according to Voigt[125] nothing points to the contrary, then it can be said that the Congress party's decision leading to the failure of the mission was due to Bose's influence. When Hauner calls Germany's India-politics in his book *India in Axis Strategy* 'the complete failure on the part of Nazi Germany to exploit the revolutionary potential of India'[126] and Bose's propaganda as 'personal failure', is this, to say the least, an undifferentiated statement?

Berlin was greatly satisfied with the mission's failure. Ribbentropp congratulated Bose and thanked him for his efforts. He let it be known that he attributed the English failure partly to Bose's activities.[127] Goebbels knew: 'At present Bose is the best horse in our stable.'[128] At the height of the euphoria, the propaganda minister is even supposed to have suggested to the scriptwriter Thea von Harbou, who made the feature film *The Indian Tomb*, to shoot a feature film with Bose as hero.[129]

Naturally, Sir Stafford Cripps did not have a good opinion of Bose. When Orwell asked his opinion of Bose he called him 'a thoroughly bad egg'. Cripps presumed correctly that Bose had escaped via Afghanistan and now pursued his propaganda from Germany. However, he countered Orwell's remark that he considered Bose to be 'subjectively pro-Fascist' with: 'He's pro-Subhas. That is all he cares about. He will do anything to help his own career along.'[130]

THE JAPANESE DRAFT OF THE DECLARATION ON INDIA

The Japanese considered the time suitable for a joint declaration regarding India and the Arab countries when the failure of the Cripps Mission was to be expected. They presented a draft but let it be known at the same time that they were open to negotiations regarding individual formulations. The slogan 'India to the Indians, the Arab countries to the Arabs' had been taken over from the previous German drafts. The declaration did not contain an explicit guarantee for an independent India. It stated simply: 'Japan, Germany and Italy do not have the ulterior motive to replace Great Britain in India and the

Arab countries.' The text concluded with the vague promise that the three powers would 'gladly render all possible support to the Indians and the Arabs if they were allowed to assist them in gaining their independence.'[131]

The Japanese considered the inclusion of Arabia as well as India important even though they had no intention of marching into the Arab countries. So far, the Foreign Office had not entertained the idea of treating the Indian and the Arabian question in the same declaration.[132] The German ambassador in Tokyo could gather the information that with the mention of Arabia, the Japanese government wanted to avoid the demarcation of power spheres, which would be to Japan's disadvantage.[133] Mussolini was in favour of accepting the Japanese draft at once and without essential changes,[134] even though it was more a propagandistic manifesto than a declaration of independence. Blasco Lanza d'Ajeta, cabinet chief of the Italian Foreign Ministry, explained to the German ambassador in Rome that the opportunity for issuing a joint declaration should not be missed as the Japanese had now finally agreed to it.[135]

Woermann discussed this with Keppler and the diplomatic expert for Arabian propaganda, Fritz Grobba. They agreed that one certainly could combine both declarations in one issue but considered the Japanese draft as not suitable for being 'too journalistic' and also 'not very concrete'. Woermann presented an edited version of the Japanese draft that again contained the explicit recognition of independence and considered Indian and Arabian political expectations in a concrete manner. Indian politicians received the warning: 'These [the Tripartite Powers] have no cause to touch India if India does not chain her destiny to the sinking power of America and England.'[136] Ribbentrop now had to try to finally convince Hitler that the declaration was necessary. In a long 'Note to the Führer' which he wrote on 16 April 1942, he gave a detailed explanation as to why he was in favour of the Japanese proposal. Taking up the matter of Hitler's known reservations, he wrote:

> The declaration as proposed by the Japanese does not contain a political decision in the sense that it would ultimately rule out an understanding at the price of India. On the contrary, Japan's commitment contained in the draft to the principle, that Japan

did not want to continue with England's legacy in India, could even be of advantage for an agreement with England in case that such a possibility would after all still arise. Otherwise, I am of the opinion that it can only have a favourable effect on the preparedness of English circles for peace, if now in these circles we point out once more the danger threatening India.[137]

Ribbentrop argued skilfully: a declaration by the Tripartite Powers for Indian independence did not mean that England should give up India; it stated only that Germany, Italy and Japan would not make any claims on India. He knew that Hitler had nothing against British rule in India if England only gave him a freehand in Eastern Europe. Therefore, he presented the declaration as a means that would eventually force an agreement on the English. Bose would have been horrified had he known about this argumentation.

However, Hitler was not to be convinced. The Führer's permanent representative of the foreign minister, Diplomatic Expert Walter Hewel, reported that Hitler did not see the point why he should be part of such a declaration just because the Japanese wanted it. When Hewel tried once more to present Ribbentrop's arguments to Hitler, the Führer mentioned only that he first of all discuss the entire matter with the Duce. Moreover, the matter was not as important as the Japanese and Italians made out.[138]

Now the Japanese government slowly became impatient and started pressing for an early decision. Berlin only informed that the proposal was in the process of being thoroughly examined and that this could take some time.[139] On 29 April 1942, Hitler and Mussolini met in the Klessheim castle near Salzburg. Ribbentrop and Ciano were also present. Hitler was already going to finish the meeting after both the heads of state had discussed various problems, when Mussolini reminded him that the question of the declaration on India and Arabia was still outstanding. Thereupon Hitler and Ribbentrop entered into a discussion regarding this matter within earshot of Mussolini. Hitler declared that his position was governed by memories of the First World War. In all likelihood, Germany could have had a special peace agreement with Russia at that time had she not declared Poland to be a separate kingdom. If now the Tripartite Powers were to issue a declaration on India and Arabia, then this could easily lead to the strengthening of England's willingness to resist, as she saw her empire in danger.

Ribbentrop remarked now that England would make peace only when she saw herself cornered to such an extent that there were no chances left to win. Hitler disagreed; a declaration without necessary military backing would not only be useless but dangerous as well. The Japanese could certainly intervene militarily in India, but the Axis Powers only had interests of a theoretical nature there. Mussolini now wheeled around to Hitler's point of view. Japan could issue the declaration on her own accord to which the Axis Powers would then agree. At the given time, a declaration would at the most be purely 'platonic' only. Ribbentrop replied that nevertheless a joint declaration regarding India would signify that the Axis Powers also had a say in this matter. On the other hand, Japan had made this proposal quite some time ago and might suspect an agreement with England if the Axis would further delay consent. The Reich's foreign minister suggested informing the Japanese that a positive stand was taken in the matter of a joint declaration on India, but that the point of time for the actual proclamation would have to be kept open. Mussolini liked the idea. He was of the opinion that Japan would have to be allowed to issue a declaration on India on her own. Hitler, however, said the Japanese ought to remain patient a little longer. After all, they in their turn had often made the Axis wait quite some time.

This discussion bore no concrete results. The protocol, written by interpreter Paul Schmidt for the files of the Foreign Office, concluded with the sentence: 'Finally the suggestion of the RAM (i.e. Ribbentrop) was accepted, that the matter should first be discussed orally with Oshima by bearing in mind the Führer and Duce's opinion.'[140] It seems that Mussolini did not quite comprehend this decision because his protocol reads: 'With regard to the declaration desired by Japan about the independence of India and the Arab countries, it has been agreed upon, that Japan, being on the borders of India, can issue this declaration, and the Axis consent to it.' To issue a declaration for Arabia would be premature as long as the Axis did not stand south of the Caucasus.[141] So Mussolini had recorded his own contribution to the discussion only. The comparison of his protocol with the German one gives rise to the assumption that the Italian did not clearly understand that the Germans regarded the declaration on

India and Arabia not as two separate issues, but as a single, indivisible problem.

The Japanese now received the information from the foreign minister that the Führer and the Duce principally agreed to a joint declaration. However, they did not consider the given time suitable. The reason stated: it served no purpose to issue such declarations at a point of time, when the means for their realization were not adequate. A declaration therefore would either be wasted or give rise to rebellions that could easily be squashed by the British.[142] Mussolini and Ciano explicitly supported this diplomatic note.[143] Keeping in mind Mussolini's protocol of the discussion with Hitler, his consent can thus only be interpreted that he had mainly the declaration on Arabia in mind. But as it was a case of a double declaration, the declaration on suffered the same fate.

Bose travelled to Italy and together with Ciano met Mussolini on 5 May 1942. Bose managed, during the long discussion, to convince him that a declaration on India should be issued at once.[144] On the strength of this, the Italian ambassador presented a note to the Foreign Office requesting a reconsideration of the decision made in Salzburg in the face of a nearly complete occupation of Burma by the Japanese. Mussolini suggested that the Japanese should, on their own, issue a clear declaration on India to which the European partners had to give consent only. Thus the Duce tried to accomplish what according to his protocol had been agreed upon with Hitler, namely, to leave the declaration on India to the Japanese and to postpone the Arabian one.

But now it was Ribbentrop who did not agree. He did not want to go back on the diplomatic note, which he had sent only ten days earlier, so as not to create an impression of unstable politics.[145] When after a week the Italian ambassador again enquired, he referred to the agreement made in Salzburg.[146] With this, Bose's endeavours concerning the declaration had failed for the time being. Each proposal in this direction, as for instance the one made by the German ambassador in Kabul in June 1942,[147] was abruptly dismissed by Ribbentrop.[148] Only in October 1943, when Bose founded the provisionary government of a free India, was the Axis to recognize the same on Japan's request.

Ribbentrop's note clearly expressed that the opinion, which had been arrived at eight days ago, should be adhered to. Curiously,

Hauner in *India in Axis Strategy* gives the interpretation: 'Ribbentrop tried to achieve the revocation of the Salzburg decision.'[149] He also adopted the view that Hitler forfeited his only chance for a final victory when he waived the declaration on India. Hauner argues that Japan and Germany could have united all anti-British forces of the world under their leadership, had the declaration been issued. Therewith he underestimated the effect of propaganda. As the Congress leadership obviously was not inclined to accept the leadership of the Tripartite Powers, a declaration of independence would probably have been ineffective as long as Japan and Germany could not see it through with military intervention.

BOSE'S MEETING WITH HITLER

After Bose had met Mussolini, the long-planned-for meeting with Hitler could not be postponed any longer,[150] even though Ribbentrop did not consider an audience opportune just then.[151] In any case, Bose's presence in Berlin could no longer be kept a secret after the propaganda-offensive. For instance, the German ambassador in Bangkok had already been asked whether Bose could accept leadership of the Indian expatriates.[152]

To begin with, Bose was asked on 27 May 1942 to meet Ribbentrop who explained to him why the German Reich could not issue a declaration on India for the time being. The Tripartite Powers had agreed in principle; only the date was still open. He himself had at first favoured issuing the declaration but had then accepted Hitler's opinion, that the action would make sense only if it could also be seen through with military operations. It would be a different matter should Japan now proclaim India's independence. At the given time, Germany and Italy could not expect any advantages from such an action. Bose should remain patient and wait until German troops had reached south of the Caucasus.[153] Naturally, Bose knew that this was hardly to be expected. The only interesting information for him was that he could meet Hitler in the afternoon. Bose had waited a long time for long for this opportunity, for such a meeting would enhance his position as a political leader. After his arrival at the Führer's headquarters, Bose called Hitler an old revolutionary in his greetings. With this, he probably wanted to create a common platform for the talk. He thanked Hitler for the support he had received in Germany and asked Hitler to help him with advice as an old and experienced revolutionary.

Hitler now started on a long monologue, explaining why he did not want to issue the declaration on India. It was his guiding principle as a politician not to promise anything that could not be carried out later. He had always been careful with inciting violence for shaking off foreign rule. India was very far removed from Germany.[154] The way to India would only be over the dead body of Russia. He expected Germany to have reached India's borders in one or two years only. Therefore, he could only give Bose the advice to go to Japan and carry the revolutionary battle into the country himself from the frontiers of India. British rule could be broken only if the people themselves arose simultaneously with an attack from outside the country.[155] Bose had already learned German but preferred to speak in English in order to avoid misunderstandings. His interpreter Paul Schmidt translated, as Hitler could not understand English.[156] Bose had two requests to make. First, Hitler may please explain to the Indian people the meaning of the remarks about India in *Mein Kampf*. Second, India needed Germany's moral and diplomatic support so that she might not have to depend solely on Japan. Hitler explained that the paragraphs in question had been written against a purely internal political background to demonstrate that he considered passive resistance after the Indian example not to be a suitable method for German conditions. He would give support to India, but only economical, as his country's power reached only as far as his sword.

One of Hitler's remarks gives us an idea as to the role he possibly liked India to play after the war, and that was 'eliminating British influence, avoiding Russian influence, trying to induce Japan to come to any agreement with respect to Russia's eastern border.' According to this, India would have become a buffer between the power blocs: liberated from England, shielding the remaining parts of conquered Russia from the Indian Ocean, and limiting Japan's influence to East Asia.

To be sure, Bose was proud of the fact that he was the first Indian politician to have been received by the Chancellor of the German Reich like a head of state. He saw in the meeting a public recognition of the Indian independence movement.[157] For the rest, however, the audience was a disappointment for him. He is supposed to have remarked later that he considered Hitler to be a German version of the Fakir of Ipi. It had been impossible to have a logical discussion with Hitler.[158]

Bose also met Himmler and Göring on this occasion. Göring displayed a jovial behaviour and promised Bose air force training. Himmler surprised Bose by talking about the Upanishads and Kalidasa's *Shakuntala*. The head of the SS seemed to be quite knowledgeable in respect of Indian cultural history. He was also well informed about the current political and economic situation. Vyas notes in his memoirs: 'Unlike the other Germans, even non Nazis I had come across, Himmler was the only man of consequence in the Third Reich, who seemed to accept India's right to independence as a matter of fact, rather than a mere exigency.'[159]

When on 29 May 1942 the Italian Foreign Ministry announced that the Duce had received Bose, the German press also came to know of Bose's meeting with the Führer. The press received an instruction to avoid any reference as to how Bose had come to Germany and how long he had been there. They should only stress the point that Bose's visit was very welcome in Germany. While mentioning that for the first time Hitler had met a representative of the Indian nationalists, any attack or comparison with Nehru or Gandhi was to be avoided. In particular, they should not create the impression as if Bose's arrival in Berlin had been the signal for a general revolution in India. It should, however, be made clear to German readers that Hitler's ideas had the power of attraction even in India and that Germany was on the side of subjugated peoples.[160]

THE FOUNDATION OF THE SOCIETÀ AMICI DELL'INDIA

On 29 April 1942, the Società Amici dell'India—Society for the Friends of India—was founded in Rome. This was the first opportunity for Schedai to publicly work as freedom fighter for India, as so far he had been allowed to carry out his campaign in secret only. He now had a title to print on his visiting card and an institution for his letterhead. The Società Amici dell'India was basically an interstate association like the Amici dell'Ungheria, Amici della Spangna and the Amici della Romania—friendship societies for Hungary, Spain and Rumania, supported by the Ministry for National Culture in the interest of cultural relations with those countries. However, the association had a far greater meaning for Schedai: it gave him an official status. This was important for him, as after all his rival Bose in Berlin held the status of ambassador and was addressed as 'Excellency'. The foundation of the Società Amici dell'India should therefore be interpreted as the re-valorization of Schedai and his Indian colleagues by the Italians.

The Ministry for National Culture took great pains to invite foreign journalists. In particular the Japanese accepted and noted down each word of the speeches with great interest. The Grand Mufti, Gailani, and the former king of Afghanistan, Amanullah, attended the ceremony.[161] Bose sent Nambiar who read out a short greeting.[162] He could not come himself, as he was still incognito.[163] Rash Behari Bose cabled a greeting.[164] The ceremony took place in the large hall of the Istituto Italiano per il Medio ed Estremo Oriento (ISMEO). As it were, the institute accepted partnership of the new society. Its president, Giovanni Gentile, declared in his speech:

> We like to look upon this Society for the Friends of India as the daughter association of our institute. The institute expects from the society support and promotion of its studies and activities it intends to carry in this part of the Orient. We are convinced that the immediate approaching end-victory will open these parts for Italy's intellectual life.[165]

A well-known personality of Italy's public life, Consigliere Nazionale Ezio Maria Gray, accepted the presidentship of the new society. Schedai's comrade in arms, Ajit Singh, became vice-president. Gray was vice-president of the Camera dei Fasci e delle Corporazione, which functioned in the Fascist state as a representative of the people, and as a legislative organ. He invoked in his speech the historical ties between Italy and India, reaching back to the classical antiquities. He bemoaned the exploitation of the subcontinent through British soldiers and merchants and stressed the point that Italy had no political and territorial ambitions in this part of the world. He avoided thereby any mention of the actual happenings in India and of Italy's concrete India-politics. He described the purpose of the society with the following words: 'Let us jointly utilize it in order to get to know each other better, in order to prepare fertile soil for our nations, and realize on this soil after the common victory the ancient pact between Rome and the Orient.'[166]

Schedai's speech captured the listeners' attention when he mentioned that in 1926 he had met the late Arnoldo Mussolini, the Duce's brother, and that he had won him over as a friend of India. He then introduced the society's programme: once or twice a month he intended to invite the public to scientific lectures about India. The society's activities should be extended after the war to other large cities of Italy. The society would then further promote the political, economic and cultural relationships between both the countries. Until then, it would contribute in convincing the Indian people to look upon Italy and her allies as friends.[167] The Italian diplomatic representative in Bangkok reported that the expatriates in Southeast Asia were thrilled about the society. The Thai press reported on the ceremony, and the transmissions of Radio Bangkok directed towards India spread the news.[168]

THE FORMATION OF THE INDIAN LEGION

Even as a youngster Bose had been interested in military matters. He took part in training courses as a student, later he organized the Volunteer Corps, the cadre troop of the Congress party. In Berlin he recognized the opportunity for the formation of a military unit with Indians as a core unit of the future army in independent India.[169] During his talk with Ribbentrop on 1 May 1941, Bose suggested for the first time to bring the Indian prisoners of war, who had surrendered to the German army in North Africa, into action in the fight for independence. He explained to the minister that he expected them to be immediately prepared to fight against England. An Indian troop on the German side would then exert an extremely strong propaganda-effect on the other Indian units in the British army. Thus the British would lose confidence in these troops and would not be able to bring them into action without reservation.[170]

Bose thought the troops should be employed in the following way: at first, twenty-five to thirty-five well-equipped divisions of the German Africa Corps should fight their way through to the port of Basra. After that, Bose's soldiers, together with the rebellious tribes of the northwest frontier as well as deserters of the Indian army, would march into India.[171] Such a proposal of an Indian Legion was not at all off the track. Foreign voluntary units were no rarity in the Wehrmacht and the Waffen-SS. During the course of war, men from all European countries, as well as from Arab countries and the Asian Soviet Union, served in the German armed forces. There existed the Germanic SS for volunteers from the Netherlands, Belgium and Scandinavia, the French grenadier division in the Waffen-SS 'Charlemagne', and the Russian liberation army under the command of General Andrej Andrejevich Wlassow, to name but a few. Even a British Free Corps was under consideration. It was estimated, that at least 1.5 million foreign nationals fought for the German Reich in the Second World War.[172]

At times, even Hitler did not consider an advance into India by the Wehrmacht an improbability. When, in the summer of 1942, the army group A advanced into the Caucasus and got ready to invade the plains south of the mountain range, Hitler announced according to the memoirs of his armament minister Albert Speer, 'There we can draw up our troops undisturbed and establish supply depots. Then in one or two years' time we will start an offensive into the underbelly of the British Empire. With negligible force it will be possible to liberate Persia and Iraq. The Indians will greet our divisions enthusiastically.' He could not be sure though of the latter assumption. After all, Gandhi had said: 'If the Nazis come to India, the Congress will give them the same fight that it has given Great Britain.'[173]

Alexander Werth writes in his memoirs, that by 1940 the High Command of the Wehrmacht had already decided to send a commando troop to the Indian frontier.[174] Bose's arrival presented a chance to put this plan into action. Already by the end of April 1941, the defense officer of the cavalry, Captain Walter Harbich, received instructions to visit Bose in his hotel, the Esplanade, and converse with him on India's geographical, political and religious questions. This meeting was followed by several more until Harbich received the order in January 1942 to start with the training of Indian volunteers in Camp Regenwurm near Meseritz in the administrative area of Frankfurt on the Oder.[175]

The Reich's foreign minister enquired from Keppler only on 16 October 1941 about 'the range of possibilities of bringing into action

Indian prisoners of war who had fallen into our hands for propaganda purposes, if need be.' He enquired from the high command of the Wehrmacht 'how many Indian prisoners do we actually have,' and whether these Indians could be put into action in the Near East against units of the Indian army. He envisaged thereby using them 'for radio purposes in case of a possible advance into the Caucasus and Iran, etc.'[176] It is noteworthy that at the time of this instruction, Indian prisoners of war had already been working for the German radio for several months under the Foreign Office's supervision. Probably Ribbentrop's ideas extended this limited employment and he already had the formation of an Indian Legion in his mind.

December 1941 saw the first concrete steps undertaken in forming the Indian Legion. Bose was prepared to cooperate under certain conditions only, namely, that Indian soldiers should receive the same military training by instructors of the German army like German recruits.[177] The legion, however, ought to remain a self-reliant unit and should not be mingled with German ones. They would fight against British forces in India only or on the way thereto. He also demanded for his men the same pay, same uniforms and provisioning as the German soldiers. The general army administration was instructed to prepare the formation of the troop in close cooperation with the intelligence service. Nevertheless, the initiative was taken by the Foreign Office. From the very beginning, the legion was not conceived as a military enforcement, but one to only serve propagandistic purposes. It should be an infantry unit and be equipped with the same arms and other equipment as corresponding German units. The legion was to be put to action at the Caucasian front. Bose objected to have the Indian troops put into action in North Africa. He wanted the legionaries to march towards India only.[178] German instructors were provided for, who trained the Indians also in the handling of special weapons such as anti-tank and anti-aircraft guns and light field artillery. During training the troop was to be commanded by German officers only, to be replaced later on by suitable Indian officers and non-commissioned officers.[179]

At that time, about 1,200 Indian prisoners of war were accommodated in Camp Annaburg, situated about 150 kilometres southeast of Berlin.[180] They were provided with the same food rations like German soldiers and received pocket money in addition. They could also avail of the possibility of earning some additional money through work outside the camp. They received Indian food through parcels delivered by the Red Cross. In spite of these facilities, friction occurred between the Indians and the German supervising staff, who insisted on strict observance of the camp rules.[181]

Bose's visit to the Annaburg camp

When Bose paid a visit to the camp on 21 December 1941 in order to recruit volunteers for the Indian Legion, the tensions, bottled-up by the prisoners of war for the past months, were let loose. Incited by non-commissioned officers loyal to the British, who saw in Bose's propaganda a request for betrayal, soldiers started to disturb the speech. They could not believe that it was actually the famous politician who stood in front of them, and took it for a bad trick the Germans were playing on them. The commanding officer of the camp, Major Kurt Krappe, drew the consequences. He threatened the prisoners prior to Bose's next speech on the following day that the guards would resort to shooting should they again show indiscipline. In any case, the Indians must have thought the better of it overnight, because now they received Bose with loud cheers. Meanwhile the news had spread that one of the Indians, who knew Bose from Calcutta, had recognized him.[182]

Bose realized that he had to carefully prepare his recruitment action in order to win over at least part of the prisoners of war for the Indian Legion. Therefore, he selected fifteen men from among the Indian students living in Berlin and the prisoners of war, to form the core of the troop. On 27 January, they received a solemn farewell at the Anhalt railway station, from where they departed partly to the 'Regenwurm' camp near Meseritz for military training and partly to Frankenberg near Chemnitz that was to become the first garrison of the legion.[183]

Meanwhile, 200 prisoners of war, most likely to be suited for the legion, had been selected in Annaburg. Sixty-eight of them were transported to Frankenberg. Bose's trusted persons started canvassing. They could finally convince twenty-one Indians, and the rest were moved to another camp. Additional groups were taken from Annaburg, so that until June 1942, 362 men in seventeen batches passed through, of whom eighty-three asked to be enlisted. Forty-six volunteers were won over from Camp Lamsdorf in Upper Silesia, which had 156 Indian prisoners.[184]

Problems of recruiting volunteers

It became obvious that the Indians were almost indifferent to political arguments. They were much more open to religious questions. The Hindus were prepared to enlist in the legion if they did not have to eat beef there, the Muslims worried about being served pork. A German officer, trying to recruit prisoners of war in North Africa, noticed the positive reaction of Hindus to the swastika on his uniform, which they recognized as a religious symbol. They enquired thereupon, whether in Germany they would have access to the Vedas, their holy scriptures.[185]

The formation of the legion proceeded rather slowly in the beginning of 1942. Non-commissioned officers who had served in the British army for many years and who had developed a strong sense of loyalty towards the British crown, often engaged in counter-propaganda.[186] The army decided to look upon the formation, for the time being, as an experiment and to postpone oath-taking and investiture of the volunteers for the time being.[187]

The Indian Legion recognized neither the military ranks achieved in the British army nor the enlistment periods. Each volunteer had to start anew as private. The first promotions to lance corporal took place after five months. It took even longer to become a non-commissioned officer or an officer. This did not make the legion very attractive for deserving non-commissioned officers of the British army. Sis Ram, a VCO of the Indian army, was at first involved in recruiting volunteers. However, he soon lost all interest when Bose refused to grant him the request to be promoted at once from risaldar-major to captain.[188] One may also presume that many Indians did not find it very attractive in a very cold winter to trade a quiet camp life with strenuous exercising on a snow-covered training area. Marches over a stretch of 30 kilometres were part of daily training.[189]

Instruction officer, First Lieutenant Ulrich von Kritter wrote in his diary: 'It is not easy to pick out pioneers for new political and military aims from a mass of apathetic prisoners, who have been without military discipline for months, and who are either completely indifferent or broken up into various sections. Of course, there should be no coercion in any form. This would not be in the spirit of the

Geneva Convention nor would it serve our purpose.' Until June 1942 the legion consisted of one company only. Recruitment picked up after vehicle arrived with a number of Sikh prisoners, who volunteered.[190] Kritter could note down in February 1943:

> Recruiting improves with increasing size of the legion. [...] This may be partly attributed to a certain herd instinct. On the other hand though, knowledge of the legion's aims and tasks is increasing as well as the feeling that the legion is turning into a rallying-point for Indians in Germany. This feeling of solidarity alone can contribute greatly to the growth of the legion. A few days ago, His Excellency Bose could cable his congratulations to the 2,000th legionary.[191]

Bose's recruiters are supposed to have used force in a few isolated cases. Kritter notes down:

> The recruiters in their enthusiasm went rather too far in the case of some men. They organized a thrashing from the rest of the men when some of the recruits wanted to back out again. Such mutual methods of education seem to have an extremely curative effect on these mild people as long as they do not degenerate into brutality, which had happened in a few isolated cases only.[192]

Representatives of the Swiss protection force learnt during an inspection of the Annaburg camp that some inmates had been 'maltreated' by compatriots because they had refused to join the legion.[193] However, a later report notes that recruitment continues and 'prisoners are no longer ill-treated or subjected to brutality.'[194]

After they had deserted the British, the legion's interpreter Ernst Bannerth and the legion's medical officer Ernst Koch-Grünberg accused Abid Hasan and other Indians of having beaten up compatriots. One of the victims is supposed to have been Zain-ud-Din Abi Shah who supposedly had joined the legion only in order to persuade other legionaries to quit again. However, Koch-Grünberg also clarified that force had not been necessary: 'Most of the "volunteers" followed blindly like sheep, having no clear idea of what they were doing. They saw their friends already in legion uniform and were attracted by the sight of fine clothes, pretty girls and the possibility of a free social life generally.'[195]

German-Italian disputes regarding the prisoners of war

The number of Indian soldiers captured during Rommel's advances promised to swell the ranks of the legion. However, they were under Italian captivity. Already in the middle of December 1941 an agreement had been made with the Italians that suitable Indian prisoners of war should be sent over to Germany. Thereupon, until March only about forty Indians arrived in Germany. The high command of the Wehrmacht, the OKW, requested to bring all Indians over so that they could make the selection on their own.[196]

The Italian military agreed now to release 500 men. The remaining ones were needed in Italy. They would be put into action for matters of security, propaganda, or as interpreters.[197] In reality, the Italians wanted to form their own Indian Legion as a rival undertaking. Bose's rival Schedai was behind this project. He managed to win over 850 men for his troop. However, the Italian Legion was a complete failure. It was dissolved after a mutiny in November 1942 and the legionaries were shifted to Germany.[198] The Italians violated an agreement with the Germans, according to which the formation of Indian volunteer troops should be exclusively in the hands of the Wehrmacht.[199] For this reason, they presented their troop to the Germans as being a small special unit only.[200] Of course, they could always refer to the fact that the Germans on their part also violated an agreement by forming a troop with Arab prisoners of war, and that they in their turn did not send their Arab prisoners of war to Italy either.[201]

The disputed matter was left to arbitration on the ministerial level. Ciano declared to the German Foreign Office on 24 April 1942 that he was prepared to send 500 to 600 of a total of 1,100 Indians to Germany. The Italians themselves needed the remaining ones.[202] Keppler, however demanded all the Indians,[203] whereupon the Italians agreed to keep only 100 to 200 men.[204] In reality they sent only 500 men. Protests by the OKW did not help either.[205] Only after the Germans transferred 232 Arab prisoners of war to Italy on 26 July 1942, did the Italians sent an additional 500 men, having in mind the formation of their own troop of 200 men.[206] Trott complained that Italians had kept the best men for themselves and 'passed on to Germany only elements with a negative or indifferent mindset.'[207]

In the beginning of 1942, the Italian Foreign Office even tried to persuade Bose to come to Rome in order to supervise the formation of the Italian Indian Legion. Bose did not entertain such proposals for several reasons. In the first place he knew that the Indian soldiers did not have a high opinion of Italian officers. Secondly, he wanted that the Indian soldiers should be instructed in the use of modern weapons. These, however, were available only in the German army. Furthermore, he knew that the Germans played the leading role in the Axis.[208] The Italian Foreign Ministry refused Bose's request of going to Libya so that he could himself select suitable prisoners of war. The accommodation of the prisoners in North Africa was not yet satisfactory and the diplomatic agent Renato Prunas, chief of the overseas department in the Italian Foreign Ministry, was afraid Bose might object to this. Schedai had warned about this.[209] Apparently, this was another of his intrigues to keep Bose away from his sphere of influence.

Intelligence training in the 'Regenwurm' camp

The Indian volunteers who were sent to the 'Regenwurm' camp near the Brandenburg Meseritz, constituted there a training unit of the training regiment zbV 800 Brandenburg. This was the troop of the Secret Service of the Wehrmacht, the security. About 100 Indians received their training for action in the troubled Northwest Frontier Province of India.[210] Bose's trusted helpers Swami and Hasan had selected the participants from Indian prisoners of war in Camp Annaburg.[211]

Cavalry Captain Walter Harbich received instructions in January 1942 to train the Indians. At first he had to select suitable instructors. He considered not only military knowledge and experience in combat, but also knowledge of languages and time spent abroad. A camp library containing books on Indian history, geography and culture served for additional instruction of the soldiers.[212] On 28 and 29 September 1942, Bose visited the camp that was now known as 'Special Unit Bayadere' (Sonderverband Bajadere).[213] Harbich reported that the training progressed very well indeed as the Indians showed great interest and had already received a well-founded training in the Indian army. Therefore, he concentrated on riding instructions. According to Harbich, the officers and non-commissioned officers were allowed to retain their ranks from the Indian army as opposed to the Indian Legion. Thus the training unit had from the very beginning three Indian officers, two of them physicians, and a number of Indian non-commissioned officers.[214]

The Indians received engineering instructions and took part in parachuting and mountain rifleman training. The latter took place in Ebensee.[215] In September 1942, Swami formed another group for training in telecommunication under a Captain Ruperti, at first in Berlin and then in a telecommunication training centre of the Wehrmacht in Rösrath near Cologne. The soldiers were taught handling of radio communication sets, and receiving and sending of Morse signals.[216] After the training was completed, Harbich handed over the commando in December 1942 to a staff officer of the Wehrmacht. Unless kept for special missions, the Indians were transferred to the Indian Legion in Königsbrück.[217] These special missions turned out to be a fiasco. According to Vyas, the security flew eight commando troops into Asia. The British in Karachi captured one soldier. He had the secret code for communication with him and could not destroy it in time. The British captured two more troops before Berlin received news of the failed mission.[218]

AN INDIAN FIFTH COLUMN

Intelligence Officer Witzel could still continue his activities in Kabul after the failure of 'Operation Tiger'. Together with confidential agent Talwar alias Rahmat Khan, Witzel and Rasmuss carried out preparations for the event that German troops would march into India after victory over the Soviet Union. Rahmat Khan set out for his journey to India at the end of July 1941 with 20,000 rupees in his pocket for Bose's followers, to be used for demoralizing the military, strikes, espionage and anti-English propaganda.[219] According to the ideas of the Germans placing the order, they were to carry our extensive sabotage all over the country, 'here today, there tomorrow'.[220] However, Talwar came only as far as Lahore and did not reach Calcutta, as he thought the journey too unsafe and also because he had no contacts there. He returned to the tribal territory of northwest India where he had already established several operational bases. Thus he worked together with Miran Jan Syal in Kudakhel and with Sanobar

Hussain in Swal Quilla. These two were leaders of rebel tribes.[221]

Bose was included in the operations of the Military Intelligence. When two agents were supposed to go to Kabul, they discussed the political situation in detail with Bose.[222] After the failure of 'Operation Tiger', it was decided that Harbich's 'Sonderverband Tiger', consisting of sixty soldiers meant for deployment in Afghanistan and north India, should rather operate in Turkestan. The special unit was moved near Warsaw where they tried to recruit deserters from among Turkestanian prisoners of war.[223] It was also planned to arrange for a landing and starting ground for Condor planes[224] and to establish a permanent radio communication system with Bose's followers in India.[225] A suitable terrain was found[226] but the landing ground was never built. However, Witzel was able to have a secret depot set up where explosives and fuel were stored for the troops of the Wehrmacht. A fixed wireless communication also existed since September between non-commissioned radio operator Zugenbuehler in Kabul and the radio station in Stahnsdorf. Zugenbuehler's radio station was supposed to be ready for shifting into the frontier region. An additional mobile radio station, consisting of a petrol generator and a transmitter, was set up in the frontier region and operated by two local radio operators.[227]

Witzel worked out a plan in case German troops advanced into India. The population should be disturbed by means of psychological sabotage. This included spreading of alarming rumours and false information, inducing panic shopping, obstruction of traffic through planned misleading of the expected refugee tracks, and impediment of the government's functioning by creating an espionage psychosis. Disruptions of telephone connections and disturbing supply facilities were part of active sabotage. Besides this, individual larger acts of sabotage on communication lines and supply plants were provided for. Light signals were to indicate destinations and landing grounds for the German air force. German radio stations in the frontier region were to transmit reconnaissance results. Bose had held out to the German government the prospect of a general revolt in India, induced by the advance of foreign troops, but Witzel did not reckon with this. At most he thought it possible to harm the English through individual acts of sabotage.[228]

To be sure, Witzel and Rasmuss could not do much in Afghanistan and India without the cooperation of Talwar who showed less and less liking for the conspiracy with the Germans: the delivery of arms could be expected no more since the attack on the Soviet Union, and money alone could not achieve much in the Hindu Kush Mountains. Santimoy Ganguly and Sodhi Harmindar Singh waited for weeks in vain for the training in sabotage promised by the Italians. Over and above, Talwar could communicate with Bose only via the German embassy, and he suspected that the Germans manipulated his messages.[229] However, Rasmuss and Witzel continued to trust Talwar. They mentioned in their reports to Berlin sabotage acts, 500 deserters in the border region, and German civil internees giving advice on sabotage to Indians.[230]

Bose also thought he could use Talwar as messenger for his followers in India. He sent detailed instructions for revolutionary operations via the German embassy:

- Seditious propaganda should undermine trust in currency as well as induce soldiers and civil servants to desert. The newsreels by Radio Azad Hind should be spread through whispering campaigns and handbills, even the cows roaming India's streets freely should be utilized as 'sandwich man'.
- Industrial sabotage should not take place. On retreat, the British should be stopped from carrying out destructions. A go-slow campaign should impede war economy.
- Japanese and German armed forces should be greeted as friends on advancing into India. Agents should be ready at the east coast, in Burma, and at the northwest frontier to support the invaders. The code word 'silver moon' was to be the contact code.
- The party should prepare lists of ministers for each province as well as registers of friendly and hostile persons. Hostile persons were to be immediately arrested on retreat of the British.[231]

Talwar however preferred not to be seen too much. Kabul became too hot for him and he kept his distance from the Germans after Uttam Chand had been deported by the Afghan authorities, in spite of—or due to—the fact that the German ambassador had used his influence in his favour.[232] Trott expressed his disappointment in Berlin: 'Attempts to establish a regular relay of messengers with the help of

Rahmat Khan (Talwar) have failed so far, also all attempts to establish a radio communication across the border region with the Bose-people in India.'[233] But Rasmuss and Witzel continued to put their trust in Talwar, most probably because they did not have another confidential agent in India. Thus they consulted him regarding the course of the Quit India Movement[234] and planned the construction of the landing ground with him.[235] On 29 November 1942, the British criminal police arrested Talwar in Lahore when he was in the process of preparing a report for the Germans about his journey to Bombay. Talwar made himself known as a double agent in the service of Germany and the Soviet Union. During interrogation, he willingly and without delay revealed details of his operations as agent and the German secret code. The police noted with satisfaction: 'He is prepared to go back to Kabul and continue his contact with the Axis, reporting to the Russians in Kabul and to the British if and when he returns to India.'[236]

Now Talwar was not only a double but a triple agent. He worked even with the colonial masters when he, strictly speaking, wanted to drive out of India to avoid being arrested for high treason. This meant for the Germans that the enemy was well informed about their secret operations in Afghanistan. It seemed Talwar was not quite happy though with the triple role he played. In his memoirs he did comment in detail on his contacts with the Soviet embassy in Kabul. His arrest by the British, however, is not mentioned even with a single word. The Germans were unsuspecting. On 18 January 1943 Talwar handed over his report to Rasmuss exactly as if nothing had happened, and he had a spirited conversation with Witzel about the political situation in India.[237]

Initially, the Italian minister Quaroni had also worked together with Talwar until Rasmuss forbade the agent to have contact with the Italian.[238] Quaroni preferred to gather his information about happenings in India through careful study of the press. He used half of his budget for secret service activities to buy newspapers. He feared that aggressive conspiratorial activities would only endanger his position in the country and was useless anyway as long as none of the Axis troops was advancing. He could only dismiss the attempts of the Germans as is evident from the protocol he gave the British ambassador in Kabul during interrogation, after the Italian government had switched over to the side of the Allied:

As regards the German Legation Herr Rasmuss and his acolytes showed a rather surprising technical inefficiency in the conduct of their work, their chief fault being a failure to take sufficient precautions for secrecy. Much worse than this, however, was their neglect to base their plans on the higher requirements of the politico-strategical situation of the Axis. This meant, in effect, that they should confine themselves to unobtrusive espionage, and at all costs avoid getting into trouble. In fact they did nothing but look out for it.[239]

The Germans carried on with their sabotage and seditious plans in the spring of 1943 as well, and finally got into great difficulties with the Afghan government. The Afghans became more and more inclined to give in to British and Soviet pressure. The Allied would have really liked it if the Afghans had completely severed diplomatic relations with the German Reich.

The Continuation of India-Politics until Bose's Departure

ose's decision to go to East Asia was governed by the same reasons that had made him give up his reticence while involving himself actively in German propaganda for India. He presumed that with Japanese help he could achieve considerably more than in Europe. On the face of it, it seemed the Japanese military could advance as far as India. An impressive number of Indian expatriates waited for him in Southeast Asia to take over the leadership of their organizations. Hitler agreed to the journey but its realization proved difficult because of the war conditions. It took months before Bose could embark on his journey. German India-politics continued during this waiting period.

NEGOTIATIONS FOR BOSE'S JOURNEY TO SOUTHEAST ASIA

When Bose celebrated his birthday with his Indian assistants in January 1942, he remarked that his next birthday would definitely not be celebrated in Berlin. He intended to continue his fight from a place nearer to India.[1] In February 1942 Bose presented a plan for propaganda and sabotage activities in India to the Japanese military attaché in Berlin. At the same time he expressed his urgent desire to fly to Rangoon.[2] Ribbentrop refused Bose's departure.[3] Naturally he did not want to let go of the Indian who had just declared himself willing to assist in propaganda activities as long as this action was in full swing. The Japanese on their part also had reservations allowing Bose to take over the leadership of Indian expatriates in their sphere of influence. They suspected Bose to be under German influence and that he would grant them economic privileges after India had gained independence.[4]

But finally they had to concede that the Indian expatriates did not accept their favourite candidate Rash Behari Bose as their leader.[5] The Indian Independence League, which stood under the influence of Japan, led by Rash Behari Bose, finally merged with the independent Indian National Council, and the council wanted to be under Bose's leadership.[6] Ribbentrop, though, did not favour Bose's plan at that particular time. He did not want to be played off against the Japanese by Indian expatriates.[7]

Bose sent a letter to Ribbentrop on 22 May 1942 requesting his permission to go to the Far East: 'Not only the cause of India, but our common cause as well, will be best served by my presence in the East, as near to India as possible.'[8] He could refer to Mussolini who favoured his plan as well. The Italian government was of the opinion that Bose could serve the interests of the Axis Powers in East Asia better than in Berlin.[9] Bose called on Woermann the following day and explained once more the reasons for his plan. He would be able to work much more effectively from Burma than from Berlin. The majority of Indians in Southeast Asia desired *his* leadership and not that of the other Bose who stood under Japanese influence. He mentioned Mussolini's offer to fly with an Italian plane in a non-stop flight from Rhodes to Rangoon. Woermann refrained from commenting on the itinarary.[10] Keppler, however, declared that he considered Bose's departure to be premature. The time was not ripe for a successful revolution in India.[11] Woermann did not agree with these arguments. Bose was best able to decide on the right time, and this was the best in the Far East. The undersecretary of state though was not sure whether the Japanese would actually welcome Bose and suggested to Ribbentrop to ask them first before letting Bose embark on his journey.[12]

The Reich's foreign minister told Bose at a meeting on 27 May 1942, that he was not against the journey but thought travelling by plane too dangerous. He offered transportation by submarine directly from Germany to Rangoon. He would have to exercise some more patience though as the preparations would take some time.[13] Hitler, who met Bose on the same day, was also willing to make the journey possible. He too advised against taking a plane and suggested using a submarine instead.[14]

Mussolini's offer to take Bose by plane to East Asia was based on the military convention by the three powers effective from 18

January 1942. The convention provided for an air connection between Europe and Japan. Hitler was disinterested and Air Minister Hermann Göring was strictly against it as he lacked the necessary machines; but Mussolini, who also held the position of air minister, was all in favour of the project. The Italian air force and the Linee Aeree Transcontinentali Italiane (LATI) already started planning for flights in January. Almost like a dress rehearsal a plane flew on 9 May 1942 over the capital of Eritrea and dropped pamphlets, announcing Italy's final victory. The plane did make a safe landing in Ciampino near Rome on the following day, but all three engines failed when it was taken to the workshop, situated 20 kilometres away in Guidona. The machine crash-landed and four passengers were hurt. This incident made Hitler and Ribbentrop lose faith in the technical abilities of Italian aviation. The Italians and Japanese nevertheless made common preparations for the intercontinental flight.[15]

After the propaganda action about the Cripps Mission had been successfully completed, it seemed Ribbentrop did not need Bose any more. Keppler's reservations did not convince him. Woermann succeeded instead with his argument that Bose could work more effectively in Asia against the British. Goebbels was of the same opinion: 'But his moving to Bangkok is more purposeful because, when he stays in Bangkok, he is not viewed so much as an emigrant as when he stays in Berlin or elsewhere in the Reich.'[16]

The delegates of Indian expatriates from East and Southeast Asia met in Bangkok on 15 June 1942. The Japanese tried very hard to give moral support to the Indians. They had specially invited the German and Italian ambassadors to attend the meeting so that together they could reassure the Indians that the Tripartite Powers would not make any claim on India whatsoever.[17] The conference participants paid special attention to the representatives of Germany and Italy.[18] Rash Behari Bose was elected president and expressed special gratitude to the two diplomats of the Axis Powers for their friendly and encouraging attitudes.[19] The German ambassador, however, noticed that the Indian expatriates hardly supported Rash Behari Bose. Subhas Chandra Bose could take over the leadership were he to go to East Asia.[20] The delegates agreed on a resolution of thirty-five points. The thirty-first point provided for Subhas Chandra Bose's coming to East Asia.[21]

A power struggle was in the making: the two Boses had a

discussion by telephone on 3 July 1942 and Rash Behari suggested to acknowledge Gandhi as supreme leader in India's freedom struggle.[22] Next day the Bangkok papers reported in bold letters that the two Boses had agreed to acknowledge the Mahatma as spiritual head.[23] At that time the Japanese still hoped to be able to use Gandhi or Nehru for their politics, as ambassador Oshima explained a few months later.[24] Subhas Chandra, however, was alarmed about the manner in which his namesake claimed to the Japanese an allegedly complete agreement with him.[25] He wanted therefore to send a telegram to Bangkok, suggesting combining all Indian nationalists of the world in one organization only. Ribbentrop, however, forbade him to do so as it would have contradicted Japanese opinions too much.[26] The Italian ambassador in Tokyo came to know that the Japanese did not want Bose's presence yet in Asia.[27]

The British military hoped to be able to prevent Bose's arrival in the Far East. The Special Operations executive in a cable to the Indian government suggested instigating the Indians against Japan through newspaper articles published in China. These articles should report that the Germans wanted to get rid of Subhas Chandra Bose and that the Japanese wanted him only because they did not quite get on with Rash Behari Bose.[28]

Ciano understood that a politician like Bose did not want to remain in exile if he could work much more effectively in his native country or from a nearby location. To force Bose to stay in Europe would in his opinion have meant losing his friendship. And that would have rendered him useless anyway.[29] The Italian foreign minister even tried hard to make the journey possible. He offered a flight to Asia. Bose could have embarked on his journey to Japan at the end of June from Rome.[30] The first Italian intercontinental flight during the war to East Asia started on 29 June 1942. After touching down in Saporoschje on the Dnjepr River and in Baotou in Inner Mongolia, the flight reached Tokyo on 3 July 1942. The return flight in the same month was also successful. The Japanese, however, did not like the Italians to fly over the Soviet Union because of the Japanese-Soviet non-aggression pact.[31]

Ribbentrop still considered a non-stop flight too risky. If the plane had to make an emergency landing, he kept Ciano informed, Bose might fall into British hands. He hinted, though, that there would be 'another possibility to help Bose to reach East Asia'[32] shortly. Ciano was annoyed. Bose's continued stay in Europe served no purpose and was detrimental to his image in his native country.[33] Preparations for 'the other possibility' came to naught. The Japanese navy refused to assist in preparations for transportation by submarine.[34] Bose contacted the foreign minister on 23 July 1942 and pointed out the successful transcontinental test flight of the Italians.[35] Ribbentrop told him he could fly if he wanted this so desperately.[36] The Japanese government also finally signalled their agreement that Bose could come to Japan with the next Italian flight.[37] The Italians and the Japanese differed on the choice of the best flight route. The Italians preferred the shortest route. The Japanese insisted on a more southern route that would avoid flying over the Soviet Union.[38] Finally Ciano requested Bose to commence his journey after 15 October 1942 at a date still to be fixed, but for technical reasons alone and without luggage.[39] Bose agreed and requested at the same time to be allowed to see Ciano and Mussolini so he could bid farewell.[40] This request was at first even granted.[41]

Ribbentrop received Bose on 14 October for an official farewell. Ribbentrop explained to him the objectives of Japanese politics. Japan was interested in revolutionizing India because she felt threatened by the British. A conquest of the country, however, was not a realistic political possibility. India would become a free country in a world led and shaped in Europe by the Axis Powers and in East Asia by Japan. After that they discussed a future collaboration in propaganda for India. Bose should continue to stay in touch with the Foreign Office via the embassies in Tokyo and Bangkok. In case German troops crossed the Caucasus, Ribbentrop held out the prospect of using parachute troops in northwest India.[42]

A short while later it was announced that the flight had to be postponed but would start within the next few days. Bose waited several weeks in vain.[43] The Italian Foreign Ministry informed only in the middle of November that the flight had to be postponed by three to four months as the Japanese did not have the medium-wave radar equipment the Italians considered to be absolutely necessary. They had to be installed first.[44] The Japanese did not want to agree to a renewed flight over the Soviet Union because of their non-aggression pact. The southern route did not have the required technical preconditions.[45] The audiences with Ciano and Mussolini were also cancelled. The

Italians now did not want Bose any more in Rome.[46] Bose did not give up hope and wrote to Ribbentrop: 'Viewed from the standpoint of a common world strategy, it would appear that the importance of India in the common struggle against the Anglo-American powers has increased considerably.' Therefore he had to reach East Asia as soon as possible and would request the foreign minister to make the journey possible, either by plane or submarine.[47]

The Japanese navy was prepared to send a submarine into the Indian Ocean. A German submarine was to transfer important war materials to the Japanese.[48] Bose could avail of this opportunity even though the Japanese navy superiors were reluctant at first as internal regulations forbade transportation of civil persons on a warship during wartime. Bose refuted this reservation with the argument that he was not a private person but in superior command of the Indian liberation army.[49] Strictest secrecy had to be observed as the journey would take a long time. Only the Italian Foreign Ministry and Mussolini had to be informed. All others were told that Bose was on an inspection tour. Listeners to Azad Hind did not notice his disappearance either as Bose's voice had been recorded.[50] Bose used the same Italian passport issued to one Orlando Mazzotta, which he had been given for his escape from Kabul as travelling document.[51]

On 26 January 1943 Bose gave a speech at a public function on the occasion of India's Independence Day in front of six hundred people. He visited the Indian Legion for the last time two days later. Together with Keppler, Nambiar and Werth he went to Kiel on 7 February 1943 and spent the night there. Abid Hasan, who was to accompany him on the passage, met him at night. At the crack of dawn on the following day, the two Indians boarded the submarine type IX.[52] His wife Emilie Schenkl and daughter Anita, born in November 1942, stayed behind.[53]

To the Far East in submarine

U 180, under the command of Lieutenant Commander Werner Musenberg, reached the North Sea through the Skagerak, made a wide circle around the British Isles north of the Faroe Islands, and in the beginning of March 1943 took fuel from a submarine tanker. The submarine crossed the Atlantic in a southerly direction at a speed of 140 nautical miles per hour. On 18 April 1941, east of the Cape of Good Hope, the *U 180* sunk the British motor tanker *Corbis*.[54] Bose and Hasan watched how the crew left the ship: the English soldiers secured the only lifeboat for themselves, while the Indian and Malay sailors had to make do with rudderless floats, providing them hardly a chance for survival.[55]

Bose utilized the forced leisure during the passage and translated his book *The Indian Struggle*. He also prepared his talks with the Japanese prime minister Tojo and discussed various problems of Indian politics with Hasan. The future of the African colonies after the collapse of the British Empire was one of the subjects; others were whether Shakespeare should still be taught in Indian schools after independence, and what type of uniform should be worn by women in the Indian National Army.[56] As agreed upon, the *U 180* met the Japanese sub-marine cruiser *I 29* on 23 April 1943. A rough sea impeded for a few days the exchange of passengers and freight. Only four days later a rubber dinghy took Bose and Hasan to the Japanese submarine. Two Japanese engineer officers changed over to the *U 180*. The *I 29* reached Sabang on Sumatra on 6 May 1943.[57] Bose arrived in Tokyo by plane ten days later. Before boarding, Bose had cabled to Hitler, thanking him for support and hospitality.[58]

An additional group with Swami as leader managed to get to the Far East in a blockade runner, the *MS Osorno*, that put out to sea on 23 March 1943 from Bordeaux. Three German diplomats, one engineer and a businessman who wanted to go to Shanghai, were part of the group. A submarine attacked the ship before the coast of North Africa, and she was chased at the equator by an American cruiser. She managed to escape at a speed of 27 knots. The *MS Osorno* reached Batavia (now Jakarta) on 20 May 1943 and proceeded from there to Yokohama. Hasan went to meet Swami there and took him to Tokyo, where he also met Bose.[59]

BOSE'S ACTIVITIES DURING THE TIME OF WAITING

Bose continued with his activities while waiting for an opportunity to travel to the Far East. He worked untiringly for the realization of the working plan he had drafted in May 1942. He prepared in all seriousness for taking over power in a free India. He designed, for instance, the stamps for use after independence. The stamps depicted military and folkloristic motifs and bore the inscription 'Jai Hind'. The

Berlin Reich's printing press printed up to ten million pieces of the ten stamps of different values produced by a German graphic artist.[60] The founding of branches of the Free India Centre (ZFI) was one of the projects still outstanding. Bose's detailed plan of work had provided for branches in twenty countries of Europe, Asia and America.[61]

Planned founding of ZIF branches

Bose approached Renato Prunas on 4 June 1942 as a fist step for realizing this ambitious goal. He suggested the installation of another secret transmitter, in addition to the one already operated by Schedai, that could broadcast programmes in Bengali, Gujarati or Marathi. The sender should function under the name Swatantra Bharat Radio. Besides that, he also wanted to publish in Italy a journal in English, and the vernacular version of his journal *Azad Hind* published in Germany. He also considered the publication of a weekly newspaper. Within the framework of his plans for the government of the future independent India, he thought of sending some Indians to Italy for studying land reform as well as malaria and tuberculosis control. He wanted three or four of his assistants to move to Italy in order to realize his ideas.[62]

The resonance of Bose's project in Rome was poor. The Italians did not want to outright refuse the founding of a ZIF branch—maybe out of consideration for the Axis partner. The Italian Foreign Ministry, however, did not consider the installation of an additional transmitter so very urgent. After all, they already maintained Schedai's secret transmitter besides the official programmes of the Roman short-wave transmitter. They did hold out the project, however, in order to publish an Italian edition of the journal *Azad Hind* through the institute there for the Far East, but it never came to pass.[63] Prunas was willing to accept his proposal of sending one of his Bengali assistants to Rome, but the competent department in the Ministry for Popular Culture preferred selecting a Bengali from among the Indian prisoners of war on its own.[64]

Even though the Italian Foreign Ministry was busy at that time working on plans for increasing activities in the Orient, and attaining a leading position in this field, they were not interested in working with Bose. They preferred to hold on to Schedai even though Prunas and other leading personalities did not credit him with political understanding and thought him suitable only for propaganda activities. Bose had gained the impression during his earlier contact with Italy that they were very much open to his ideas. Now he had to register with disappointment that the Italians preferred his rival Schedai.[65]

The situation in France was different. The founding of a branch of ZFI in Paris was entirely left to the discretion of the German military authority in occupation. In January 1942, Bose travelled to the French capital to prepare the organization of his office there.[66] He presented a plan for working in France to the Foreign Office on 10 June 1942. The extension of his activities to the neighbouring occupied country, he explained, was very much necessary before Schedai could extend his field of action there. He suggested that the Paris branch should spread anti-British propaganda in collaboration with the German embassy and exert influence on the Indians living in France. He proposed his compatriot Madhavo Rao as director.[67] Rao was given the task of organizing the office, the objective of which was limited to publishing and distributing a French version of the journal *Azad Hind*.[68] As the construction plans for the office were shelved a few months later,[69] Rao's activities consisted mainly in arranging functions and get-togethers for the Indian Independence Day on 26 January 1943[70] and for the Amritsar Day on 13 April 1943.[71]

After Nambiar had presented a plan of the ZFI in September 1943 for organizing a branch in Paris,[72] the branch was solemnly inaugurated on 26 January 1944 in the presence of representatives of the Indian colony, the German embassy, the Japanese consulate, and the chargé d'affaires of the Fascist Italian Republic.[73] The office did not last long. When the Allied Powers advanced towards Paris, it had to be closed on 11 August 1944. Rao, his assistant Bannerji Lal, and the French lady secretary fled to Berlin.[74]

Training of Indians in government and party offices

The study of the political system of his host country was another of Bose's concerns. He thought this would give him ideas for the formation of the future Indian constitution. He had already observed developments in various countries during his travels in Europe in the 1930s. The labour service of the Reich was one of the institutions that interested him. He deputed an assistant of the ZFI to thoroughly study the manner of working of the labour service, with a representative of the department for external affairs of this institution, followed by a visit to one of the labour service camps.[75] Bose also wanted some of his younger assistants to participate in instruction courses for leader recruits for the Hitler Youth Organization.[76]

During talks with Ribbentrop on 14 October 1942, Bose enquired about the possibility of having a small police troop trained in Germany as core for the future Indian political police.[77] Apparently, Bose had mentioned this already on 15 July 1942 to Heinrich Himmler, the Reichsführer SS and head of the German police.[78] It seems the methods of the German police had impressed Bose so much that he would have liked to apply these in India. He repeated his request shortly before his departure. He had the support of Ribbentrop and Keppler who approached Himmler directly.[79] Some selected soldiers of the Indian Legion were sent in February 1943 to Berlin for a course in police training.[80] SS-Gruppenführer Ernst Kaltenbrunner, chief of the Reich Security Head Office, decided that the Indians should be trained 'more as police and less as SS'.[81]

Establishment of additional clandestine radio stations

Bose approached the Foreign Office with the request to permit him the expansion of his clandestine radio programmes, after he realized that the Italians would not concede to him the new possibilities for his activities. He based his proposal on the fact that now enemy transmissions for India had been started from Teheran, Chungking, Tashkent and Boston. Bose wanted to direct a programme called National Congress Radio in Hindustani, Bengali and English to the followers of the Congress party, instructing them in the continuation of the non-cooperation movement in India. A Waziristan Radio with programmes in Hindustani and Pashto was to be directed towards the rebel tribes in northwest India.[82]

Bose had himself spoken a few times on Radio Azad Hind and had openly sided with the Axis Powers. Now he was worried the broadcasts could have lost credibility with some of the listeners and be viewed as instrument of Axis propaganda. Broadcasts from the National Congress Radio reported on happenings in such a way as to make listeners think the broadcast came from within India.[83] The name was cleverly chosen as Congress Radio, the underground transmitter of the Congress party, as if it actually existed in India.

During the August uprisings, transmissions commenced from various points in Bombay and could be received up to Madras. The police managed only in September 1942 to locate it.[84]

Bose could operate his new radio station by the beginning of September: Waziristan Radio was on the air daily for a quarter of an hour and National Congress Radio for half an hour. Radio Azad Hind continued to transmit daily for two hours.[85] After some time the transmission times were even increased and the programmes repeated once daily, so that in August 1943 the programmes of the three stations were on the air for a total of six hours daily.[86] The Italians came to know of the new stations only after Quaroni reported to have heard them in Kabul.[87]

Travelling in Europe

Through Keppler's kind intervention Bose was able to make the acquaintance of two guests of state from Slovakia. First he met Prime Minister Vojtech Tuka and President Josef Tito. Tuka showed great interest in Indian culture and requested a copy of the Bhagavadgita. They invited Bose soon after the meeting to visit their country. This gave Bose an opportunity to undertake a short journey through Europe. He travelled to Slovakia in November 1942 and visited France, Belgium and the Netherlands afterwards. He met Pierre Laval, the president of unoccupied État Français, in France and held a press conference in Belgium with Belgian and French journalists. The round trip was completed with a visit to the Indian Legion in Holland.[88]

GANDHI, THE 'HINDENBURG OF INDIA'?

Goebbels received Bose on 22 July 1942 to discuss with him the underlying principles of propaganda for India. The propaganda minister was actually in charge of interior propaganda but he observed the India-activities of the Foreign Office with great interest, judging by the frequent entries referring to Bose in his diary. The propaganda on India, after all, did not only serve a foreign political purpose but Bose's collaboration with the Axis Powers was also highlighted in Germany. Bose had created such an impression on Goebbels that he wrote later in his diary: 'He is full of praise about our national socialist propaganda work and claims that these in particular have made the Reich and National Socialism represented by me popular in India.'[89]

Bose gained sympathy for this flattery. Goebbels judged Bose as 'to make an extremely intelligent and flexible impression and he has it in him to become a great leader of the people.'[90] Bose's hope of having the proclamation on India published through contact with the influential minister was an illusion. Goebbels held on to the opinion of Hitler who had told him that one could proclaim the freedom of a nation only if one also had the power to enforce it. In this connection Goebbels remembered the independence declaration having been issued when the Africa Corps advanced: 'We also operate with our Egypt declaration somewhat in a vacuum. It would have been better to have waited with this declaration until we had at least Alexandria. Like this it can do us at present more harm than good.'[91] Anyhow, the officials in the propaganda ministry who were always at loggerheads with the press department of the Foreign Office were now, after the meeting, less unwilling to work together with the ZFI. Goebbels obliged Bose by seeing to it that less exotic and misleading articles about India appeared in the German press.[92]

The Cripps Mission had failed because of Gandhi's unyielding attitude but his anti-German and anti-Japanese attitude gave Berlin still enough cause for worry. Gandhi had announced in February 1942 in an article in *Harijan*: 'If the Nazis come to India, the Congress will give them the same fight that it has given Great Britain.'[93] Keppler had so far insisted that Gandhi should not be attacked but he suggested in the beginning of July 1942 a strategy change. He was afraid Gandhi would ask the Indians to resist a Japanese invasion and in this case might side with the British. Keppler therefore suggested warning the Indian listeners of the radio propaganda against any compromise with England as this could result in a Japanese invasion. They should not follow Gandhi should he call for a compromise with the colonial masters.[94] With this, Keppler also expressed Bose's opinion. Bose would have preferred from the very beginning to continue the political altercation with Gandhi in his short-wave transmissions. He viewed Gandhi in a similar role as Paul von Hindenburg's when the National Socialists took over power. He wanted to acknowledge the respect the Indian people had for him and honour him as a person but declare his method of passive resistance as outdated. In this way he hoped to be able to incite the Indians to a violent uprising against colonial power. Trott believed Bose capable of being successful with these 'two-edged polemics'. He therefore suggested allowing Bose to differ with Gandhi in his secret transmissions. However, Gandhi should not be attacked in the official short-wave transmissions and in the German press.[95] The German foreign minister gave his permission for this change in the propaganda line.[96]

THE QUIT INDIA MOVEMENT AND THE AUGUST UPRISING

The German diplomats' worries about Gandhi's attitude proved soon to be unfounded. The All-India Congress Committee (AICC) passed on 8 August 1942 in Bombay the Quit India Resolution in reply to the offer by the British government, which Cripps had conveyed. This resolution included the demand for immediate independence so that India could defend herself against the Japanese. Gandhi and numerous other Indian politicians were incarcerated after this, resulting in week-long disturbances and violent encounters between Congress followers and British security forces. The leaders of the Congress party were arrested. The people reacted with active resistance: in the six to seven weeks after 9 August 1942 people all over the country revolted. According to official estimates, in the first week after imprisonment of the politicians alone, 250 railway stations as well as more than 500 post offices were damaged or destroyed, and 150 police stations attacked. For weeks on end all trains were stopped in Bihar and the eastern part of UP. In Karnataka alone 1,600 cases of cutting of telephone wires were counted.

The colonial masters soon retaliated brutally. Police and the military opened fire in 548 cases on unarmed people. Even low-flying planes shot on demonstrators. The British took hostages, imposed penalties of a total of nine million rupees, tortured suspects, and burnt down entire villages. More than 60,000 people had been arrested by the end of the year. Twenty-six thousand were convicted, and 18,000 arrested under the Defence of India Rules.[97] This violent outburst was in actual contradiction to Gandhi's principle of non-violence. In spite of this he refused to condemn the rioters in this situation. He viewed the violence as reaction to the much greater violence practised by the colonial power. Gandhi's followers argued that their violence was directed only against buildings and telegraph poles but not against people. Others candidly confessed that violence was against their principles but they let it happen nevertheless.[98]

Bose had foreseen this development and had approached Ribbentrop with a proposal a few days before the AICC session. He informed him that he now wanted to support Gandhi and his confrontation course energetically over his secret transmitter. He requested to spread his announcement as far as possible through the German media.[99] Consequently, the Indian uprising and Gandhi's leadership were not only utilized for the transmissions directed towards India but also for the propaganda meant for Europe, America and Germany. This reality in India was particularly highlighted in this connection.[100] Bose read out his address on 10 August 1942 in the Hindustani programme of the German short-wave radio network. He declared his solidarity with the All-India Congress Committee and the captured politicians:

> While the British Government is professing to fight for freedom and democracy, it is casting into prison the leaders of the nation that is striving for national freedom. This should furnish the last argument necessary to convince impartial men and women all over the world that Britain is fighting for her own selfish imperialism. [...] Every single Indian must take part in this struggle, no matter what the suffering and sacrifice may be. Indians in India and abroad must march shoulder to shoulder and must fight till the last British imperialist is driven out of India and the flag of independence is hoisted once again on our sacred soil.[101]

Meanwhile Bose's presence in Germany and his collaboration with the Axis Powers had been officially made known. He had announced on 17 June 1942 in the Hindustani programme of the German short-wave transmitter: 'About five weeks ago I addressed you last over another radio, the "Azad Hind Radio". Since that I have travelled quite a lot and am now here in the very heart of Germany.' He had accepted Hitler and Mussolini's support as they were enemies of India's only enemy, the British Empire. The dictators' internal politics were not his business; they concerned the people of these countries. In any case, would not the British fight side by side with the Soviet Union without consideration for ideological differences?[102]

He now had to clarify to his followers that England's enemies were India's friends and that he himself could fight for India's freedom even from faraway Europe. He explained to his listeners in a radio speech on 19 August 1942:

> Friends, when you are in the fight, you will certainly feel encouraged to hear that Indian news today are on the front page of the world press and Indian reports, however, the most interesting items of radio broadcasting all over the world. [...] It is also obvious that in this fight against British imperialism, India does not stand alone. All the powers of the world that are now fighting Britain are arrayed on the side of India and in spite of all the manoeuvres of Anglo-American propaganda, public opinion throughout the world sympathizes with us in our struggle. [...] If at any time you want help from abroad, you have only to ask for it. Your countrymen abroad will then rush to you with all the assistance you may need and you may ask for. [...] I naturally feel unhappy today that I am not at home to participate in this campaign but it will not be long before I am at your fight again. [...] It will be my duty to only utilize the international situation for the achievement of India's independence, to keep the wide world informed of all the facts of [the] Indian situation and to secure from the enemies of Britain all the sympathy and help that India may now need.

Bose continued with a whole series of detailed advice for daily sabotage, boycott of British goods and passive resistance. Finally, he appealed to the fighting spirit of his listeners, to the will to win the battle, and warned them not to fall for the colonial masters' false promises of freedom and democracy.[103]

The effect Bose's appeals had can be gauged from police reports of the provincial governments. Punjab reported that urban citizens became more and more interested in the propaganda.[104] It was generally assumed that the Axis Powers would win the war.[105] 'There is no doubt also that enemy broadcasts have had a very great effect,' reported the UP government.[106] They mentioned propaganda pamphlets calling people to listen to the enemy broadcasts and stating the times of transmissions. The district administrations were ordered to confiscate radio sets used for spreading enemy propaganda.[107] The report from UP proves the desired effectiveness of Bose's transmissions: 'Subhas Bose's propaganda has undoubtedly had the effect of identifying the Congress more and more with the Axis with the result not that sympathy with the Congress had decreased but that there is now a more friendly feeling towards the enemy.'[108]

In Bengal it was rumoured that Subhas Chandra Bose and Rash Behari Bose were prepared to march with 10,000 soldiers into India.[109] The government of the Central Provinces and Berar reported that the Indian news of the enemy broadcasts had found enthusiastic listeners among intelligentsia.[110] Even those not hostile towards the colonial government would pass on the news of the enemy broadcast.[111] The government threatened to confiscate radio licenses used for 'undesirable purposes' to prevent gatherings of people for listening to the transmissions.[112] The government of Orissa reported that the enemy broadcasts were particularly valued as source of news about the course of the uprising. Here, too, the police started confiscation of radio sets,[113] just like in Bihar.[114] The following report came from this province:

> Reports from several sources emphasize the great harm that is being done by enemy broadcasts which are responsible not only for prolonging resistance to the steps taken to quell the Congress 'rebellion' but also for the many false and defeatist rumours which are prevalent. These broadcasts are freely listened to everywhere with their stories of bombardment of Assam, aeroplanes flying over Calcutta and 'national' armies waiting on the frontiers of India.[115]

The Foreign Office registered with pride that the British were very worried about the effect the secret stations had on the Indian population, when in August 1942 German troops captured in Africa two secret reports of the Indian Intelligence Service.[116] The British radio network could not but react to Bose's propaganda in its programmes for India. George Orwell commented: 'If we look at the Axis propaganda especially directed towards India at this moment, it boils down to the pretence to be fighting against imperialism. For Germany to call Britain imperialistic is at best the pot calling the kettle black.'[117]

The tie between Indians and the British was finally severed

after the Quit India Movement and the August uprising. There was no looking back for the national movement. The demand for independence was no longer an alternative choice. The subject of each further negotiation with the colonial rulers now could only be the transfer of power. The credit to Bose was, as it were, that he took over leadership at a time when the Indian leaders were sitting behind bars.

THE GERMAN-INDIAN ASSOCIATION IN HAMBURG

In May 1942, the Indian physician Devendra Nath Banerjee who was working for the Hamburg Tropical Institute initiated the establishment of a German-Indian Association.[118] Hamburg citizens supported the proposal.[119] Contact with Indians seemed profitable in order to have a point of contact for economic relations after the war. The business people of the port city were attracted to the huge market of the subcontinent. Ribbentrop agreed to the founding of the association. Its activities should be limited to cultural, economic and social affairs, in other words, political problems should not be attended to. Like the Indian-Central European Association in Vienna and the India Committee of the German-Orient Association, it should also join the alliance of interstate associations and establishments under the administration of SS-Obergruppenführer Werner Lorenz.[120]

Bose on his part tried to revive the Indian-Central European Association. He had founded this association in 1934 together with the Austrian Commercial Councillor Otto Faltis in Vienna. However, by 1936 it ceased to function. Out of consideration for Bose, the association was not dissolved completely. After the annexation of Austria, Faltis requested the Foreign Office in vain for financial support.[121] Soon after his arrival in Germany, Bose had contacted Faltis, asking him to work as advisor.[122] Bose suggested expanding the association to the whole of Germany and moving its head office to Berlin.[123] When Bose heard about the plans for founding a German-Indian association, he asked Faltis 'that he should establish an Indian-European Association embracing this new establishment as far as possible and, if necessary, function also as collection centre for the economic traffic Europe-India.'[124] Bose did not get through with his proposals. The Indian-Central European Association remained intact besides the German-Indian Association without, however, embarking on any activities worth mentioning. Faltis even had new brochures printed by the middle of 1944, canvassing for new members.[125]

Bose was somewhat annoyed that the German-Indian Association was arranged as a purely German affair without any Indian in its administration. He suggested naming it 'German Association for India'.[126] Nevertheless, he did not miss the opportunity to make his appearance before numerous high-ranking personalities at the solemn inauguration of the German-Indian Association in Hamburg on 11 September 1942. Besides Keppler and Lorenz, Karl Kaufmann, the Reichsstatthalter of Hamburg, as well as representatives of the propaganda ministry, the Wehrmacht, the NSDAP, and the German and Italian consulates, participated in the function. Bose could note with pride that the saffron-white-green flag of the Indian freedom movement was waved like a symbol of an independent state, equally entitled, besides the swastika flag[127] and that the chamber orchestra of the German radio station Hamburg performed the song *'Jana gana mana'* as Indian national anthem for the first time.[128] Bose's assistant Pappu Balkrishna Sarma still remembered in 1971, how the Indian flag was fluttering over Hotel Atlanta and the strong impression this symbol had made on him: 'I remember well how we walked along the streets and looked back from time to time at the national flag fluttering over the biggest hotel. Really it was a good moment in our life.'[129]

The First Lord Mayor of Hamburg, Carl Vinzent Krogmann, mentioned in his speech 'the identity in many ways' of the Germans and the Indians: 'We are called the nation of poets and thinkers. Your people also are a nation of poets and thinkers who have given the world immortal monuments in literature and philosophy.'[130] Bose spoke in a similar vein, mentioning the interest German intellectual giants showed in the cultural achievements of ancient India. He delivered his speech in excellent German:

> When the British conquered our land, they did their best to depict everything Indian as inferior as possible. In this psychological moment when India needed moral assistance, German poets and thinkers discovered India and her culture. This is a fact we can never forget, and it is this cultural tie, free from all egoistic and material interests, that has furnished, until the present, the foundation for German-Indian relations.[131]

The speech was also broadcast to India via the German Hindustani radio network.[132] The solemn functions appeared to have been extremely harmonious and were conducive to German-Indian collaboration. Trott thanked SS-General Lorenz later: 'Our Indian colleagues feel slightly dwarfed by the supremacy of the Nordic people and were therefore particularly pleased that you treated them as comrades.'[133]

The activities of the German-Indian Association, in accordance with the Foreign Office, remained limited to Hamburg and its surroundings. When the vice-president, Professor Franz Heske, wanted to hold lectures about India in the name of the association in other cities of Germany, Keppler told him that it was in keeping with the politics of the Foreign Office, 'not to engage in elaborate propaganda for Indian matters in the Reich as this is not worth the effort for promoting our Indian politicians and might only result in undesirable conclusions by the German people.'[134]

The 'Indo-Germanic Study-Group'

By the middle of 1942 the Sonderreferat Indien started worrying about the motivation of the Indians working together with the Foreign Office. Finding suitable lodgings had become difficult in the third year of war. Possibilities for leisure-time activities were also limited. In this situation Keppler made an application to the main building inspector for Berlin, Albert Speer, for a building as 'homestead', where the Indians could meet their compatriots and German acquaintances in their leisure time. He considered a villa with ten to twelve rooms to be appropriate.[135] Unfortunately, his endeavours were in vain. At a chance meeting with Professor Walther Wuest, rector of the Munich University, at the Führerhauptquartier where he had accompanied Bose to an audience with Hitler, the idea came to him to make use of the SS-headquarters 'Ahnenerbe'.[136] Keppler had in the Berlin building of 'Ahnenerbe' some rooms arranged for the 'Indo-Germanische Arbeitsgemeinschaft' (Indo-Germanic Study-Group).[137] The inauguration took place by the end of 1942 in the presence of Wuest. The Indians did not quite accept the new establishment, as they had not been involved in the preparations. Thereupon the rector lost interest and cancelled all further functions.[138]

The Chinese restaurant Kwang Tung was the social centre for the

Indian students. The actress and producer Thea von Harbou invited them every Wednesday evening at 7 p.m. for dinner. It is said that she also supported the students with up to twenty thousand Reichsmark per month. The background to this generosity was her love affair with the Indian, Ayi Ganpath Tendulkar, who had returned to India after his doctorate. Thea von Harbou wanted to follow him to his native country and get married to him there. Prior to his departure, he had asked her to look after the Indians living in Berlin.[139]

Plans for a German translation of Bose's book

The Indian Struggle, describing the freedom struggle during the time from 1920 to 1934 from Bose's point of view, was published in 1935 by the London publisher Wishart & Company. On Bose's request, Keppler suggested to the Reich's foreign minister a German translation, supplemented with a description of the years 1934 to 1942.[140] Bose's secretary and partner Emilie Schenkl had already been working on a translation.[141] Ribbentrop agreed.[142] Alsdorf, however, had reservations: the German reader, not being familiar with the conditions of the country, would not be able to understand the description of the political developments in India. The unmistakable critic of Gandhi's politics also did not comply with the Foreign Office's language regulations. Therefore, Bose's book not only had to be translated, but also thoroughly revised. A prolonged dispute, where even a lawyer had to be consulted, arose now between the Soderreferat Indien and the Union Deutsche Verlagsgesellschaft about the nature of the revision.[143] The publication of the book somehow could not take place in the turbulent wartime, even though Keppler had written a foreword.[144] An English edition of the supplemented version was published after Bose's death. An Italian one entitled *La lotta dell India* without the supplement for the years after 1934 appeared in 1942 in Florence.[145]

PROBLEMS OF THE ITALIAN PROPAGANDA

In these months, the Italians had more problems than success with their propaganda for India. Back in 1941, Schedai had already repeatedly complained to the Foreign Ministry about the Italian radio company and its deficiencies in the broadcasting of the programmes of

Radio Himalaya. There were breakdowns in the studio and Quaroni reported that the transmissions were inaudible in Kabul. Finally, Schedai had even announced that he was going to leave for Germany. [146] Thus, the chief of cabinet in the Foreign Ministry, Blasco Lanza d'Ajeta, contacted the Ministry for Popular Culture and urgently asked to solve the technical problems and to guarantee the transmission of the programmes. [147] Celso Luciano, chief of cabinet in the Ministry of Popular Culture took care of this matter personally and arranged the transmissions to be broadcast on a more suitable frequency. [148]

Schedai's conflicts with the Germans

Keppler and the experts on India in Berlin complained about sharp personal attacks on Bose in Schedai's radio transmissions. He also did not adhere to the valid language regulations with his aggressive remarks about Gandhi and Nehru. Radio Himalaya went off the air in 1942 but more because of technical reasons than German intervention. [149] When Werth and Bose, during discussions in Rome in July 1942, tried to bring about Schedai's suspension, the Italians pacified them: one could not expect an understanding of larger political connections from the Indian, but he did useful work as propagandist. [150] The Japanese also liked Schedai's style. The Japanese ambassador in Rome, Toshikaze Kase, invited him on 24 June 1942 to the embassy and urged him to take up broadcasting again. [151] Thereupon Lanza d'Ajeta approached the Ministry for Popular Culture, and Radio Himalaya came on the air again from 2 July 1942. [152]

Schedai remained a thorn in the flesh for the Germans: in October 1942 the German embassy finally managed to persuade Ciano to suspend all his activities. [153] Schedai saw himself above all criticism and suspected Bose of intrigue, accusing him of being jealous of his success. [154] Lanza d'Ajeta complied reluctantly. He was evidently embarrassed at having to yield to the pressure of the Axis partner. He claimed in a cable to Kabul that it was only a temporary disruption due to Schedai being indisposed. [155] As a matter of fact, a few months later Radio Himalaya was on the air again. Schedai immediately made himself unpopular in Berlin again, for he now started to propagate Pakistan's division from India. [156]

Reorientation and grand plans

Critique came not only from the German side but from the home camp as well. Quaroni criticized the poor effect of the propaganda for India. Mario Lucidi, head of the radio department for the Middle East, composed thereupon a ten-page memorandum with a plan for the expansion of India-related activities. He complained, that for a long time he had submitted repeated proposals and suggestions for improvements. The Foreign Ministry or the Italian radio network EIAR, however, had constantly ignored them. Radio Himalaya and the Hindustani programme of Radio Rome had only one speaker each, Schedai and Ajit Singh. If one of them was absent, one could only resort to sending music. He had wanted to use Indian prisoners of war as speakers, but it did not work out for the simple reason that civilian clothing was not supplied to them. Besides, clear instructions by the Foreign Ministry for the shaping of the programmes were also not forthcoming. It was also not clear which competences Schedai actually had and which ones he only claimed for himself. He suggested increasing the personnel of his department. He wanted some ministry officials as well as Indian staff members, to be selected from the prisoners of war. The expanded programmes should include two news transmissions in Hindustani, two in Persian, two in Pashto, one each in Bengali, French and English. The Bengali programme could be alternated with a Tamil transmission, the one in Pashto with a Punjabi one, and the Hindustani transmission could be supplemented with news in Marathi and Gujarati. Lucidi stressed the point that Schedai and Ajit Singh should now receive exact instructions and that they should adhere to the line taken by Italian politics in tune with Germany and Japan. Working together with them in any way would not be possible.[157]

In January 1942, an Italian delegation came to Berlin, trying to persuade Bose to shift his headquarters to Rome. They wanted the Indian Legion to be organized and trained in Italy and not in Germany. The Italians told Bose the Germans were interested only in 'Lebensraum in the East'. Asia's future after the victory of the Axis Powers would be decided upon in Italy. Bose, however, did not accept the offer. He wanted for the Indian Legion the best possible training with modern weapons, and these he did not expect in the Italian army.

He also saw that Germany played the leading role in the Axis. Vyas saw Schedai's hand behind this headhunting mission: he had wanted to incite Bose to come to Rome so that he could control his relations with the Italian government.[158]

The Italian activities on India were marked by a spirit of reorientation in the first half of 1942. In March 1942, a voluminous memorandum was submitted to Mussolini with the title 'Economic possibilities and resources of India'.[159] Werth noticed during his visit in July 1942: 'It seems, Italian government departments are already preparing this year to lead in the field of Orient activities in Europe, and they have already started to apply themselves to the task of training suitable personnel for mastery of the Orient later on.' With this in mind, the activities of the ISMEO are to be intensified. The number of students should be increased by next year from forty to five hundred students, two hundred of them officers of the Italian higher ranks.'[160]

ISMEO during the war

The Istituto Italiano per il Medio ed Estremo Oriente (ISMEO) did not interrupt its activities when the war broke out but rather increased them. Mussolini had granted to the institute in July 1940 the status of the Mobilitatione civile. With this its activities were considered essential to the war efforts.[161] Besides the main office in Rome and the branch in Milan, the ISMEO established additional branches in Genoa, Turin, Venice, Trieste and Bari in 1942. The institute offered courses of two-year duration and subsequent courses of education courses in oriental languages and cultures. In 1942 the following languages were being taught: Bengali, Chinese, Japanese, Hindi, Malay, Persian, Tamil, Urdu and English. The courses conveyed knowledge in commerce, accountancy, geography, politics and culture.[162] In the academic year 1941-2, eighty-five students were enrolled.[163] Large commercial firms, banks, shipping lines, insurances, associations, universities and cultural establishments sent the participants. The ISMEO now published, besides the cultural journal *Asiatica*, an economic information service and organized an information centre for commerce and economy. A study centre for indigenous medicine existed as well since 1937. A museum for oriental art and a bibliographical information centre were also part of the ISMEO.[164]

In June 1943 the president of ISMEO, Gentile, organized a special economic section consisting of military personnel under the management of an officer. This section, together with the Red Cross, was supposed to compile a list of all Italian prisoners of war in India and to find out, which of the men could be used for the re-establishment of commercial relations after the war.[165] The realization of this plan remained in the initial stage. After Mussolini's ouster in July 1943, ISMEO ceased to function. The board of directors met again only on 22 November 1947.[166]

Prisoners of war in propaganda activities

From the very beginning, work with Indian prisoners of war had been on the agenda of Italian propaganda on India. Since the middle of 1941, Schedai was urging the authorities in the Foreign Ministry with whom he used to interact to allow him entry to the camp, but the Italians hesitated. On 3 February 1942 he drove to camp Avezzano near Rome but was refused entry.[167] On 9 April 1942 he went again, this time accompanied by a first lieutenant of the prisoner of war administration and a major of the War Ministry's propaganda department. Now the camp commandant let them enter. Schedai observed that the fifty inmates were not provided with sufficient bread and vegetables. He suggested supplying them with books in English and Indian languages, screening propaganda film for them, and installing a radio set so that they could listen to Radio Himalaya. They should also receive news and be allowed to send messages to their families over the radio.[168]

Work with the war prisoners progressed now. Lucidi could select four Indians for propaganda work by the end of July 1942: Anwar Hassan was to be a speaker for the Hindustani radio, Abdul Rahman for the Punjabi one. Har Gopal Uppal was given the job of listening in to German and Turkish Hindustani transmissions, while Niranjan Singh should assist Schedai in the Uffizio India. The men were released from captivity and given the status of volunteers in the Italian army.[169]

The 'Garibaldi scheme'

Just as Indian war prisoners were kept in Italian camps, so were their Italian counterparts in camps in India. The first Italians to be taken to

India were soldiers having been captured by the British during the first
North African counter-offensive from December 1940 onwards. More
followed after the British had occupied Italian East Africa. Though
their exact number is not known, it may safely be assumed that it was
anything between 80,000 to 90,000 in 1943[170].

Should such a large number of men captured in battle not
be deployed as a 'fifth column'? The Italians actually managed to
somehow supply the prisoners with propaganda leaflets for distribution
among the locals at a suitable opportunity: 'Italian prisoners of war
travelling in a troop train on 9 March dropped pieces of paper on the
platform at Dehri-on-Sone (Dalmianagar) depicting a double V sign
over the names of Subhas Bose, Gandhi, Hitler and Mussolini,' the
police reported to Delhi from Bihar.[171] The Indian Political Intelligence
(IPI) reported in August 1942:

> In February 1942 reports were received from different parts of
> India that Italian and German prisoners of war passing through
> to their various camps indulged in propaganda which, from the
> uniformity of procedure, appeared to have been carefully planned
> beforehand. In each case pro-Axis slogans in English, Arabic and
> Hindi, some handwritten and others duplicated on small sheets
> of paper, were placed in cigarette packets and thrown among
> members of the public assembled on the platforms.

The prisoners had also demonstrated at the stations of Ambala and
Jalandhar. Once, even Indians had joined them. The IPI suspected
that the actions were directed from Goa. Two agents, Robert Koch
and Robert Hepp, were said to have made contact via radio from the
Portuguese colony with the internees and captives, and distributed
propaganda literature issued by the German embassy in Lisbon.
As long as Portugal remained neutral, the British decided not to
interfere.[172]

Inspired by the August Uprising, General Ricciotti Garibaldi,
a direct descendant of the nineteenth-century hero of Italian unity
Giuseppe Garibaldi, worked out a somewhat eccentric plan which he
submitted to the War Ministry: he wanted to go to Burma together
with his brother Peppino and incite from there guerilla warfare by
deploying Indian nationalists and rescued Italian prisoners of war.[173]
'The name Garibaldi, not unknown to Indian patriots, could be an

incentive for carrying out these plans,' the general wrote to the head of the Italian general staff, Marshal Ugo Cavallero.[174]

The plan made detailed provisions: a group of selected officers was to be sent to Rangoon or Mandalay. From there they would establish contact with the Italians in POW camps, after discussions with the Japanese and with the help of Bose's organization. At first they would locate the camps and then plan with the inmates their escape. Men from the Indian underground would then take the soldiers to a rallying point where the Japanese would provide them with arms and equipment. They would then either form their own unit, join the Indian rebels, or serve as 'protection elements for Italian interests and Italian pockets in occupied territories in case of a general revolt.'[175]

Mussolini sanctioned the plan.[176] In any case, he had been waiting impatiently for a Japanese attack on India: 'If Japan now would finally decide to march in to India, grand and unforeseen happenings could occur,' he told Ciano.[177] The Italian Supreme Command commented: 'The task General Garibaldi set for himself could be of practical use, particularly from the moral point of view, even though it creates great difficulties.' However, the military attaché in Tokyo should first find out and gauge Japan's attitude towards the plan, and the Aviation Ministry should clarify if at all it was possible to transport Garibaldi's commando by air to Southeast Asia.[178]

Six weeks later, the military attaché informed from Tokyo that the Japanese viewed such an action within their sphere of power with extreme scepticism. He also questioned General Garibaldi's suitability for leading such a commando. The entire Japanese organization in Burma and Thailand was under the command of a colonel. Therefore, it would be more appropriate if an officer of a lower rank, who could also be capable of discreetly gaining the confidence of the Japanese, would command the Italian mission.[179] With this the file ended and there is no indication anywhere that the plan was ever carried out. Nevertheless, in the beginning of 1943 Mussolini mentioned during a conversation with one of his generals that the Allied Powers had transported the captured generals and colonels from India to America only because they had been afraid of a possible action by the Italian prisoners of war.[180] The Germans came to know of the plan only when they took possession of the governmental files after Italy's change over to the Allied Powers, and gradually evaluated them.[181]

THE BATTAGLIONE AZAD HINDOSTAN

The high command of the Italian army announced by the end of July 1942 the formation of three military special units, 'in order—in case of necessity—to prepare or support operations in enemy territory.'[182] These units were supposed to include various different elements, so that they could be deployed for all sorts of possible eventualities, and constructed on similar lines as an infantry regiment. There were to be three of them: the Centro Militare A, consisting, for a start, of 100 Arabs of various countries; the Centro Militare I, consisting at first of 200 Indian volunteers, and the Centro Militare T, made up initially of 200 to 300 Italians, former residents of Tunisia familiar with the country and the language. The units were to be under direct command of the high command. A special schooling was to be provided for, including parachute training as well as training in single combat and telecommunication. The high command put Lieutenant Colonel Massimo Invrea in charge as commander of the Reggruppamento Centri Militari to which the three centres were subordinated.[183] The three special units were stationed near Rome. The country seat Villa Marina on the Via Casilina was allotted to the Indians.[184]

The plan for these special units can be traced to a suggestion by the Grand Mufti and Gailani. The two Arab leaders wanted to organize troops consisting of Arabs and were prepared to let them work for the Italian secret service. These volunteers should first receive military training in centres specially arranged for this purpose by the Italian army.[185] When the Italians now requested the Germans to transfer 400 Arab prisoners of war from their camps to Italy, they found out 'with a certain astonishment', that the Germans on their part were also busy to form an 'Arab Legion'. Thereupon the Italian Foreign Ministry stopped the transfer of the Indian prisoners of war the Germans required for forming the Indian Legion.[186] The Grand Mufti had suggested the recruiting of Arabs not only to the Italians but also to the Germans.[187] After some deliberation, both sides finally agreed to send the Arab prisoners to Italy and the Indian ones to Germany. Both parties, however, kept a small contingent each for themselves. The sources do not reveal how and why the suggestion of the Arab leaders to organize troops consisting of Arabs came to include also Indians and Tunisians. It shows once more, however, that the Italians viewed their India-politics merely as an extension of their Islam- and Arab-politics.

The prisoner-of-war camp no. 80

Acting on the initiative of the Foreign Ministry, the general staff of the Italian army arranged, in March 1942, a special camp for the Indian prisoners of war—the prisoner-of-war camp no. 80—at the country seat Villa Marina in the Roman Campagna.[188] At first the Indian prisoners whom Schedai had convinced during his camp visits to fight for India's freedom on the side of the Axis were housed here. The Italian military command had used a ruse to remove the camp from the supervision of the Red Cross: official location of the camp was not Rome but the island of Elba. In case the inspectors of the Red Cross had demanded a camp inspection, it would have been refused as a journey by sea was not permissible at present for security reasons.[189] The Indians were not given arms as long as they were still POW officially. Training for this reason was initially limited to sports only.[190] After some time they received the uniform of Italian paratroopers.[191] They marched in their new uniforms to the prisoner-of-war camp Avezzano to aid Schedai to win over new volunteers.[192]

Formation of the Centro Militare I

On 11 June 1942, the high command of the Italian army gave strict instructions: the selection of willing volunteers should be fast. Soldiers suitable for parachuting or close combat training, or those who could serve as informants or interpreters should be selected. At the same time, 'fellow travellers' should be indoctrinated through continuous propaganda to convince them that they are on the right side. The Centro Militare I should initially consist of a rifle company with machine guns, and a machine gun company. The objective was the training of the volunteers so that they in turn were able to train friendly partisans in the use of supplied weapons.[193] Schedai and his colleagues were in charge of selecting and recruiting the volunteers. The Indian prisoners of war were transported from North Africa to Italian camps where Schedai could have a look at them. The selected men then congregated in the Villa Marina, the POW camp no. 80, where the Italian trainers prepared them for joining the Italian army.[194]

On 1 August 1942, the Centro Militare I started functioning with forty-four Indian volunteers, four Italian officers, and eleven Italian non-commissioned officers and ordinary soldiers. Initially, Captain Rodolfo di Carvalho took over the command. All Indians had signed the following vow:

> I swear to fight for the independence of India and for the honour of the Indian national flag. I swear to carry out the commands of my superiors, Italian as well as Indian. I accept the Italian law and military rules and pledge to observe them. I consider myself to be an ally of Italy in her fight against the common enemy.[195]

The small troop started at once with military training. Major Luigi Vismara took over the command on 16 August 1942.[196] Eight days later, another 100 Indians joined the unit.[197] Training took place, evidently without any problem. On 1 September 1942, the first batch of Indians had been promoted, after an examination, to the rank of non-commissioned officers.[198] By the middle of September, the planned division into four rifle platoons, three machine-gun platoons, and one parachute squad was effected, and the parachute squad ordered to take part in the parachute training course at the Scuola Militare di Tarquinia.[199]

The three special units of the Raggrupamento Centri Militari were given new names: the Arabs were now Gruppo Formazioni A, the Tunisians Battaglione d'Assalto T, and the Indians were called, most impressively, the Battaglione Azad Hindostan.[200] The Indian soldiers wore collar insignia in the colours of the Indian National Congress—saffron, white and green. The cap badge depicted the emblem of the Raggruppamento Centri Militari, three arrows in a bundle.

Disciplinary problems

Immeditaely, on arrival of the first Indians to the POW camp no. 80, Lieutenant Rizzi noticed something peculiar: 'Our Indians are in the military sense abnormal.' Only some of them could salute properly, and talk and behave like soldiers. The others behaved like civilians, in an orderly fashion but decidedly non-militarily. They did not create at all the impression of having been close to death and in active combat for months. Most of them behaved, not only with the Italian officers but also with Schedai, without any military manners; they just displayed the deference due to a respected person.[201] They were apt at learning during training, they followed politely the trainer's commands, but did not show much motivation. They simply stopped cooperating when they lost interest. The trainers had to accept that it was of no use to insist on discipline in such cases.[202]

Rizzi found an explanation for this phenomenon when he registered the volunteers. A large number of the Indians stated as their profession tailor, cobbler, driver, hairdresser, cook or kitchen help. Rizzi asked Niranjan Singh how this could be possible and was told that these men were not soldiers in the actual sense but camp followers. These followers did not take part in combat and had not been under military training. They were simply used to doing their own specific jobs and otherwise to behaving in an orderly fashion.[203] The Italian trainers had to note now with frustration that not even one-third of the Indians in their unit were proper soldiers. The rest were hardly of any use in war and certainly not suitable for parachute and single combat training: 'We realized that it might be possible to open a day hotel but certainly not organize a battalion if the number of these camp followers remained constant. The presence of these artisans instead of dedicated soldiers deferred the commencement of this unbelievable undertaking.'[204]

Rizzi informed Schedai confidentially about the unsuitability of the recruits.[205] Schedai, however, was of the opinion that the lack of military effectiveness did not diminish the value of the Indian unit of volunteers. Schedai had little knowledge of military matters and was also not interested: 'For him it sufficed to know that the Indians were forming battalions and divisions for the liberation of their country. This alone was an extremely important word for propaganda.'[206] When Rizzi met Bose he observed that, contrary to Schedai, he certainly had some understanding about the art of war. Rizzi carefully broached the subject of the camp followers and was surprised when Bose told him that the German Indian Legion did not have any men in this category. Schedai listened to this conversation with studied unconcern. He obviously did not want to admit that he had selected the wrong persons. Rizzi suspected that Bose and the Germans had kept the best soldiers for themselves and left only the 'rest' for the Italians.[207]

But the Italian personnel were also not suited for this task. Schedai critized Invrea, the commander of the Raggruppamento, that he could not adjust to the mentality of the Indians and treated them like Italian recruits. He could not see the connection of worldwide propaganda. For Invrea, there was only a battalion of volunteers whose training was a failure. The trainer could achieve much more, but they had to apply intelligence, sensitivity and tact.[208] Invrea on his part critized Schedai. He was accused of having made false promises to the volunteers with regard to their service in the Italian army. He was responsible that the Indians saw their job only in marching triumphantly into their country leaving her liberation to the Axis comrades. He had lost their confidence when they realized his deceit.

> He did not behave sincerely and honestly with the volunteers. His behaviour towards them was not correct because he did not adhere to a clear line, maybe due to lack of experience in military matters. He is a man who seems to me to be caught in narrow spiritual boundaries, limitations and most probably he will never be able to shake off his limitations.[209]

It seems the Italian officers did not have much of an understanding of Indian culture. Transcribing the Indian names into Roman script on registering the volunteers was already an insurmountable difficulty.[210] Also the language problem could not be solved. Orders were given in English which many Indians did not understand, or pretended not to understand when they did not like it.[211] Instead of letting the trainer learn Hindi and employ interpreters like the Germans did in the Indian Legion, they simply put Italian lessons on the timetable.[212] Rizzi mentions in his memoirs that Invrea was never interested in the religion and custom of his recruits.[213] Thus entailed a lack of understanding: 'I think there never was a more eccentric unit as the Centro Militari I.'[214] Not suprisingly, the Indians had no confidence in their Italian superiors. When the soldiers were sent to the training area Tivoli, which meant that they would be soon deployed in action, the mood worsened. They started arguing and quarrelling among themselves. Rizzi records: 'They were all united in one matter only: they were fed up with us.'[215]

Mutiny and disbanding

The Indian soldiers of the Centro Militare I (CMI) refused on Tuesday, 10 November 1942, to form up for the morning roll call. They declared that with this action they wanted to protest against a possible deployment in Libya. Major Vidmara called the Indian non-commissioned officers and asked them whether they realized that this was a case of mutiny? When they answered in the affirmative and the volunteers continued to remain in their barracks, the major had the men give up their arms and the barracks surrounded. The Italian members of the CMI, a platoon of the Centro Militare A, and some carabinieri took over surveillance. Actually, at that point of time a deployment of the Indians in North Africa was not under discussion, but the military command was not prepared in future to exclude such a possibility completely.

A captain of the CMI went to Tarquinia to arrange for the disarmament and premature return of the volunteers who just then took part in a training course for paratroops. Vismara had five Indian non-commissioned officers and one former non-commissioned officer of the Indian army, whom he considered to be the ringleaders, arrested at the Centro Militare T. By noontime, Lieutenant Colonel Invrea reported personally to the Commando Supremo and sent a written message to the general staff of the army. The major pondered over the motivation behind the mutiny and came to the following conclusion: There had never been any signs of indiscipline. The Indians had also no reason to complain about their treatment by trainers and superiors.

> On the other hand, rumours about a possible movement to North Africa arose simultaneously with the start of the British offensive. Gradually, they grew more and more persistent against all logic, as the English offensive proceeded. These impressionable, inconsequent and fickle people saw the war as easily lost for the Axis as they saw their victory at the time of advancing to Alexandria. Gripped by panic, they presumed it would be better for them to have the prisoner of war status again. The military situation, and only that, can have induced the volunteers to an otherwise absurd and inexplicable behaviour.[216]

Two days later, the Supreme Command ordered the disbanding of the CMI retrospectively from 10 November 1942. All volunteers were now prisoners of war again. They should be taken to another camp, best in North Italy where they could not come in contact with other prisoners and also would not get the preferential treatment the other Indian prisoners of war had the benefit of. They will have to be under strict surveillance and have to work hard. The Italian personnel and the facilities of the CMI were transferred to the Centro Militare T.[217] Eleven Indians were later selected for employment in the Centro Militare A.[218] This procedure had been decided upon at a meeting between the SIM (Italian Military Intelligence) and the Foreign Ministry. They lost no time in agreeing that the experience could not continue 'without the close collaboration of an Indian confidant in order to control the moods and inclinations of the enlisted volunteers.'[219]

On 16 November Subhas Chandra Bose, who happened to be in Rome, and was waiting for his flight to Asia in an Italian plane, came to meet the commander of the Raggruppamento.[220] The commander's war diary does not reveal the topic of the conversation but it may be presumed that Bose wanted to arbitrate beween the Italians and his compatriots. Evidently his endeavours were not appreciated as the war diary of the Centro Militare T does not mention a visit by Bose.[221] Lieutenant Colonel Invrea did not even let him see the Indians, presumably because the Supreme Command had already decided to disband the battalion. On the following day the Indians were taken to Udine, to prisoner-of-war camp no. 57.[222]

Two hundred and sixty-five Indians served ultimately in the battalion.[223] They were later on taken over by the Germans. Most of them joined the Indian Legion of the Wehrmacht.[224] Later, Bose criticized the poor leadership of the Italians in a memorandum that he composed prior to his departure to the Far East: 'The Indian Legion in Italy disintegrated because the political training of the corresponding officers had been neglected, even though the legionnaires were good from a military point of view.'[225]

The unpleasant episode apparently had no negative effects on the Indians remaining in Italian captivity. In the summer of 1943, when the Swiss diplomat Rudolph I. Iselin visited the POW camp no. 91 having Indian inmates, he commented: 'This is a fairly good camp.' The Italians would take care that each Indian would be able to eat in accordance with his religious strictures.[226]

Reasons for the failure

The Italian experiment of forming a legion of Indians failed completely. The propaganda value of the undertaking in the fight against the English was zero. They disgraced themselves instead before the Germans, and in the conflict about opinions of leadership in Asian politics they were the losers. Why were the Italians not capable of organizing a troop from Indian volunteers whereas the Germans managed to do so to quite a considerable extent?

The Germans also were confronted with mutinous Indians when the Indian Legion was to be moved from the training area Königsbrück to the North Sea and the Indians feared deployment in combat. But the Germans, in contrast to the Italians, managed to control the mutiny and restore discipline. The legion was never used for combat but nevertheless fought successful battles at the propaganda front line. Newsreels depicting Indians in uniforms of the Wehrmacht created the impression that the whole world supported the German Reich in her 'battle against Bolshevism'. The Germans too had their difficulties with the Indians, but they tried hard. The military took the help of experts in order to come to terms with the mentality of the volunteers. They searched out Indologists and people with Indian language skills for the Indian Legion. The German instruction personnel had to learn at least a few words of Hindi. An Indian calendar of festivals existed as also, Indian cuisine, and an instruction manual in Hindustani: instruction officers like Lieutenant Rizzi had been selected only because they knew some English. Yet the Italian government had already established the ISMEO in the thirties for educating experts on Asia. That means there must have been Italians knowing Indian languages. But they were not employed where they were needed: a clear sign of faulty organization.

The Italians depended instead on Schedai and his people, and that was the mistake. Bose also had considerable difficulties in recruiting the prisoners of war for the Indian Legion. But he succeeded in enthusing his compatriots with the charisma of an experienced politician. Not so Schedai, since he lacked this charisma. The Italians in the Foreign Ministry and the Supreme Command realized that Schedai was not the right man for such an undertaking. Therefore, they decided to quickly break up the experiment before the mutinous Indians could cause any harm. The failure of the Centro Militare I as compared to the relative success of the Indian Legion, demonstrates the importance of Bose's role. If the Germans had not had an Indian politician of Bose's calibre but only a confidant of Schedai's type, then their experiment would surely also have failed.

THE INDIAN LEGION IN KÖNIGSBRÜCK AND THE NETHERLANDS

The Indian Legion—its official name was now '(Indisches) Infantrie-Regiment 950'—by the middle of May had already grown to such an extent that the Frankenberg camp had become too small. The troop moved on 15 July 1942 to the training area near Königsbrück, a small town situated about 80 kilometres southeast of Dresden. Königsbrück had been one of the largest German military training areas and was partly vacant after the war had started. The legion, which had grown to the size of a regiment as time went by, found sufficient space here. The area was also suitable for training in all types of weapons.[227] The Indian special unit had so far been trained in Meseritz. It was now merged with the legion and moved to Königsbrück as well.[228]

Recruiting for the legion continued. The recruiting officers had problems with counter-propaganda by prisoners of war loyal to the British. For this reason, the new arrivals from Italy to Germany went straightaway to Königsbrück instead of first to the prisoner-of-war camp Annaberg. There they underwent a short but intensive propaganda treatment. Those prisoners, who did not enlist as volunteers, passed on to the prisoner-of-war camp Mühlberg. From the 5,677 Indians who came in seven batches between June 1942 and January 1943 from Italy to Germany, 2,430 joined the legion.[229]

Swearing-in of the legionnaires

The first solemn swearing-in ceremony of the legionnaires took place in September 1942. Accompanied by representatives of the OKW and the Japanese military attaché Colonel Yamamoto, Bose visited the camp for the ceremony.[230] The Indian soldiers took the oath on his name and on Hitler. An officer first read out the form of oath in German and then in Hindustani.

> I swear by God this sacred oath that I will give unconditional obedience to the Führer of the German nation and people Adolf Hitler as supreme commander of the Wehrmacht in the liberation struggle of India under the leadership of our leader Subhas Chandra Bose. I will any time be prepared as a brave soldier to lay down my life for this oath.[231]

After the oath had been read out, Bose quickly added: 'I shall lead the army to India when we march together.'[232] Evidently, he wanted to make it quite clear, with the addition, that the command of the Indian Legion was not with Hitler. On the other hand, taking oath in the name of Hitler was necessary for including the Indians in the German Wehrmacht. Without the protection of the German Reich, their status would be that of irregular volunteers only, and they would not be any more entitled to treatment as prisoner of war in accordance with international law. Nevertheless, the legionnaires did not consider themselves German soldiers but fighters for a free India.

They were invested in German uniforms with the national insignia of the German Reich. Like other foreign associations, the legion, however, also had its own characteristic sign. Each legionnaire wore a badge on his right upper arm in the Indian national colours orange-white-green with a springing tiger, with 'Freies Indien' written above.[233] The legion had also its own regimental flag in the same design: a saffron-white-green striped tricolor with the springing tiger, and the inscription 'Azad Hind.'[234]

Hindustani as command language of the legion

The language of command for the Indian Legion was Hindustani. As the German training officers did not know this language, interpreters were required. The interpreter department of the OKW in Meissen trained specialists for the Indian Legion. Professor Paul Thieme, professor and head of the department for Indology at the Halle University, conducted the lectures there. The English-language *Hindustani Conversation Grammar* by St Clair Tisdall served as textbook. Hindi was taught there until the end of February. Evidently, not many people in Germany were conversant in Indian languages at that time. Therefore, only a slight knowledge was already sufficient for enrolling in the interpreter course. The then infantryman Rudolf Hartog, for instance, relates that he taught himself the rudiments of Hindustani as a patient in a military hospital on the recommendation of his brother Hans, who served as Indologist in the legion. It sufficed for the entry test.[235]

Each German training officer had to acquire a basic knowledge of Hindustani. Ernst Bannerth, chief interpreter of the legion, gave the lessons.[236] The Indian legionnaires, who were called up for officers' and non-commissioned officers' schooling courses, were on their part obliged to learn German. German classes were arranged for them. Personal contact with the German population nearby also contributed to the fact that soon many Indians started speaking quite good German. Even the ordinary soldiers were eager to learn the foreign language. Kritter noted in his diary: 'I often see the brown fellows sitting there in the evenings with notebooks, busy learning vocabulary.'[237] The military commands had to be worked out first, as it was the first time that Hindustani was being used as command language. No other army in the world had used this language before. The staff of the legion was entrusted with translating the German commands into Hindustani. The end result was the publication in 1943 of a military dictionary German to Hindustani, which lists, on 228 pages, commands and all types of special terms in German and Hindustani. The editors explained in a foreword the principles of their work, which necessitated at times the coining of new terms:

> The already existing language of the Anglo-Indian army (Urdu) was taken as basis for the dictionary, as it is supposed to serve the military by content and size. Wherever English expressions were used in this army, and this is the case with nearly all technical and tactical terms, these were replaced with Hindustani terms. Special importance was given to keep the language as national popular as possible, and preference was given to pure Hindi. Only for those cases where the Arabic-Persian or English loan word is already commonly used, have these been retained. For some terms, new words from the existing Hindustani vocabulary had to be created the use of which has yet to be carried through (e.g. call for 'March' which is otherwise used only for 'action, presentation'). Of course, the literal translation of the German term had to make place for an explanatory translation to facilitate quick understanding. [...] The generally understood form of Delhi's colloquial language has been used as pronunciation.[238]

The Indian lower-rank leaders were supplied with a two-language training manual as teaching aid.[239] Bannerth published a collection of private letters in Hindustani with detailed explanation of the scripts for Urdu and Hindi. Evidently, this publication was meant as aid for the postal censors.[240] As textbook for the language instruction, the staff of the legion compiled an *Outline of the Hindustani Grammar* with a vocabulary all German training officers were expected to know. 'Also this work is to be a contribution for strengthening the bond of friendship between the Great German Reich and the Indian freedom movement,' said the foreword.[241] The textbook *Lehrbuch der Hindustani-Sprache* by the two interpreters of the legion, Bannerth and Otto Spiess, published in 1945 by Otto Harrassowitz, may also be counted as one of the results of the Indian Legion's scholarly work.[242]

The regimental journal *Bhaiband* was also published in Hindustani. The editors were Bannerth up to July 1944 and after him Paul Thieme and Kurt Hoffmann. Bannerth had all editions printed in two scripts, Nastaliq and Devanagari. All the texts had to be written by hand. After that, the Latin script favoured by Bose and which could be machine-typed, was used.[243] During interrogation by the British Bannerth describes the editorial work as follows: 'We tried to get people to write articles on various virtues, such as obedience, self-sacrifice, sobriety, but here again they merely produced well-worn phrases: interest in the paper was confined to the news items, and these were always bad for propaganda.'[244] In order to counteract the westernization of the Indians, Bannerth illustrated the journal with pictures of Indian deities, mosques and sceneries, and resisted the changeover to the Latin script. His plan of organizing a traditional Indian theatre failed due to lack of interest in the soldiers.[245]

The Bhaiband station was another means for political schooling. The legionnaires could hear daily news, the report of the Wehrmacht in Hindustani and also Indian music. The station started transmitting in May 1944 but had to stop three months later when the legion retreated.[246]

Mixing of ethnic groups, religions and castes

The choice of Hindustani was not the only concession to the Indians that took into account the legion's character as 'propaganda troop'. In addition, the special requirements of the various religious communities were met as far as possible. As the Hindus refused beef, so also the Muslims did not eat pork. The legionnaires were provided ritually slaughtered mutton. The numerous vegetarians had to be given additional vegetarian food. The Indians received Indian spices and other food items not available in Germany in their Red Cross parcels, which were still sent to them even though they had ceased to be prisoners of war.[247]

This type of provisioning was quite expensive but it was possible in this way to keep together members of various religions and ethnic groups in the same units, platoons and groups. This was a difference as compared to the British army where the individual castes and ethnic groups had their own units. It was in keeping with Bose's political programme which saw the Indian Legion as a model for a modern India. This close living together of the various groups was of course not free from conflicts, but mutual understanding was supposed to be promoted in this way. Certain inconveniences due to the random formation of the units, not only because of various food habits but also because of different timings for prayers and festivities, were consciously accepted.[248]

However, not everyone was in favour of this procedure. A German non-commissioned officer wrote in a personal letter to Adam von Trott zu Solz about the Indians: 'With us they only become spiritually uprooted half-Europeans who in the end hold nothing sacred any more.'[249] Bannerth expressed himself extremely critically about the Indians' ethical conditions during his interrogation by the British: 'The completely new European surroundings destroyed in the minds of the Indians almost everything they had formerly revered. Bose's policy of bridging religious differences led to the disappearance of religion generally.'[250] An Indian soldier expressed himself in retrospect differently later: 'There was complete harmony among our ranks. We respected all religions and faiths. There were full facilities for anybody and everybody to worship freely and religious functions were celebrated jointly.'[251]

They saw to it that the men strictly followed all religious rules. Muslims had to abstain from smoking and partaking of food between sunrise and sunset during the month of fasting. To leave the observation of their particular religion's customs to each individual believer might have resulted in tension between the orthodox and the less orthodox ones.[252] Sikhs consider shaving the face a grave sin. When some of them shaved by emulating European habits their fellow Sikhs reacted violently. In order to keep peace in the camp, the command of the legion had no other option but to become executers of religious rules. They strictly forbade the Sikhs to shave. To offend against this ruling meant that the clean-shaven Sikh soldier was incarcerated because of disobedience until his beard had grown again.[253]

EXPERIENCES IN INTERCULTURAL LEADERSHIP

Under these circumstances, leading the Indian units was a special challenge for the German training officers. Officers who had experience in dealing with people of other countries were preferred. To find suitable non-commissioned officers, however, was not so easy. They soon had to find out that the concept of Prussian discipline did not correspond to the Indians' concept. The daily roster at the line-up of the company in the mornings, for instance, was not at once accepted but first an opinion was obtained from the soldiers and its reasonableness checked.[254] The Germans had no other option but to adjust to the different mentality of the Indians. The 'Leadership principles' of the legion states:

> In spite of their intelligence, Indians are open to influences of a pedagogial and, in certain ways primitive, nature. The appeal to reason usually fails as one can hardly find a starting point. [...] Joking and persuasion are essential aids. It serves no purpose to give commands the execution of which will most probably create difficulties, so far as it is a matter of less importance; it never serves a purpose to fight out a principle for insignificant things. [...] Orders to be given simply and clearly, orders once given must be enforced. On no account must the superior give the subordinate the impression that he is unsure; otherwise, the authority is shaken in its fundament. [...] The personal relationship of the superior should be determined by his understanding for the troop. The tenor of the relationship, however, should be distance and composure. Orientals see in this almost the criterion for superiority, while a superior throwing fits of anger and abuses loses esteem to quite an extent in their eyes. The individual soldier must be given opportunity for a private talk, it is worth it when the superior—particularly in the beginning—spends much time, trouble and patience for such talks; the soldier feels he is being understood when he thinks that he has the superior's ear.[255]

The German training officers who had hardly encountered foreign cultures before, now had to grapple with problems they had never before thought existed. 'What peculiar questions arise,' Kritter wondered and wrote in his diary about the clash between a Prussian non-commissioned officer and a group of Sikhs. Common bathing had been on the plan and the Unteroffizier was on duty for supervision.

> Suddenly the Sikhs refuse, goaded on by a particular orthodox one, to take off their underpants. Their faith would not allow the complete baring of both legs, they were allowed to change their underwear only alternately from each leg taking off the worn underpants and putting on the new one. One never knows with them if they do not hide a completely different opposition behind such pretexts. As the non-commissioned officer on duty refused to put up with this, considering parasitic infections and the necessity of a thorough cleansing, he demanded respect with a typical Prussian dressing-down. As a result, a revolt threatened. Another officer was called who managed to smooth the ruffled feathers. The military procedure of ordering and obeying, that is normally used, has to be replaced therefore for these exotics with a somewhat more individual treatment.[256]

Of course, too much leniency entails only new dissatisfactions and makes the necessity of a skilful middle path the more important. The officers noticed that traditional punishments such as confinement and prison had no effect on the Indians at all. The command of the legion therefore requested OKW to permit stricter punishments. For the first time, four legionnaires who had been punished repeatedly were taken in December 1942 to the penal camp Zeitheim where Russian prisoners of war were kept. The training officers were relieved that they were permitted to inflict this hard punishment:

> The conditions so far were indefensible. If one of the gents considered duty too strenuous or if he did not like one of his superiors, he appeared in the orderly room and declared: 'I want to go back to the prisoners' camp.' If such fellows were kept in the confinement cell, they rather enjoyed the few days' suspension from duty and raked about undesirable discontent in the legion after their release. If one were to absolve them from their oath and release them to the prisoner's camp, one would have to be afraid that more would follow this bad example

and evade their duties as legionnaires in such a simple way. Therefore, a penal camp is the only possibility of a noticeable sanction, and political considerations that one might perhaps have to consider, have to take a back seat against such military cardinal problems.[257]

However, the relationship between Indians and Germans were not marked by discontent and frustration. Legion Officer Hans Franzen described in his memoirs the peculiar relationship: 'In spite of all the trouble we had with the Indians, we loved them, their graceful beauty, their enigmatical eyes, their charm, their intelligence, their spirit. Of course, we loved them [...] as their masters [...]. They also loved us, they were loyal to us, and we had become their fate.'[258]

The Indians became restless after Bose's disappearance in February 1943. For example, fifty men of the eighth company resorted to hunger strike, Red Cross parcels excepted.[259] The legion's command was apprehensive about allowing such lack of discipline and requested the OKW to permit special punishment regulations. Indians offending against military rules and regulations should initially receive corporal punishment to serve as a general deterrent and then be put in a concentration camp. The command was of the opinion that even a military prison would not have the desired deterrent effect.[260] A special company consisting of seventy Indians and twenty Germans was formed instead in the summer of 1943. Captain Franz Ludewig, who had been transferred to the legion because of his dentures and rude behaviour, was in command. The Indians wore legionnaire uniforms without badges of rank. They received sufficient provisions and sometimes a Red Cross parcel. They were allowed to write and receive letters but were confined to barracks. Instead of taking part in the instruction courses, they had to do farm and other outside labour. The special company remained in Königsbrück until the war ended.[261]

Since open mutiny arose when the legion was to move to the Netherlands in April 1943. Numerous legionnaires refused to prepare for the move. When they joined the legion, they had been promised that they would be deployed only in India or on the way to India. Representatives of the Free India Centre could not dispel the soldiers' reservations either. Bose himself could not use his influence as he was already on way to East Asia. The legion's command decided to have the mutinous soldiers court-marshalled. They were sentenced to penal servitude and prison, but this did not end the protests. Discipline was restored after patient propagandistic persuasion. The legion's command explained to the soldiers through confidants that their behaviour was not conducive to India's liberation struggle. The German instruction officers were bitterly disappointed with them. This way they ensured that one company after the other pledged their loyalty to the commander, Colonel Krappe. After that, the transfer could be accomplished without any difficulty.[262] Two battalions arrived on 30 April 1943 at the training area Beverloo in Belgium in order to complete their training. In May 1943, Batallion I took over the security of the Westwall in the region from Ijmuiden up to Zandvoort near Haarlem. Batallion II was stationed on the island of Texel. Batallion III remained for the time being in Königsbrück and moved in July 1943 to the training area Oldebroek near Zwolle in the Netherlands.[263]

Since the Indian soldiers had taken the oath on the Führer they were subjected to the same discipline as all others belonging to the Wehrmacht. A legionnaire who perhaps one day did not feel like fighting for India's freedom any more could not simply be released. An Indian soldier who stayed in Berlin for some time without having taken leave had to be punished for desertion. However, the legion's commander was pragmatic in its dealing with Indians, as Kritter relates in his diary:

> There are well-founded doubts, however, whether German regulations for military punishment could be applied to the Indians in spite of their having taken the oath on the Wehrmacht. Of course, if the exemplanary punishments became known, it might result in non-assessable repercussions with the other legionnaires. Therefore, such happenings have been taken care of by means of compromise solutions by tacit deportation of the concerned soldiers, or they were disposed of under the pretext of being unfit for military service for health reasons. In less serious cases a prolonged, strict detention also helps at times, and it has often happened that a penitent fellow returned as an absolutely useful and willing soldier to the company after three weeks, confinement to barracks with barely sufficient food.[264]

The relationships between legionnaires and German women were a ticklish chapter. Like all soldiers in the Wehrmacht, the Indians also were allowed outings to the garrison town. Contact with the female population was unavoidable. However, too close a contact was in contradiction to the National Socialists' race-political notions. But the officers could hardly forbid the Indians to have contact with German women because of their racial inferiority. They would never have understood such a snub. The propagandistic value of the legion would have been lost. Therefore, the German officers hoped that German women on their part would not allow any intimate relationships.[265] Nevertheless, the Saxon women were easy game for the Indian Romeos with the help of exotic titbits from the Red Cross parcels:

> It has already started in Frankenberg where the legion was stationed for the first few months of its existence. The girls unfortunately are completely unrestrained and undiscriminating. Not only the imposing beards and colourful turbans of the Sikhs have a magical attraction for them, even the greasiest Moslems, no matter how unsympathetic they look, have the greatest chances with them. One cannot yet estimate how many little bastards are already on the way.[266]

The local NSDAP officials complained. The officers of the legion pacified them by pointing out that the Indians were after all Indo-Germanic, i.e. Aryans.[267] If that did not suffice, the legion's command always mentioned the superposed propagandistic nature of the troop as appeasement. The Indians should not be made to feel as second-class soldiers. In the end, the women were blamed.[268] The Free India Centre managed in two cases in 1942 to procure the marriage permit from the Reich's Home Office for two Indian volunteers who wanted to marry German women. It was difficult to convince the officials. They gave permission only after many hour-long negotiations, spread over one year.[269]

After moving to the Atlantic coast, the Indians were not as lucky with French women as they had been with the Saxon and later on with the Dutch women. The command arranged therefore for a troop brothel called Phulvari (flower garden). A first brothel for Indians had already existed in Holland on the insistence of the army administration. Besides other reasons, they wanted to avoid that the

Indians might discuss official secrets during their rendezvous.[270] The female personnel in France created some problems initially as French prostitutes in coastal cities considered intercourse with coloured men below their dignity.[271] Actually, they did the Indians injustice, as one of the prostitutes testified: she praised the Indians' artifices of love sky-high. Leopold Fischer, who had to supervise the 'flower garden' once as Unteroffizier on duty, states: 'It was lively and amusing, and I never noticed any of the revolting coarseness and vulgarity inseparable from a German military brothel.'[272]

On 1 October 1942 the first Indians were promoted to non-commissioned officers.[273] This created some new tension as the Indian NCOs were formally of equal rank with the German ones, but they could not become training officers. This equalization with the 'Bimbos', as the Germans called their Indian comrades, caused a lot of bitterness with the German non-commissioned officers. One NCO complained to Trott:

> Nowadays the Indian NCOs even have their meals with us in our dining hall: the things they get to hear there! What sort of impression will they get from the German officer and NCO corps when they notice how disrespectfully the latter talk about their officers because they imagine themselves to be constantly slighted and ineptly treated. The legion is divided into the officer corps on one hand and the Unteroffizier corps, the troops and the 'Bimbos' on the other. This seems to me and all of us an impossible situation, particularly, as there is so much propaganda about the supremacy and superiority of the Germanic race.

The promotion did correspond to the propagandistic concept of the legion as an army of free India, but not at all to the daily distribution of duties in normal army routine. Now the Indian Unteroffiziere on their part reacted touchily to each real or imagined slight. Kritter noted down following incident:

> Today we had a lot of trouble during the 25-kilometre pack march. Without my knowledge, the Hauptfeldwebel ordered last evening. That the Indian NCOs had to march with full equipment but not the Germans. Next morning all Indian section leaders lined up without packs. They did not react when

the order was once more repeated. Thereupon, Sergeant Major Schwarze dismissed them and let them stay in the camp. When I came to the orderly room at 8.30 a.m., the company [was] already on its way without section leaders. I summoned all to the office and, to start with, chased them without packs. Open mutiny according to German concepts, the mood is precarious. However, I could not possibly incarcerate them all. [...] It was of course a great mistake of the Hauptfeldwebel to take such fundamental decisions on his own. Unfortunately he is not bright enough to understand that such treatment not only serves no purpose but unnecessarily increases the inner resistance of the Indian NCOs.

The penitent Indians got away with a few days' cancellation of leave. In addition, for the next march, Germans as well as Indians alike had to march with full equipment. Like this the German Feldwebel had reason to swear and the Hauptfeldwebel had to accept the embarrassing fact that he could not carry his orders through.[274] Leopold Fischer, who gained close contact with the Indians due to his language skills, came to a sobering conclusion in his memoirs: 'The legionnaires were not slow in comparing their new masters with their old, and the British came off better in this rating, because although they were oppressors by definition, British officers had at least been tactful in their relations with Indian troops, whereas the attitude of the Germans was tactless and overbearing.'[275]

At the end of July 1943, the first Indians passed the sergeant's course and were promoted. The OKW still hesitated to promote Indians to officers.[276] The legion's command, pressed by Bose, did apply for the promotion of Indians from NCO to officer. The OKW however insisted on the principle that each prospective officer would have to prove himself first in enemy fire.[277] Finally, Bose carried his point through with the generals: on 1 October 1943, fourteen Indians were promoted to lieutenants, two more followed later. Two Indian medical men were nominated to the rank of medical officers.[278]

The End of India-Politics
after Bose's Departure

T he Japanese submarine I-29 brought Bose and Hasan in
the beginning of May 1943 to the island of Sabang, north
of Sumatra. Bose proceeded by plane to Tokyo. On 27 May
1943 he called on the German ambassador in Tokyo, safe and sound.[1]
Two days earlier, he had already called on the Italian ambassador.[2] In
Japan, Bose initially kept contact with the Foreign Office and the Free
India Centre through the German embassy in Tokyo. Without Bose's
participation, the India-politics of the Axis Powers declined.

BOSE IN THE FAR EAST

The Japanese made Bose's presence in Japan known through a public
communiqué only after the Japanese imperial parliament's session
on 18 June 1943. The Japanese government combined this with an
acknowledgement of India's independence. Bose could then speak over
the Japanese radio to the Indians.[3] The German government waived
a communiqué of their own and had the Japanese one published in
the German media.[4] Mussolini declared on 24 June 1943 before the
National Directorate of the National Fascist Party: 'Bose, who is not
starving himself, is before India's gates,'[5] alluding to Gandhi's hunger
strike with this remark. He conveyed to Tojo through the German
ambassador in Tokyo that he admired his politics and combined his
praise with the advice: 'Tell him also that I consider the most concrete
assistance for Bose, whom I know personally and consider capable of
fulfilling the task he set out to do, as urgent and necessary.'[6]

Bose organized his headquarters in Singapore where he took
over leadership of the independence movement upheld by the Indian

expatriates.[7] He reorganized the Indian National Army (INA), the Far Eastern counterpart to the Indian Legion. Goebbels commented on Bose's activities in East Asia: 'He organizes his movement exactly according to National Socialist example and calls himself Führer.'[8] The Japanese had founded the INA in the beginning of 1942 with captured Indian soldiers from the British army. It had grown to the strength of a division. The founder of the INA was Mohan Singh, a captain in the Indian army, who had disengaged himself from his troop on retreating and deserted to the Japanese. The Japanese made him general of the Indian volunteer troop. On 1 September 1942, Singh could form the first division with 16,300 men. By the end of 1942, 45,000 Indian prisoners of war had enrolled voluntarily. The Japanese, however, wanted only a core troop of 2,000 soldiers, whereas Singh wanted to increase the INA to 20,000 volunteers. Both sides were at variance with each other. Singh refused to be part of the Japanese commando structure, whereupon the Japanese dismissed and arrested him. The troop lost its importance after this.[9]

Bose succeeded through broadcasts to enthuse Indian expatriates in Southeast Asia for the freedom struggle. Business people started donating money. Young men volunteered for the INA. He gave the demoralized officers new self-esteem and combined the various political directions and religious communities of the Indian expatriates under his leadership. After Mohan Singh's arrest the strength of the INA had fallen to 13,000 men. Bose wanted to increase the number of men to 50,000 and was at variance with the Japanese about this. However, they were now willing to agree to a force level of 30,000 soldiers.[10]

The Foreign Office tried to keep in touch with Bose. They even considered establishing a consulate in Singapore for this purpose only.[11] Bose on his part tried hard to send one of his people as representative to Rome as he feared that the Italians could lean towards the Pakistan movement that desired an independent state for the Indian Muslims.[12] The diplomats did not succeed in influencing the Japanese allies through Bose. Bose was lost for the Axis Powers' India-politics. In spite of this, his activities were carefully observed. In this way, he still played a role in Germany until the end of the war. Keppler explained to the Reich's foreign minister 'that Bose's eye-catching success in East Asia supported also German India-activities in as far as it strengthens the morale of the Indians here and gives there work a new uplift.'[13] The effect of the propaganda by the Axis Powers in India after Bose's arrival in Southeast Asia, however, could not be compared any more with the one during the August Uprising in 1942. According to the police reports of the provinces, the Axis Powers lost their prestige with the Indian population after their defeat at Stalingrad. The report from Sindh dated February 1943, states:

> The newspapers give full publicity to the Russian success and widespread admiration for the Russian army is expressed. The significance of the German reaction to the news has also been appreciated. One result that has been noticed is that Axis propaganda is losing its influence and listinging-in to the German radio is becoming less popular.[14]

The news spread rapidly through Japanese and German broadcasts that Bose had taken over leadership of the INA and intended to march into India. However, the Bombay police noted: 'There is nothing to suggest that anyone in this Province takes this "army" seriously.'[15] Orissa reported that Bose's announcement of an invasion had not made any impression.[16] Anyway, the Japanese broadcasts with Bose's voice at least created amusing or sceptical interest,[17] while the German and Italian ones were completely ignored.[18]

An India proclamation at last

On 21 October 1943, Bose proclaimed in Singapore to a congregation of 50,000 Indian expatriates the formation of a provisional government of free India, consisting of five ministers, eight representatives of the INA, and eight civilian advisers. The Japanese government recognized this government that immediately declared war on Great Britain and the USA. With the approval of the Japanese government, the provisional government took over sovereign rights of the Andaman and Nicobar islands under occupation of the Japanese navy. Actual administration was left in the hands of the Japanese military, but Bose was allowed to hoist an Indian national flag in Port Blair and appoint a governor. He renamed the group of islands Shahid and Swaraj Islands, i.e. Martyr and Independence Islands.[19]

The German Reich recognized Bose's government on Japanese request.[20] Thus, Germany became one of the first countries to recognize a free India before her actual independence. Fascist Italy followed suit: on 1 November 1943 Mussolini as head of state of the Repubblica Sociale Italiana recognized Bose's government.[21] Therewith Bose finally had achieved what he had fought for in Europe so long. That Hitler, who had always resisted the proclamation in support of India's independence, finally agreed to the recognition, was most probably out of consideration for the allied Japanese. Goebbels noted: 'The Japanese engage in very clever politics in the territories occupied by them. They could teach us a thing or two.'[22]

The march to Delhi

When in March 1953 the Japanese army invaded India from Burma, soldiers from the INA were part of the invading troops. The sole intention of the Japanese for undertaking the operation 'U-Go', was impeding the planned Burma offensive by the Allied Powers and securing the territories occupied by them east of the Chindwin River. Bose wanted more: while the Japanese secured their positions, the INA was to march on. Bose chose the old battle cry of the 1857 mutiny: Delhi chalo! (Onwards to Delhi!) The appearance of free Indian soldiers was to incite rebellion everywhere on the way against the colonial rulers until finally Bose would march triumphantly into Delhi. The crowning finale of the march to Delhi was to be a victory parade in front of the Red Fort.

Tojo announced on 22 March 1943 before the Japanese parliament that Bose's government would take over sovereignty of all occupied Indian territories. Moirang in the princely state of Manipur was the first town where soldiers of INA hoisted the Indian tricolour on 14 April 1943. Initially, the Japanese troops advanced rapidly, but they could not conquer Imphal, the capital of Manipur. The British sent additional divisions and their air force. The Japanese troops broke down completely with the onset of the monsoon. On 16 July 1943 the high command gave orders for retreating. Bose did not give up hope and decided to continue fighting with the INA. However, the troop was much too weak to be able to stand up to the British advance into Burma. To Bose's horror, individual attacks resulted only in a large number of men crossing over to the enemy. The Indian soldiers on the British side did not join the INA either. Even though the greater part of the INA gave their best and fought valiantly gaining the admiration of the Japanese officers.[23]

TURBULENCES IN AFGHANISTAN

One should have thought that the intelligence base Kabul would have lost its importance after the defeats of El Alamein and Stalingrad. The German troops retreated. An advance of the Wehrmacht into India, that seemed possible even in the summer of 1942 during the Caucasus offensive, was now absolutely out of the question. Far from it, on 20 March 1943, Rasmuss and Witzel passed on a new order by Bose to their confidant, Talwar. He was to undertake concrete preparations for the landing of a plane and accommodating twenty people in tribal territory. Further, he should gather military information, plan a rebellion, establish friendly contacts with the Japanese, and prepare for a landing of submarines on India's coasts.[24]

This could only mean that the intelligence intended to support a Japanese attack on East India with an advance to the northwest frontier. Talwar presumed that the Germans wanted to overrun south Russia and then march into India.[25] However, he accepted the plan and proceeded to the tribal territory to start preparations. Talwar and his co-fighters considered the military failures of the Axis Powers and lost interest. Besides that, he was doubtful whether the Germans and not Bose had actually given the orders. Talwar preferred to remove himself to India. He returned only in September 1943.[26] With this, much to the frustration of the agents, the military plans were shelved for the time being.

In June 1943 Witzel cabled to Berlin that the seditious activities had reached their nadir after Bose's people had to wait too long in India for the advance of the Axis troops or at least for arms supply.[27] Talwar's attitude after his return in September 1943 did not inspire much confidence. He had come to know in the meantime that Bose was in Southeast Asia and presumed he had fallen out with the Germans.[28] He gave the Germans to understand that he could continue working with them only if he could have direct contact with Bose. To oblige him, Witzel introduced him to the secret service officer of the Japanese embassy. However, he did not have any instructions from Bose for him either, and consequently Talwar went back to India.[29]

Now the British started to create difficulties for the Germans in Kabul. They had meanwhile found out that the diplomats of the

Axis Powers in Kabul not only created disturbances in the tribal territories of the northwest frontier but they also incited the people of Turkestan against the Soviet Union. Therefore, the British Foreign Ministry suggested to the Soviet leaders a common protest to the Afghan government. In October 1941 the British and the Soviets had already managed to achieve the departure of all Germans and Italians from Afghanistan, except the diplomatic corps. However, at that time the Afghan parliament had explicitly guarded against breaking off diplomatic relations with the Axis Powers.[30] The British ambassador in Kabul, Sir Francis Wylie, handed over on 27 May 1943 a list to the Afghan prime minister. The list contained the names of thirty-six Afghans he considered as agents of the Axis Powers. He demanded the immediate arrest of three of them, and that the remaining ones should be kept under surveillance. In addition, he gave the 'urgent advice' to reduce the diplomatic personnel in the embassies of the Axis Powers to a minimum, and requested to prevent the Axis Powers from procuring larger sums of Afghan currency, which they used for the support of subversive elements. The Soviet government made a similar petition to the prime minister.[31]

The Afghans did arrest an Axis agent but refused the expulsion of any diplomats.[32] When the British explicitly demanded the expulsion of Witzel, Doh and Anzilotti, the Afghans claimed to have known about their intrigues for a long time.[33] At the same time, they pressurized the Axis Powers to voluntarily recall embassy staff not liked by the British.[34] However, they waited until Wylie had left the country, in order to save face.[35] The Foreign Office and the intelligence decided to recall the intelligence agents Witzel and Doh.[36] The British allowed the two Germans and Anzilotti free passage through India for their return journey.[37] Now Rasmuss alone took over the responsibilities of the two intelligence officers. Together with the wireless operator of the intelligence, Corporal Zugenbuehler, he kept the wireless connection with the tribes intact.[38]

However, his days in Afghanistan were also numbered: on 25 October 1943 a Swiss engineer by the name of Egler visited him. Egler asked him to see a German-American journalist who had a very important message from India for him. The fake journalist introduced himself as Colonel Michallow of the Soviet Union and told him that he knew everything about the subversive actions of the Germans. He knew of the wireless connection with the tribes, Witzel's seditious pamphlets and all of Talwar's reports from India. He asked Rasmuss to work for the Soviet espionage service. He could continue with his India activities but would have to change them into agitation against Hitler. Otherwise, he would hand over the entire material about him to the British and demand his removal to the Soviet Union where they would treat him as a war criminal. Rasmuss did not allow himself to be blackmailed; he reported the meeting to his superior, Minister Pilger.[39]

The incident did not create surprise in Berlin. Rather, it was presumed 'that the English, Russians and Afghans had kept the entire activities of the embassy under surveillance since long.' Under these circumstances, it was much too dangerous for Rasmuss to operate as double agent. His recall was the best solution.[40] The British were annoyed about the Russians' action: Talwar had now become useless for them as a double agent. They could not do anything about it though. As they had just demanded the expulsion of Axis diplomats, it would look very odd if they were to speak against Rasmuss's recall.[41] As if this were not enough, in November 1943 Pilger learnt from the Afghan Foreign Ministry that Quaroni had revealed all secrets of the Axis Powers to the British.[42] The Italian ambassador had given the British all desired information regarding his activities on the side of the Axis, after Mussolini had been forced to resign his post and his successor Marshal Pietro Badoglio had surrendered to the Allied Powers.[43]

When Talwar returned to Kabul by the end of April 1944, Pilger asked him to explain himself. He wanted to know how it was possible that the Russians and the British were so well informed about the German embassy's secret intelligence activities. Talwar was evasive: the wireless operator of the embassy, Doh, had lost a parcel with secret documents from him in February 1943. The Russians most probably had found it. In addition, if Pilger doubted his loyalty he did not have to work with him any more. The ambassador evidently accepted his explanation and requested him to help him with the preparation for the landing of the plane.[44] The intelligence planned to send Witzel— meanwhile promoted to captain—again to Asia. He was to land by plane with three comrades and an Indian guide in the northwest frontier territory, somehow manage to reach Delhi, and organize a radio station there.[45] Berlin was convinced that a mass rebellion could be ignited if a direct radio connection existed between Bose and his supporters in India.[46]

Nothing came of this plan though. In the following months Zugenbuehler and Talwar still met occasionally, but Talwar preferred now to keep contact with the Japanese as these could convey Bose's messages directly to him. Talwar left Kabul by the end of April 1945. He came to know about the end of the war in Delhi and retreated to the tribal territory to continue fighting against the British. He settled down in the Indian part of Punjab after independence where his family had gone.[47] Until the end the Germans did not find out that it was Talwar who had betrayed their secrets to the enemy all the while. In Berlin, he even created 'the impression of great reliability and trustworthiness because of his straightforward description of even unfavourable happenings and developments.'[48]

THE PAKISTAN CONTROVERSY IN THE FOREIGN OFFICE

As long as Bose stayed in Germany, India-politics on the whole was going on according to his concepts. Bose was an energetic advocate of the idea of a united Indian nation comprising all people of the subcontinent irrespective of their religion or language. Consequently, he was against the movement aiming at the foundation of a separate state Pakistan for the Indian Muslims. German propaganda on India always supported a united nation and condemned the Pakistan movement as the result of the politics of British rule following the principle of divide et impera. Italian India-politics also followed this language regulation under German influence.

The Foreign Office did not accept this line unanimously. The officials in charge of propaganda for Arab countries would have liked it, if the propaganda in India worked towards the unity of all Islamic powers. Keppler, however, adopted Bose's position decidedly and had the party of the Islamic separatists, the Muslim League, and their president Muhammed Ali Jinnah condemned in broadcasts as British-friendly collaborators.[49] He carried his point of view through. Ribbentrop also approved of the resolution by the Working Committee for Oriental Questions, that there should be no Islamic propaganda directed towards India.[50] This principle was once interrupted when the

Grand Mufti of Jerusalem gave a speech to Indians on 22 August 1942 that was transmitted to India as a German-Italian joint programme.[51] This action had as its objective inciting the Muslim Indians with the help of a religious authority to participate in the August rebellion and the Quit India movement started by Gandhi. To avoid the danger of the Grand Mufti using this opportunity for undesirable Islamic propaganda the speech was strictly censored before the broadcast.[52]

The liaison officer of the Reich's foreign minister to the foreign organization of the NSDAP, Minister Ettel, was not at all competent for propaganda in India. However, he suggested a bare two weeks after the broadcast that the Grand Mufti should once more speak to the Indian people, this time with an appeal to the Muslim League to collaborate in the struggle for freedom with the Congress party. Keppler returned the memorandum with the handwritten note: 'I would request you to leave the treatment of the India question to me.'[53] Ettel was offended and complained to Secretary of State Weizsäcker. He pacified him and told him his attitude was correct and he had been perfectly right in acting the way he did. However, it happened that Keppler had something against the Grand Mufti because in this matter he was under the influence of Minister Grobba, the Foreign Office's expert for the Middle East.[54]

Bose did not think much of the Grand Mufti's participation in activities related to India. He warned Ribbentrop against any further deployment of religious leaders. A mixture of religious elements in propaganda was dangerous as it might divide and confuse the Indians.[55] Keppler also objected to any further attempt to let Islamic authorities broadcast to India. This was not part of his propaganda conception.[56]

After Bose's departure, the advocates of an Islam-related propaganda on India tried to carry their ideas through. Keppler had to prove his point with a detailed description of the 'propagandistic comprehension of the Indian Muslims'. He explained that in his opinion too strong an appeal to a confessional special group could easily contribute to a hardening of the differences. Though the radio station Azad Muslim Radio did address the Muslims separately, the programmes strictly avoided religious arguments. One should not equate Indian Muslims with the Muslim League. On the contrary, the League was a tool in the hands of the British. Keppler finished his exposé with the warning: 'Any dallying with the Pakistan movement would bring in Hindu opposition for us.'[57] Press and radio had instructions to omit any praise of the Muslim League and as far as possible keep silent on the subject of Pakistan.[58]

In the beginning of May 1943, that is a few weeks after Bose's departure, a proposal came from the Sonderreferat Indien, not only to omit any dallying with the Pakistan movement but also to explicitly oppose a Muslim state altogether. German propaganda on India was to depict the advocates of the Pakistan idea as 'seduced and misled victims of English Muslim politics.' The propaganda broadcasts should not contain any negative comments on the religion; they should highlight the national attitude of most Indian Muslims instead.[59]

Hans-Georg von Studnitz, the official representing the news and press department in the Sonderreferat Indien, disagreed. In spite of their minority status, he considered the Muslims the politically stronger part of India's population that would rule the country after independence. Working together with Islamic forces would prepare a confident collaboration for post-war times. Moreover, the Pakistan project would bring unrest to India, which would be inconvenient for the British during the war. Besides, to take a stand against Pakistan would annoy all Muslims and impair Muslim politics.[60] Melchers, the expert on India and the Orient in the political department, also warned against attacking the Pakistan movement that could have unforeseeable consequences for the Arab propaganda.[61] Keppler defended himself. An attack on Jinnah, the Muslim League and the Pakistan movement did not go against Muslims. He always stressed the point that the Pakistan movement worked in the interest of the British. He and the others in his support did not attack the religion of Islam as such, nor did they take an open stand against the idea of a pan-Islamic block. He argued that a state based on religion as Pakistan was, contradicted the National Socialist Weltanschauung that provided for states based on nationality and race. He demanded that German India-politics should take a stand against the Pakistan movement.[62]

The department for the Middle East and India of the news and press section favoured a compromise. The secretary of the legation, Hilmar Bassler, suggested spoiling Jinnah's image by calling him 'the English hireling', without, however, equating him with the Pakistan-movement. No stand should be taken either for or against Pakistan.[63] This corresponded exactly to the ruling agreed upon in December 1942 with the Italians and which became the basis of propaganda activities. Keppler gave in and agreed reluctantly to waive propaganda against the Pakistan-movement. He proposed directing all propaganda equally against all Indians supporting Britain's war, that is, also against Jinnah.[64] The India Committee, encompassing experts on India from all departments of the Foreign Office, agreed in a meeting on 20 May 1943 to this language regulation.[65] A week later the German press published articles on a meeting of the Muslim League where Jinnah had attacked Gandhi.[66]

The controversy about the propaganda for Pakistan broke out only after Bose's departure. This shows to what extent his presence determined the political line of German propaganda on India. Overall, to be sure, he had to submit to the strategic interests of the German government, but he could certainly exert influence within this framework. India-related activities became rudderless without Bose. Keppler had so far extensively represented Bose's ideas, but he could not execute the ideas alone. Even from the Far East Bose saw to it that Pakistan would not win friends in Europe. For instance, by the end of June 1943 he requested the Italian ambassador in Tokyo not to allow the press in his country to depict the Pakistan movement as the voice of Indian Muslims.[67]

Notwithstanding all this, the Sonderreferat Indien (SRI) continued working as best as possible. The German Institute of Foreign Studies published in 1943 the volume *India and Ceylon* by Ludwig Alsdorf in its series 'Kleine Auslandskunde' (Short Guide to Foreign Studies) as outcome of his activities in the SRI.[68] However, India-related activities lost all importance later when the constant motivator, Adam von Trott zu Solz, left as well. After the assault on Hitler on 20 July 1944, Trott was arrested as one of the conspirators and accused by the People's Court (Volksgerichtshof). His superiors, also Keppler, immediately distanced themselves from him, but Nambiar and Alexander Werth, the vice director of the SRI, stood by him unselfishly.[69] However, they could not prevent his execution on 26 August 1944. Werth carried on with the SRI until Soviet soldiers took him prisoner of war on 25 April 1945.[70]

END OF THE FREE INDIA CENTRE

The Free India Centre continued functioning under the management of Nambiar until the end of the war. They continued the publication of the journal *Azad Hind*, and distributed it in Germany, Italy, France and other West European countries. Azad Hind Radio broadcast daily for two hours in six languages, National Congress Radio daily in four languages, and Azad Muslim Radio daily for twenty minutes in Hindustani. All programmes were repeated once daily, so that the Centre's secret transmitter functioned daily for a total of six hours. All programmes gave exact instructions for rebels in India and appealed particularly to young people, farmers, workers, soldiers, sailors and police officers. They gave special attention to Muslims and exhorted them to show solidarity with the national struggle. Bose's declarations were given prominence in the programmes. They particularly focused on the ill-treatment of Indians in South Africa and of sailors in American and British service, as well as the food shortage in India.[71] The Centre even started a new series as late as in 1943. The Heidelberg publishing house Vowinckel published its first volume, Girija K. Mookerjee's *The Indian National Congress*.

The Centre moved its office in August 1943 to Hilversum in the Netherlands as working in Berlin became increasingly difficult because of the frequent air raids. Its new location was the hotel Heidepark. The radio department resided in the Palais Moenikenberg next door. 'Life was peaceful, almost like a holiday,' Vyas describes the mood there.[72] In spite of the move, transmissions continued without interruption. The secret transmitter could now use the strong Hilversum transmitter, which had transmitted programmes to the Netherlands Indies before the war.[73]

The Centre remained there for one year. In August 1943 an air raid destroyed the Berlin office and nearly all files. The Centre was allotted new rooms in Charlottenburg. Moreover, the situation in Holland became increasingly unsafe. In the night of 26 August 1944, the Indians left Hilversum and shifted to Helmstedt.[74] There the Centre used the radio station Oebisfelde until 9 April 1945 when the Americans were only 50 kilometres away. Even though the Indians stayed in a good hotel, the constant interruptions from air-raid sirens were very irritating.[75] When the complete breakdown of the German

Reich was inevitable, the Indians discussed their further actions. Some thought it sensible to flee from the British to the Soviet occupation zone. Fifteen of them proceeded to Leisnitz in Saxony. Three other, Vyas one of them, decided to stay in Helmstedt and wait for the arrival of the British.[76] They did not know that a special unit of the British forces was already on their trail.

MUSSOLINI'S GREAT EXPECTATIONS

After the dissolution of the Centro Militare I, the Italians had hardly any practical scope left for their India-politics. Schedai, however, did not want to remain idle and started searching again for suitable prisoners of war, still left in Italy, for assisting him in radio broadcasts. The Foreign Ministry gave him permission for selecting ten compatriots from the Avezzano camp,[77] but they never had a chance to operate—after the Ministry for Popular Culture decided in August 1943 against an expansion of transmissions to India.[78] Now a different wind was blowing: Victor Emanuel II, King of Italy, had dismissed Mussolini on 25 July 1943 after the Fascist Great Council had passed a no-confidence vote. The new government under Badoglio incarcerated the former Duce in the mountain fort Gran Sasso. The Allied Powers had occupied Sicily in the meantime, and Badoglio capitulated on 3 September 1943.

The Americans and the Italian officials announced the capitulation only five days later. The Allied forces landed in Brindisi and rapidly advanced towards the north. The German military immediately took position north of the front line. German paratroops rescued Mussolini from his prison on 12 September 1943. He on his part now declared the king as dismissed and announced the republic, later to be called Republica Sociale Italiana (RSI). The ministerial council of the new state met on 27 September 1943. Italy was now divided: the south occupied by the Allied Powers remained a kingdom; the German-occupied north was a new Fascist state.

Ajit Singh evidently expected the defeat of the Axis Powers.[79] He applied in April 1943 to the Foreign Ministry for Italian nationality. It seems he wanted to avoid being branded a traitor by the British. After Mussolini's ouster, he worked for a few weeks more for the Italian radio. He was prepared to speak against Fascism in his transmissions but always ended up in polemics against the British whom he called the worst fascists. Badoglio, however, would not tolerate anti-British propaganda and Ajit Singh had to stop broadcasting in August 1943. When he heard about the capitulation, he escaped to Venice to avoid capture by the British. He returned for some time after Mussolini's rescue, went again to Venice for eight to ten months, and moved finally to Milan where the British arrested him on 2 May 1945.[80]

Schedai also went first to Venice and then to Milan. Radio Himalaya was gone, but the Ministry for Popular Culture appointed him to compile news for India for the Italian radio.[81] He started re-establishing the association Amici dell'India in January 1944. Fernando Mezzasona, minister for popular culture, and Serafino Mezzaloni, foreign minister of the Fascist Republic, favoured his endeavour. They considered it so important that they personally looked after the matter.[82] The Foreign Ministry kept a sum of 225,000 lire from membership fees for the association in safekeeping,[83] and the Ministry for Popular Culture supported the activities financially.[84] On 7 September 1944 the Association for the Friends of India started functioning again, officially as Sezione milanese.[85] Schedai managed to flee when the Allied forces advanced into Milan,[86] the British, however, finally caught up with him.[87]

Mussolini was again Duce and head of the government, but the real power, in fact, was with the German Wehrmacht. He could only wait and hope for the war to end. He was formally the head of the Italian Republic but he did not have much authority as such as no other countries besides the vassals and allies of the German Reich had recognized his government, not even Spain. The fact that Mussolini eagerly nurtured contact with the provisional government of free India should therefore not be understood as pure goodwill for Bose. For the Duce, this was one of the few possibilities to be active in foreign politics. When Bose declared the government of free India, Mussolini himself formulated the letter of recognition, as a handwritten pencilled draft in the files of the Foreign Ministry proves.[88]

After the 'March to Delhi' had started, the Japanese ambassador enquired in April 1944 whether Mussolini would recognize an Indian government established by the Japanese in occupied territory.[89] Mussolini agreed at once.[90] He sent an encouraging telegram to Bose: 'I am sure that you will achieve your goal and liberate your people from the imperialistic slavery of the British. The slogan of the RSI and the people is: India to the Indians.'[91] The Duce did not forget the anniversary of the proclamation day of free India either and sent Bose a congratulatory telegram.[92] Bose on his part paid his respects to Mussolini and called on the RSI embassy during a visit to Tokyo.[93] When Nambiar planned to visit the units of the Indian Legion in Italy, the Duce agreed to receive Nambiar in Salò.[94] However, the visit never took place because the planned dispatch of additional parts of the legion was delayed. Moreover, shortage of fuel played a part during the last six months of the war.[95]

Mussolini did not just observe the happenings in India with interest while he sat more or less idle in his residence at the Garda lake. As the independence movement gained momentum, he even gathered hope that the British Empire, and therewith the power of the Allied Powers, would break down after all. In this connection, the article 'L'India agli indiani' (India to the Indians) that appeared on 26 March 1944 in the *Correspondenza Repubblicana*, is very revealing:[96] 'The event that happened can be a decisive factor for the course of war and unforeseeable developments. The tireless and heroic Japanese armies of the Tenno, together with the Indian Chandra Bose, have crossed the eastern border of India,' reads the introduction. The Japanese had written the slogan 'India to the Indians' on their banners, and with their assistance the Indians, who alone were too weak, would finally be able to shake off the British yoke. He proceeds to explain to the readers that India is a world on her own with a boundless variety of races, religions, languages, and the abundance of nature. In spite of this diversity, the independence movement under the leadership of Gandhi, Savarkar and Jinnah had united against the British. The politics of the British had increased the difficulties arising from the diversity of this huge country, but the Indians would solve these without foreign help once they had gained liberty. The text concludes with a promising outlook for the future:

> From passive resistance that could not solve the problem but only brought it to the consciousness of the world, one proceeded to attack with the force of national weapons against the foreign oppressors. These are black days for London now. Chandra Bose is a man of unusual energy. When the Anglo-American forces

start retreating, which is likely to happen, the Indian masses will light the torches of rebellion. Meanwhile the Indian frontiers have been crossed. The wheel of fate is moving. The Indian phase has been inaugurated after the Pacific one, in this war full of the unforeseen and unsuspected.

Mussolini's biographer Renzo De Felice points out that it would be too simple to read only self-deception in these words. Rather, he recognizes three characteristic points of Mussolini's political thinking. The first is the importance Mussolini gives to India as the heart of the British Empire. The second is the assessment derived at through the happenings of the summer of 1942—that the Indian independence movement required the support of the Japanese. Finally, the third is the conviction that the future is open any time and allows any possibility.[97]

DEPLOYMENT OF THE INDIAN LEGION

German India-politics had lost importance after Bose's departure and finally petered out completely, but the largest undertaking of propaganda on India remained intact until the end of the war: the Indian Legion had grown to the strength of a regiment by 1943. It remained the 'showpiece' of the propaganda even though it was not of great military importance. The mutiny in Königsbrück had undermined the confidence of the superior military officials in the combat value of the legion. Moreover, the legionnaires had apparently told the Dutch during conversations, when they were stationed at the North Sea coast, that they would help the Allied Powers in case of an invasion to drive the Germans out from Holland.[98] The appertaining superior command did testify in an evaluation that the legion was well trained and was probably a good combat troop, but they made it clear that a deployment might be risky:

> The applicability of the Indian battalion depends on the few German officers they rely on. If these officers become a casualty through death or wounding during action, one cannot perceive how the Indians will act. They might then possibly even fight against us. […] To use an even stronger commitment of forces of foreign formations in the Corps-range is extremely hazardous,

even dangerous. The third battalion already means more of a disadvantage than an advantage.[99]

The climate of the rough North Sea coast was not suitable for the Indians in the long run. On advice by the medical officers, the legion moved to a climatically more favourable section of the front after the cold and depressions became more frequent. The Wehrmacht gave the Indians the southernmost position at the west front they could offer at that time. They were allotted a section of the French Atlantic coast south of the Gironde estuary near the locality of Lacanau, which they had to protect against a possible invasion.[100] The close contact the Indians had established with the Dutch population may have been an additional reason for shifting.[101]

Coast protection in the south of France

The deployment of the legion for coast protection was not in keeping with the ideas Bose had written down in a memorandum shortly before his departure. He had written that the troop ought best to be used in Iran or Iraq, but never in Libya or in Russia. He would have preferred though if the legion did not have to fight at all but only received thorough training in the handling and use of various weapons. In this way, they could form the core and leadership of the new army of a free India after independence.[102]

The military situation, however, did no more permit any deployment in the direction towards India. Though the German Africa Corps had reached Egypt in the summer of 1942, and the German Caucasus offensive could reach the uppermost peak of these mountains, after the defeats of El Alamein and Stalingrad, however, it was obvious by the spring of 1943 that German troops would never reach India. The Indian Legion started moving to the south of France in September 1943.

The entire legion had reached there on 18 October 1943 and Oberbefehlshaber West took over command. He allotted the Indians a coastline of about 60-kilometre length east of Bordeaux for surveillance. The regimental staff stayed in Lacanau. The units built 'resistance nests', with sand and wood along the coast, equipped with guns. The Indians worked hard and earned praise when General Field Marshal Erwin Rommel visited the western defence line of the legion in February 1944 for inspection.[103]

Mission in Italy

Only the ninth company was put to use in Italy in January and February 1944. According to a report by Captain Walter Toedt, the company commander of the unit, several legionnaires wanted combat after some had already fought with German units in Italy. In the beginning of 1944, the ninth company, strengthened with volunteers from other units of the legion, moved by train to Italy. The company consisted of 202 men, twenty of them Germans. In the region near Pescara (Abbruzzi Mountains), the 278th infantry division and the division's light infantry battalion 278 took over command of the company. The Indians had the task of protecting and camouflaging disengagement movements and reconnaissance. In July 1944 the company had to build positions in the Apennine Mountains. In August 1944 the Indians took over the safeguarding of rearward connection lines in the Ravenna region. According to Toedt's report, the legion proved in Italy 'that some of the subaltern men knew their jobs as soldiers.' However:

> The higher-ranked troop officers were not always satisfied. Moreover, various legionnaires were discontent because they realized the futility of the actions and wondered what would happen to them in case one or the other of them were captured by the Allied. These understandable thoughts created some disagreements amongst the legionnaires so that a recommendation to the authorities seemed advisable for moving the company back to the regiment formation. [...] It can be stated as summary that the company proved its worth in skirmishes because of arms superiority; in large-scale fighting with heavy weapons, however, they at times lost their nerves.[104]

A smaller group of the legion belonging to Lieutenant Jamil Ahmed had been sent to India already in October 1943 for spreading propaganda at the front among the troops of the Indian army. The men tried to reach their compatriots on the opposite side by means of pamphlets and radio transmissions under the name of Bhaiband Radio. However, resonance was poor. In spite of that, the troop stayed at the front until March 1945. They carried out their activities at first from Rome, then from the region near Como.[105]

Retreating

In the beginning, the invasion by the Allied forces on 6 June 1944 in the Normandy coast did not touch the Indian Legion at the Atlantic coast. However, as the Wehrmacht expected more landings, the Indians were committed to heightened vigilance with constant stand-by. Moreover, French partisans became increasingly active. The second battalion was ordered to search in the woods for the Maquis[106] until they received the order to join the retreating Wehrmacht. The regiment left Lacanau in the middle of August 1944. To begin with, the units met again in Poitiers and Ruffec.[107]

Partisans attacked the legion on the way. Lieutenant Kalu Ram was caught in an ambush. He became the first Indian to lose his life while fighting on the German side. In Ruffec the troop repulsed the first fierce attack by the Maquis. Feldwebel Banta Singh and Feldwebel Gian Singh earned thereby the Iron Cross second-class. Nambiar honoured them with the Vir-e-Hind and Tamgha-e-Bahaduri.[108] The legion advanced slowly towards east, partly with requisitioned civil vehicles, horse carriages and bicycles. The maquisards constantly exposed them to attacks. Many legionnaires lost their lives. Moving through the Departement Indre, passing by Bourges, via Dijon and Strasbourg, the legion finally reached Alsace in September 1944. Their new position was the training area Oberhofen near Hagenau.[109]

The Waffen-SS was supposed to affiliate all the foreign volunteer units fighting for the Germans, including the Indian Legion. Once in the Alsace, the legionnaires learned that they were now an 'Indian Legion in the Waffen-SS' under the command of the Waffen-SS. In November 1944 Oberst Krappe had to appear before Reichsführer SS Heinrich Himmler for a longer lecture. He volunteered for the Waffen-SS and could keep the command of the legion. The German officers of the legion tried their best to resist. Some, like adjutant of the legion Second Lieutenant Adalbert Seifriz, and First Lieutenant Ulrich von Kritter, had themselves transferred to the army at the Italian front. Others remained in the legion and wore the new uniforms, but refused to volunteer for the SS. The remaining ones took care that at least the obligatory tattoo of the blood group under the arm was omitted and that the changeover was not entered into their serviceman's papers. With these measures they wanted to avoid being taken for SS-men in the case of captivity.[110] Gurbachan Singh

Mangat had an interestingly different attitude to the affiliation into the Waffen-SS. He interpreted it as a positive step from an Indian point of view: 'As a token of appreciation of the Indians' acts of valour, Reichsführer Heinrich Himmler suggested that the legion be affiliated with the crack German troops, the Waffen-SS.'[111]

According to Bannerth's testimony during interrogation by the British, the Indian legionnaires initially refused to fight against the French, as after all they were not at war with France. Thereupon, the Germans allegedly promised them looting in order to incite them against the partisans. In spite of this, several Indians deserted to the maquisards. Moreover, many Indians allegedly raped French women.[112] Hartog also confirms this: 'The legionnaires could not understand that French women were still protected as after all the French had become enemies now.'[113] The command of the legion appointed a drumhead court martial consisting of a German officer and two Indians. Three rapists were caught and accused. The first was sentenced to a watched-over, fatiguing pack march of a week's duration. The second one, based on a confession, was sentenced to death because of special brutality. The third could not be sentenced as the victim in her excitement during the trial pointed to the Indian officer, sitting by as judge, and identified him as the culprit. Legion Officer Hans Franzen, a lawyer qualified for admission to the profession, stresses in his memoirs the point that the proceedings had met all principles based on law and order: 'The protection of French women was the sole motive of the death sentence. The general problem of discipline was of secondary importance as for a long time we considered the end. We could achieve that only with the threat of a death sentence.'[114]

A captain of the Indian army, who travelled through France in December 1944, following the trail of the Indian Legion, gathered information in the town of Lever. The deputy mayor and an official of the town's administration told him that the Indians had looted every house, set five on fire, and raped eight women. The Germans had done nothing to stop them. Of course, the partisans had caught an Indian three weeks later and shot him to satisfy the people. A medical man had been able to confirm the violations. Two of the victims, Marie Joblen and her sixteen-year-old daughter Madeleine had the following to relate:

At least eight Indians entered their house at about 2200 hours, 1st September 44, and the husband was threatened with a revolver and held in an adjoining room. Madame Joblen was carried to her room and forcibly raped by two Indians. Mademoiselle M. Joblen was in bed when her room was entered by five or six Indians all of whom raped her between 2200 hours and 0200 hours, 2nd September. She confirms that her sister also suffered the same fate. Before leaving the Indians collected together all the jewellery and suchlike articles that were to be found in the house.[115]

The French newspaper *Le Figaro*[116] reported on 29 September 1944 that the Indian Legion had indulged in an orgy of murder, arson and rape. The Germans had to execute two of them in order to give satisfaction to the people. A German major general who surrendered on 16 September 1944 to the Americans, admitted that the Indians had lost control and that he had offered eight million francs to a prefect as compensation for damages and losses.

On the day the article appeared in *Figaro*, the ZFI decided on counter-propaganda. Second Lieutenant Gurbachan Singh Mangat, Feldwebel Sultan Khan and Unteroffizier Rashid Mohammed were ordered to go to Berlin in order to talk over the radio about the heroic actions of the Indian Legion. Mangat reported on the retreat to Alsace. After that, listeners heard from Sultan Khan how he destroyed positions of the Maquis with a howitzer and how Second Lieutenant Sukhdev Choudhari had crawled for two miles back to the troop with a bleeding leg. Rashid Mohammed related how he stopped four American tanks with a 75-mm anti-tank gun and thus delayed the advance of an entire division for twenty-four hours. Accompanied by Keppler, an SS-general, and the Japanese ambassador Oshima the three legionnaires together with Oberst Krappe and Second Lieutenant Adolf Abdulla Khan, who were also in Berlin, addressed a press conference.[117]

The Maquis treated captured Indians in various ways. The partisans accepted some, others were treated as captives—often more roughly than the German soldiers. On 22 September 1944, twenty-nine captured Indian legionnaires were shot at the Place d'Armes in Poitiers. The India Office and the Foreign Office demanded in the beginning of 1945 a clarification about this incident from the French. They justified the execution by alleging that the Indians had terrorized the population and killed members of the resistance. One of the Indians allegedly tried after his capture to stab a French officer to death. He was shot in this action. In the following general confusion, guards and other members of the resistance had intervened and shot all prisoners. The British did not quite accept this explanation as credible. However, they waived a more exact clarification of this incident and other executions of Indians in Bourges and Levet. They saw these cases as obvious acts of public revenge, which the Indians had provoked with their excesses.[118]

In the middle of November, the legion retreated further from the advance of the Americans. The men were billeted in private homes near Bretten in the region of Pforzheim. The locals were extremely friendly towards the Indians and the soldiers enjoyed some rest for a few weeks. Gradually, the German training officers left the legion. Whosoever could be spared was sent to the front. The company officers were now mostly Indians, only the company commander, the commanders and the members of the regimental staff were still Germans. Shortly before Christmas, the troop shifted to the training area Heuberg near Sigmaringen, where the soldiers received training in close anti-tank combat. However, they did not have to fight any more: when, in the beginning of April 1945, American and French troops advanced into south Germany, the Indian Legion had to surrender arms and equipment to other units of the Wehrmacht.[119]

The upkeep of foreign troops for pure propagandistic reasons was no more defensible when arms and military equipment became increasingly short of supply towards the end of the war. At the meeting of 25 March 1945 for discussing the situation, Hitler passed adverse remarks in this connection about the Indian Legion, which at that time was still fully equipped but had never seen action:

> The Indian Legion is a joke. There are Indians who cannot even kill a louse; they rather let themselves be devoured. They will also not kill an Englishman. I consider it a farce putting those of all men against the British. Why should the Indians fight with more courage than the Indians under Bose's leadership fought themselves in India? They deployed Indian units under Bose's leadership in Burma in order to liberate India from the British. They ran away like sheep. Why should they show more courage

here? I think if one were to use the Indians for turning prayer wheels or something like that, they would be the most tireless soldiers of the world. It is ridiculous though to apply them for an actual blood fight. How strong are the Indians?—Moreover, it is nonsense. Such amusements can be permitted for propagandistic reasons, if there is a surplus of weapons. However, if there is no surplus of weapons then these amusements for propagandistic reasons are simply not defensible.[120]

The individual battalions moved towards, the south in the spring of 1945. The I Battalion even managed to come as far as the Allgäu. However, they failed to reach neutral Switzerland in order to escape capture. The last remaining German officers with the legion had no other options but to release their Indian comrades and let them fend for themselves.[121]

The Americans took most of them prisoner near Weiler on 29 and 30 April 1945. Another battalion dispersed and was picked up by the Allied forces man by man. The Indians taken prisoner in Weiler were at first taken to Marseille, then to Taranto in Italy, and then in July 1945 to the internment camp Bahadurgarh near Delhi. Others went first to Cranwich in England and in September 1945 to Bahadurgarh.[122] There they were completely isolated from the outside world for some time and—according to Mangat—interrogated with 'third degree methods'.[123]

The war-criminal process in Bordeaux

The German officers of the Indian Legion had a hard time in captivity as well. Several officers stayed in the Vaucouleurs camp, later in Baccarat, where their main worry was poor nutrition. Unteroffizier Robert Frese, writer of the 12th company, was lucky though in French captivity when he met some Moroccan guards, whom he had looked after well with ample food when they had been in German hands in 1944 as prisoners of war. The grateful Moroccans introduced Frese to the camp commander and the unteroffizier was released at once.[124]

Four officers, Lieutenant Colonel Kurt Krappe, Captain Helmuth Hamerl, First Lieutenant Erwin Iven and Captain Wilhelm Lutz were particularly hard hit. They were taken to the military prison at Bordeaux as they were held responsible for the Indian Legion's criminal excesses. They had allegedly either indulged in or tolerated murder, looting, arson and rape. The accusations were partly based on statements made by the legion's interpreter Bannerth, after he had deserted to the other side. He had heavily indicted individual officers by name with his testimonies. Bannerth disowned his testimonies only on 11 August 1949 and exonerated Krappe and the other officers. Finally, the proceedings were dropped due to lack of evidence. Hamerl was released at the end of 1948, Lutz and Iven in April 1949, Krappe only on 26 January 1950.[125]

THE BRITISH AND THE INDIAN LEGION

The Germans had tried to keep the formation of the Indian Legion as long as possible a secret from the British, but it did not work out at all. The British already knew since the beginning of 1942 that Indians were being trained in the Lehrregiment Brandenburg.[126] The news service of the India Office and the Indian Political Intelligence (IPI) came to know at the end of October, that Bose had canvassed for volunteers in Camp Annaburg. A staff member of the Swiss embassy in Berlin, who had inspected the POW camp at Annaburg as representative of the protecting power, was the source of the information. He reported further 'that turbaned Indian troops had been seen in Berlin wearing German uniforms.' The representatives of the protecting power were not allowed to enter Camp Königsbrück and Camp Frankenberg.[127]

Some information in the form of a very brief message sent from somewhere in Saxony on 8 September 1943 proved to the British that the propaganda measures of the Germans had met with success and that 3,000 Indians were under military training in Königsbrück.[128] A delegate of the International Committee of the Red Cross passed on the same information in confidence to a staff member of the British legation in Berne.[129] The IPI was already very well informed about the formation and failure of the Centro Militare I. However, they did not have detailed information about the Indian Legion. Two Indian officers, who escaped in March 1943 from German captivity to Switzerland, spoke about the ill-treatment of Indians who resisted enlisting. The British, who could not really imagine that an Indian would voluntarily become disloyal to the colonial rulers, inferred from this:

It is therefore clear that objectionable and illegal pressure is being brought to bear on Indian prisoners of war to break the spirit and induce them to change their allegiance. It may be assumed, however, that mere numbers signify next to nothing and that there must be many who have succumbed to duress without necessarily being disloyal.[130]

After the British observed the development of the Indian Legion for some months, they really became worried. They were afraid the deserted prisoners of war could become troublemakers after their return to India. The general staff for India demanded therefore that each Indian should be carefully questioned before his return and, if necessary, undergo reconditioning.[131] The British referred to the Indian soldiers and civil persons working together with the Germans or Italians as Hitler-inspired fifth column, abbreviated HIF. Indians fighting on Japan's side belonged to the Japan-inspired fifth column (JIF).[132]

Three prominent deserters eventually furnished the British with detailed information about the formation, structure and application of the Indian Legion. On 23 August 1944, the Legion's interpreter (K) Bannerth, its medical officer Ernst Koch-Grünberg and Second Lieutenant Heinrich von Trott zu Solz broke away from the legion in Ruffec. This desertion evidently was connected with the failed assassination attempt on Hitler on 20 July 1944. Adam von Trott zu Solz, India expert in the Foreign Office, had been arrested as one of the conspirators and sentenced to death by the people's court. His twenty-six-year-old brother Heinrich was transferred in April 1943 to the legion from the eastern front at the instigation of Adam. He now expected to be arrested as belonging to the same family. Koch-Grünberg, who had joined the legion because of his experience as a tropical doctor in Liberia, had lost an uncle who was hanged because of his critical attitude to the regime. Bannerth himself had been taken into custody by the National Socialists in 1938.[133]

The three officers deserted together with a German soldier and a larger group of Indians, among them Bannerth's editor colleagues from the legion's newspaper *Bhaiband*—Hassan Beg, Thakur and Jamil Ahmed. The Germans were taken to a French POW camp. The Indians were moved in four lorries on 21 September 1944. One of the lorries stayed in a locality that had been destroyed by the Wehrmacht and where Indian legionnaires had committed excesses on the locals. The Indians on this lorry were handed over to the local resistance and later shot at the market square of Poitiers.[134]

The three deserters gave the British during interrogation an extensive and detailed report on the Indian Legion. They stressed the lack of discipline in the legionnaires and the role that brutality and pressure had played on the recruiting process. They added long lists of names of German and Indian members of the legion with brief evaluation of their political attitudes, such as 'convinced Nazi', 'Nazi, but harmless', or 'not a Nazi'. In addition, Bannerth supplied a detailed description of the 'moral corruption of the Indian legionnaires'. Overall, the British had to form the impression after this exposition that the Indian Legion was an unrestrained and incalculable massed army of morally depraved characters, led by irresponsible officers.[135]

Censorship of the press

The British initially tried preventing the news of Indian deserters reaching the public. The *Evening Standard* published a photo of a Sikh wearing the uniform of the Wehrmacht; the military correspondent gave a detailed report of about 20,000 Sikhs and Hindus positioned at the Siegfried line.[136] The India Office became worried. When on 29 September 1944 *Le Figaro* wrote about the excesses of the Indian Legion in France, the military news service MI2 insisted that such publications ought to be suppressed in future.[137] The Ministry of Information gave the directive on 20 October 1944 that the media should not mention if a British or American prisoner of war became a traitor.[138] The MI2 warned that each publication of information about the numerous Indians fighting on the side of the enemies would result in widespread discussions and speculations on the subject. This would particularly discredit the British government in the USA where influential papers were very eager to harm British reputation in India. American journalists had already started to doubt the loyalty of the Indian army. If now one had to admit the existence of a deserter army as well, the response could be extremely damaging.[139]

They could not keep the story of the Indian Legion and the Indian National Army away from the public for long. The military gave up their reservations when the victorious outcome of the war was in sight. At the end of April 1945, the War Office decided to publish an official press report about the INA, after the BBC had already come to know of its existence.[140] The high command for India agreed.[141] The press declaration, which was to appear on 9 May 1945 in the morning editions, states:

> Axis propagandists, with the help of Subhas Chandra Bose, the Indian renegade politician, paid particular attention to Indians. Every effort was made to persuade them that, by joining Bose's so-called 'Indian National Army', they would be fighting for the freedom of their country. A few believed him to be a sincere patriot; others, after Pearl Harbour, the fall of Malaya and Singapore and the invasion of Burma, felt that the Allies were losing the war in the Far East and that they had better come in on the winning side. But these were a small minority. [...] But the bulk of the Indian POW stoop up to the barbarous treatment meted out to them in Nazi and Japanese camps with the same spirit which has carried the Indian army to victory in every theatre of war and earned it the praise of every Allied Commander.[142]

The declaration's objective was, evidently, to show up as failure the endeavour of the Axis Powers to break the loyalty of the Indian prisoners of war. Only a small minority had been persuaded, some under pressure, others because they misjudged the situation. The decisive inference was that the loyalty of the Indian army was beyond doubt in spite of these incidents.

Tracking the deserters

Therefore, it is not surprising that the British government paid special attention to the treatment of the Indian deserters. In December 1943 the Indian government compiled a list of sixteen pages with names of suspect civilian Indians on the European mainland. In July 1944 an edition extending to twenty-eight pages was published under the title 'Notes on Suspect Civilian Indians on the Continent of Europe'[143]. The Intelligence Bureau of the Home Department in New Delhi compiled short biographies of eighty-nine Indians as interrogation aid during the invasion and after the war.[144]

From the beginning of September 1944, an officer of the Indian army, Major de Gale, was responsible at the high command of the

Allied forces in Europe for the Indians. At the end of October, another officer of the Indian army, Captain Warren, assisted him. The objective was to catch the legionnaires as soon as possible before they disappeared among civilians, 'where they would otherwise constitute a menace in the years to come.' A group of Indian officers and English ones knowing German was to take part in the first advance on the Reich's capital to track all Indian soldiers of the Wehrmacht and the civilians.[145]

De Gale's and Warren's task was to travel at first through France in order to document the excesses of the Indian Legion,[146] and to visit the Indians kept as prisoners by the maquisards and see to it that they were treated decently.[147] In March 1945, plans for the founding of the Indian Security Unit (ISU) became concrete: one group should track Indian civilians in Germany and in territories occupied by the Germans, interrogate them thoroughly, differentiate between collaborators and loyalists, and arrest the former. The other group was to track the legionnaires and separate them from the loyal prisoners of war.[148] De Gale, now a lieutenant colonel, was in command; Lieutenant Colonel Watson was to act as liaison officer to the Red Army. Captain Warren was still part of it, together with two Indian captains of the Indian army.[149]

The vanguard of the ISU, with Lieutenant Colonel Watson and Captain Bains marched into Berlin on 4 July 1945. During the next few days, the two officers arrested eleven of the wanted Indians. Thea von Harbou, the patron of the Berlin Indians, was also arrested. Gradually, the ISU snatched up more Indians. Thereupon they searched the premises of the Free India Centre in the Lichtensteinallee and its adjacent quarters in the Brandenburger Strasse and the Fasanenstrasse. However, they found nothing but rubble. Searching through the premises of the Foreign Office and the interception station Seehaus at the Wannsee did not yield any results either. The British found numerous files with newspaper cuttings and correspondence in Habibur Rahman's residence. Nambiar's account statements were secure in the Dresden Bank. The most interesting discovery was a 35-mm film about the Indian Legion.[150] The ISU soon found out that the Free India Centre had moved to Helmstedt, where Watson arrested Vyas and two other Indians. He got three Indians, one of them Ganpuley, out of the Soviet zone when they tried to reach Königsbrück. Nambiar was located in Tyrol somewhere near Bad Gastein, Habibur with his wife and child in Oberstdorf. All of them were taken at first to Braunschweig for interrogation. The report mentions the general attitude of the prisoners: 'The general attitude of the captured civilian Indian suspects is one of readiness to talk and to explain away their actions. "His Excellency", A. C. Nambiar, makes a very poor impression as a leader.'[151]

Ajit Singh was taken to various camps in Italy, one after the other, after his arrest in Milan. He met with Ezio Maria Gray, the president of the association Amici dell'India, in a British internment camp. Together they arranged discussions and lectures on India. Later they took him to a prison in Rome where he became ill. An American plane brought him to Germany on 3 August 1945. Officers of the ISU interrogated him in Bad Salzuflen. Subsequently, they took him to Sennelager where the other Indians also stayed as prisoners. He became ill once brought out again and spent most of the time in hospital.[152]

Vyas writes in his memoirs that the Indian camp community supplied him with some additional milk rations from the special food for vegetarians so that he could keep his strength.[153] A malevolent Indian major by the name of Srinagesh, chief of the general staff of the Indian army after independence, had put a stop to that by cancelling the vegetarian food supply of the Muslims, which contained milk products instead of meat.[154] Otherwise, though, he had nice memories of the camp: 'The life in the camp was a leisurely one.' There was neither any other duty besides the roll call every morning, nor any forced labour.[155] Vyas himself was released from the camp in February 1946 and worked thereafter for the administrative refugee authority of the United Nations, the United Nations Relief and Rehabilitation Agency.[156] Ajit Singh was taken to England as a very sick man where he was treated in Hull and London. He left London by plane on 7 March 1947 and landed in Karachi the next day. On the last day of his life, he was able to witness how India regained independence. He died on 15 August 1947 in Punjab.[157]

White, grey and black traitors

The Combined Services Detailed Interrogation Centre (India) grouped the Indians after an interrogation into three categories:

black, grey and white. Those considered to be a danger for security, were 'black'. Those influenced by enemy propaganda but not posing a constant danger, were 'grey'. Those who were neither influenced nor dangerous were 'white'. The 'grey' ones were to be taken to a reconditioning camp in India and later released as 'white'.[158] The category 'dark grey' was later introduced. The 'dark grey' ones were dangerous but could be reconditioned, though it would take longer than for the 'grey' ones.[159]

In the end, however, they penalized none of the Indian deserters in Europe. The Congress party used this subject from 15 August 1947 onwards in their election campaign. The press reported on the Indian National Army (INA). The Indian public was openly sympathetic. When the British took three officers of the INA, a Muslim, a Hindu and a Sikh, to court in the Red Fort in Delhi, the entire nation watched the proceedings spellbound. The Congress party adopted the case of the accused. Nehru personally pleaded for the defence. On 3 January 1946, the sentences were pronounced: all three were found guilty of high treason, the Muslim in addition for abetting to murder. All were sentenced to exile for life. However, Commander-in-Chief Claude Auchinleck pardoned them immediately. The condemned persons were merely dishonourably discharged from the army.[160]

Demonstrations and riots in the entire country accompanied the process with Bose's brother Sarat Chandra leading. Everywhere, one could hear the INA's slogans such as Jai Hind and Azad Hind, and see Netaji's picture displayed. Riots and street battles in Calcutta and Bombay alarmed the colonial rulers. Already the Indian army's loyalty could no more be taken for granted. Even the demonstratively mild sentences in the trial of Red Fort and the announcement that the charges for high treason would be dropped could not pacify the rioters. The Congress party distanced itself from the movement when the INA fever actually seized the armed forces and the sailors of the Royal Indian Navy started to mutiny. After all, they wanted to take over a functioning army after independence. Britain's colonial power, however, had already received a severe jolt.[161]

Bose must have surmised that just a public protest would help his movement to a propagandistic breakthrough. In November 1944, he allegedly sent a coded message to Vyas to the effect that some of his colleagues and the officers of the Indian Legion should somehow manage to reach England after the breakdown of the Axis Powers and continue legal proceedings there.[162] The British decided to display a mild attitude towards the deserters under these circumstances. Nearly all the former legionnaires had left the internment camp at Bahadurgarh by February 1946, and the 'black' and 'grey' ones were finally sent home in small groups in March 1946. All were given grey shirts and pajamas as well as a railway ticket for their journey home. The camp was empty by the middle of April 1946.[163]

The Indian independence movement accepted the returned soldiers of the INA and the Indian Legion with open arms, even though they had violated Gandhi's principle of non-violence. Gandhi declared that Netaji and the INA had taught the nation the three virtues of self-sacrifice, classless unity and discipline: 'If our adoration will be wise and discriminating, we will rigidly copy this trinity of virtues, but we will as rigidly abjure violence.'[164] He called upon the INA officers to continue fighting for the freedom of India, but now without violence: 'You have to show the same degree of bravery and courage of the non-violent type as you have done in the use of arms hitherto.'[165] Based on the interrogation of the legionnaires, the British gained an entirely different impression about the legion as against the one conveyed by Bannerth. An officer, who for the purpose of making charges had to find out if prisoners had possibly been ill-treated, came to the following conclusion after having talked to a hundred soldiers of the Indian Legion: 'There is little reliable evidence that any man was ever beaten into joining the legion.'[166] Thus as soon as the legionnaires were assured that they would not be charged any more with high treason, they evidently saw no more cause to depict themselves as victims of forcible recruitment.

The ISU was relieved by the Indian Military Mission, which had its headquarters in Berlin. They did not have to hunt for Indian deserters any more but to look after the interests of Indians in Germany. From the beginning, the mission was envisaged as precursor of a future Indian consulate or trade representative. Part of their job was also assisting the scattered Indians to return home. A number of Indians who had been politically engaged on the side of the Axis Powers, however, was to be prevented from returning home.[167] On 26 April 1946, nine Indians were still in the internment camp at Paderborn.[168] In June 1946 the Indian government decided, due to political developments, to allow all Indians including the Axis collaborators to return to India. But those in post-war Germany did not return. In spite of everything, forty-four preferred to stay back in Germany.[169]

One of the German legionnaires, however, decided to move to India after the war. The story of Leopold Fischer is one of the most curious ones of the Indian Legion.[170] Fischer was born in 1923 in Vienna. He became very interested in everything Indian when he was thirteen. He joined the Vienna Hindustan Academical Association, learnt Sanskrit and Hindi, and befriended Indian students. He met Jawaharlal Nehru in 1938 in Vienna. Nehru is supposed to have said about him: 'Leopold knows more about India than all other Indians in Vienna put together.'[171] At the age of sixteen, he embraced Hinduism and called himself Ramachandra. He met Bose in Berlin in 1942. When he was called up to the Wehrmacht, he asked to be posted with the Indian Legion. There he consciously mixed with the Indians:

> On top of my very thorough theoretical knowledge [...] the unique opportunity now came of constantly hearing the Indian languages spoken and constantly using them myself. My one ambition was to be regarded by my Indian comrades as a fellow Indian. They knew me as 'Ramachandra', and although they, of course, also knew that racially I belonged to Europe, they gradually began to regard me as one of themselves.[172]

He shared quarters with the legionnaires and took part in their religious rituals, even though the regiment's command did not approve of too close a contact with the Indians and some or the other of them suspected him to be an informer. He could improve his language skills like this and learnt Punjabi and Bengali. He even arranged a Hindu temple in Oberhofen and accepted the role of purohita, the priest of the legionnaires. He could do this because of his knowledge of Sanskrit. Thereupon Fischer decided to become a Hindu monk.[173]

He pretended to be an Indian when the Allied forces captured him. He called himself Ramachandra Sharma, a Kashmiri Brahmin who had studied in Germany. He got away with this story at first. Together with the Indians, they sent him to a repatriation camp in Marseille and even gave him the uniform of the Indian army. Officers of the ISU interrogated him in Paris. The British identified him correctly only after three months and sent him to the juvenile prison in Hertford and subsequently to the internment camp at Paderborn where he met Nambiar and other followers of Bose. He returned to Vienna when they released him from captivity in January 1947. Soon after Christmas 1948, he boarded a ship to India where he joined the Ramakrishna Mission. Later on, he became a professor at the Benares Hindu University and the University of Washington and developed a special interest in tantric yoga.[174]

SHORT EPILOGUE

As India gained her independence soon after the war ended, Bose's followers not only escaped punishment, but even their home country recognized them as freedom fighters who had made an important contribution to the freedom struggle. The young nation needed people who had seen something of the world for building an efficient diplomatic service. Nehru as first prime minister of free India readily reached back to the Indians who had gained diplomatic experience as staff members of the Free India Centre. So it came about that the representative of Bose's government of free India in Berlin, Nambiar, also became the first ambassador of the Indian Union in the Federal Republic of Germany. In August 1948 he was appointed councillor of the legation in Berne; in 1954 he became ambassador in Stockholm.[175] His collaboration with Bose and the National Socialists evidently was no reason for Nehru not to send his old friend as ambassador to Bonn. Another staff member of the Free India Centre, Girija K. Mookerjee, accompanied him as press attaché.[176] The German ambassador in Sweden had already noticed Nambiar as 'he knows the German language remarkably well and he does not hide his love for Germany also in front of others.'[177] A dossier of the German embassy in New Delhi stresses the point that Nambiar had worked from 1943 onwards as 'liaison man between the German government and the Indian national movement'. However, this had been 'much to Hitler's displeasure.'[178] A note of the Foreign Office for the federal chancellor is remarkable. It was to provide 'topics of conversation' for the meeting with Nambiar when he handed over his credentials in April 1955:

As Germany never pursued political interests in India and showed interest and sympathy for the freedom struggle of the Indians, in which Nambiar also participated during his Berlin days, the relations between the two countries are in every respect friendly. India was the first country to terminate the state of war with Germany (1.1.1951) and the first country to establish at once a diplomatic representation in Bonn after the small revision of the occupational power.[179]

Thus, according to the assessment of the official of the Foreign Office who composed these lines for the federal chancellor, the interest and the sympathy Hitler's government had shown for India's freedom struggle formed the basis of the friendly relations between India and the Federal Republic. It will be interesting to find out when the files of the Indian government are made accessible for research, whether the Indians looked at it in the same way.

Even before his appointment as ambassador in Bonn, Nambiar had kept contact with his German acquaintances. Together with former German officers of the Indian Legion, he founded a German-Indian Association in 1950. He met the former adjutant of the legion and later minister for federal affairs in Baden-Württemberg, Adalbert Seifriz, several times and introduced him to Nehru in 1954.[180]

Schedai allegedly joined the diplomatic service in Pakistan after the war. Anyway, Renzo De Felice made this statement but did not document it.[181] In other respects, all traces are lost of this man. Bhatta applied from Germany for the Indian Foreign Service and mentioned his activities in the Free India Centre, besides others, as qualifications.[182] However, the application was not accepted in July 1947 as the application date had expired.[183]

Conclusion

✑

The alliance between Subhas Chandra Bose and the governments of Germany and Italy during the Second World War is an example of an alliance by three partners with completely different objectives and interests. This alliance was made only under the special circumstances of the war. The freedom movements of colonial people never had Hitler's goodwill. He actually even disapproved of India's independence. Great Britain was really the partner of his choice. However, as the British did not want to enter into a union with him, Hitler became Bose's ally without exactly striving for it. Bose entertained no sympathies for National Socialism. However, he believed in the principle: 'England's enemy is my friend.' He was prepared to collaborate with National Socialist Germany in order to reach his goal, India's independence, only as far as it served his purpose. Mussolini as the third partner of the alliance played a peculiar role thereby. Contrary to Hitler, he was open to India's freedom movement. He was convinced that India would become independent eventually, and he expected profitable export business for Italy from this. Principally, he was prepared to support Bose without reservations. However, during the course of the war he became increasingly dependant on Germany and had to keep to the Axis partner's guidelines for foreign policy.

In the beginning of his political activities, Bose developed once the idea of a special Indian form of government that should form a synthesis between socialism and Fascism. However, he distanced himself again from his appreciation of Fascism after he had gained closer knowledge of Fascism and National Socialism from personal experience, and when Germany and Italy had embarked on aggressive politics of territorial expansion. He desired contact with the governments of Germany and Italy during the 1930s (as well as with other countries, for instance Ireland). The relation with Italy was friendly but superficial. The relationship with Germany was difficult and unproductive, because Bose did not accept the racial policy of the government.

The government of National Socialist Germany did little to come to an understanding with Bose. In Hitler's opinion, India was well off under British rule. Therefore, collaboration with Indian nationalists was of no interest to the National Socialists. They were prepared to modify their racial propaganda to a certain extent only because Germany depended on India as a supplier of raw materials and as a trading area. The situation changed slowly from about 1938 when Ribbentrop became foreign minister. The desire for an alliance with Great Britain had proved unrealistic. Hitler was now prepared to accept a conflict with the British. Thereupon, the Foreign Office started to seek collaboration with Indian nationalists seriously.

The Fascist government had already tried since the 1930s to seek contact with India. Contrary to Hitler, Mussolini pursued an Asia-politics. It was his objective to secure for Italy early political and economic influence in future independent Eastern states. And again, contrary to Hitler, his viewpoint of the development was not clouded with a racially motivated contempt of Asians. The practical realization of this Asia-politics lay in establishing a reputation as protective power of the young nations, and in trying to form a trading agreement with the Indian government. The Abyssinian war interrupted these endeavours and Italy lost credibility as an alliance partner of Asian nationalists. An important reason for the war was Mussolini's desire to form a basis for economic expansion towards the East. As an alternative, Mussolini tried to establish contact with subversive forces. Iqbal Schedai as agent became a key figure of Italian India-politics.

National Socialist and Fascist India-politics differed fundamentally from each other until the middle of the 1930s. While the Italians prepared themselves for India's independence, the National Socialists considered the thought of an independent India misguided and curbed their contempt for the Indians only up to the point that it did not become an impediment for the export economy. So far, the Italians were leading in India-politics: they had better contacts, better-founded ambitions and a better reputation than the Germans. The situation changed from the middle of the thirties onwards: the Italians spoilt their hard-earned prestige through the Abyssinian war, and the Germans tried now, albeit carefully and hesitantly, to establish contacts with nationalistic-minded Indians.

Neither the Italians nor the Germans had a 'fifth column' in India when the war broke out. Neither the Fascists nor the National Socialists could rely on a party, movement or organization close to their ideology that would accept directives from them as the Communist Party of India did to some extent from the Soviet Union. If at all there existed any ideological connections between the two dictatorships and Indian parties, these were no more than inspirations from afar, often based on misunderstandings and never more than mere stimuli. In India, Fascism or National Socialism never existed in the sense of a political movement based on the ideal of the country of origin of these ideas and a perceived ideological closeness with them.

When Bose escaped from India in 1941 and requested the embassies of the Axis Powers for permission to stay, it had nothing to do with his political ideologies. He would also have gone to the Soviet Union if he had been permitted entry there. However, it would not be correct to state that the Axis Powers had been Bose's second choice. After all, he had already asked the Italian consul general in Calcutta as early as in 1940, whether he could go to Italy. At that time—Italy had not yet joined the war—his application was not accepted. However, in the beginning of 1941, he knocked at open doors. Germany as well as Italy had already started preparations for an active propaganda on India. Bose came at an opportune moment.

They needed him as figurehead for German propaganda on India. They could exert influence on the Indians only with his help. Even though Hitler did not direct his urge for expansion towards India, the subcontinent nevertheless played a role in the strategy of the German Reich. Firstly, political unrest in India could diminish the country's contribution to the British war economy. Secondly, the forces needed to maintain order in the country and thus would not be available for Britain's fight against Germany. A third point was the utilization of the Indian question in propaganda for other countries and Germany herself. With Bose's support, the German Reich could depict herself as a friend of the oppressed people and condemn Great Britain as an imperialistic power. The government could show the Germans that National Socialism had the power of attraction in other countries.

However, Bose agreed to collaborate only with certain reservations. Soon after his arrival, he placed three demands before the German government: firstly, they should recognize an Indian government in exile; secondly, they should support a rebellion of the Indian people with propaganda and arms supply; and thirdly, they should drive out the British from India with military means. The foreign minister of the Reich, Ribbentrop, could not entertain such far-reaching demands. Bose, however, stuck to his conditions as the most essential. He demanded that the German Reich should publish a declaration in which they recognized India's independence. Bose now sought contact with the Italians. The experts of the Italian Foreign Ministry had by then started some propaganda directed towards India, mainly depending on Schedai, but Mussolini and Foreign Minister Ciano hardly showed any interest. They did not quite know at that point what to do with Bose and left the initiative in India-politics to the Germans.

To facilitate working with Bose, the Foreign Office founded a special department for India, the Sonderreferat Indien, staffed with experts from various other departments. Besides looking after Bose's welfare, they were responsible for collecting information about India and give directives to India-specific propaganda. To provide working staff for Bose, they founded the Free India Centre or Zentrale Freies Indien, which had the status of a diplomatic mission. The centre started work with plans for the functioning of the government in a free India. It was mainly engaged in shaping radio broadcasts, which the staff could transmit as Radio Azad Hind, via short-wave transmitters of the German Reich, to India. The centre was fully responsible for the content of the broadcasts. The Foreign Office entertained the hope that these programmes would have a greater appeal for Indian listeners than the official ones of the German short-wave transmitter, which had to respect political considerations in shaping the programmes. A similar undertaking existed in Italy. The Indian, Iqbal Schedai, worked there in the Uffizio India and gave speeches via his Radio Himalaya. For the Italians, however, this did not constitute working for independent India but was part of their propaganda for the Islamic regions in the Middle East.

At first Bose had to work secretly as he refused to go public with the declaration on Indian independence. The Germans, however, did not want to commit themselves at that time, as they wanted to wait for a more opportune moment. Bose was put off with this argument for many months. Meanwhile, his situation became increasingly more difficult around the end of 1941, as his presence in Germany could not escape notice for longer. When he learnt of the advance of the Japanese troops towards India, he decided to give up his incognito without waiting for the declaration. German activities on India reached their peak after Bose decided to become actively involved in their propaganda for India. The first action on India on a large scale started in February 1942 with a speech by Bose via Radio Azad Hind, which the German media circulated. More speeches followed. The next large-scale action was the intensive radio propaganda which was instrumental in bringing about the failure of the British-Indian negotiations. Bose's involvement became evident in India: he reached a large public through his radio broadcasts. That Gandhi allowed the talks to fail is also not least due to Bose's influence. Bose never gave up and continued to work on the Indians during the Quit India movement and August revolts with appeals to resist the British. Indian police reports document the effect of his speeches. It was an essential contribution to the success of India's fight for freedom. Bose almost led the revolt from afar and kept it going while the other leading politicians were in prison.

The declaration on India was for some time discussed, with changing positions, between Germany, Italy and Japan. The fact that it was not pronounced even though Ribbentrop, Mussolini and the Japanese government recommended it at times was mainly due to Hitler's influence. He rejected it for two reasons. Firstly, he had nothing against British rule in India and wanted to wait with the recognition of independence until he had to give up all hope of coming to an agreement with the British. Secondly, on principle, he considered the declaration of a country's independence only of use if it was also possible to see it through. Hitler proclaimed Egypt's freedom when the Africa Corps marched towards the estuary of the Nile. German troops, however, never came near India so that a declaration on Indian independence did not seem to him worthwhile. The only point in favour of a common declaration with Italy and Japan was that with it Germany would have documented her political right to share in the making of decisions on a country that was actually in

Japan's sphere of interest. The Japanese likewise tried to have a say in the question of an Arab declaration in order not to leave the field entirely to the Axis Powers. There again, the Japanese touched upon the interests of the Italians who strived for hegemony in the Arab region. Thus the negotiations between Germany, Italy and Japan about a declaration on India, which were closely connected with negotiations about an Arab declaration, were essentially about demarcating interest spheres in the Asiatic region.

While Germans and Italians were nicely balanced in the question of the declaration, collaboration in other propaganda fields functioned badly. Italy's India-specific propaganda, particularly Schedai's radio programmes, was directed towards Muslims in India, whereas the Germans—under Bose's influence—gave priority to the unity of the Indian people. Though the Italian diplomats were prepared to adhere to the language regulations from Berlin, Schedai did not wish to adjust and created more difficulties. The Italians went against an agreement with the Germans when they founded the Centro Militare I (CMI) parallel to the Indian Legion. The allocation of Indian prisoners of war led to disputes.

The Indian Legion existed exclusively for propaganda. The intention to deploy the legion for an invasion into India had played a role at the planning stage. However, this could not be pursued any more since the unsuccessful end of the Caucasus offensive in the summer of 1942. The troop was organized corresponding to Bose's political programme. Contrary to the prevailing system in the Indian troops of the British armed forces, soldiers of various religions, languages and castes were grouped together in the same units. The troop was to be a model for the coexistence of various groups of the Indian population in an undivided nation. The command language of the legion was Hindustani, which Bose had also chosen to be the national language of free India. Like the Italians, the German instruction officers had to grapple with mutinies of the Indian soldiers. The fact that the Indian Legion was not dissolved like the CMI is mainly due to Bose's authority, the endeavour of the German officers and the employment of Indian experts. The Italians, and Schedai with them, were a complete failure in this regard.

The influence Bose must have exerted became evident after his departure in February 1943. India-politics lost its uniform line. The rejection of Pakistan was no more undisputed. Instead, some voices were raised in the Foreign Office demanding support for the Islamic separatists. The officials agreed to adhere to the former line only after prolonged discussions. The military situation was also responsible for the fact that India-politics lost importance from 1943 onwards. The Italian India-politics ended with Mussolini's dismissal. It played a role only in so far as Mussolini, as the powerless head of state of the German-occupied Republica Sociale Italiana, hoped for a breakdown of British rule in India.

While the National Socialists were influenced by racially founded considerations before the war, and therefore neither wanted the independence movement to succeed nor thought it capable of achieving its aim, the Fascists, without any such ideological blinkers, realized that India would soon cease to be a colony, and tried far-sightedly to profit from the developments. However, disappointed by the British and under war conditions, the National Socialists adopted a pragmatic attitude. Bose took advantage of this. He came to Europe in order to exploit the Axis Powers for his political struggle, and he too had to allow them to make good use of him.

Acknowledgements

I would like to take this opportunity to thank the many people who have made this book possible.

To begin with, I would like to thank my PhD supervisor, the late Professor Dr Lüth. It was he who encouraged me to tackle the project and never ceased to take a lively interest in it. But, of course, I must not forget to mention Dr Tilman Frasch, of the Institute of South Asian Studies at Heidelberg University, who, by a casual remark he dropped in one of the sessions of his seminar, first drew my attention towards what was to become the subject of my research.

Then I have to thank Professor Dr Diethelm Weidemann of the Institute of Asian and African Studies at Humboldt University, Berlin; Dr Jens Petersen and Dr Lutz Klinkhammer, of the German Historical Institute in Rome; and Dr Tilak Raj Sareen of the Indian Council of Historical Research; all of whom granted me ample time for scholarly discussion and gave me many useful hints as to primary sources and secondary works.

I would also like to extend my thanks to the staff members of the archives and libraries I used for their cooperation in this project. These were: in Germany—the Political Archive of the Foreign Office, the Federal Archive, the Library of the South Asian Institute of Heidelberg University, the branch library for Asian and African Studies of the University Library of Humboldt University, Berlin; then, in Italy (Rome)—the Historical Archive of the Ministry of Foreign Affairs, the Central State Archive, the Archive of the Historical Office of the Army General Staff, the Instituto Italiano per l'Africa e l'Oriente, the Library of the German Historical Institute, the Biblioteca di Storia Moderna e Contemporanea; in New Delhi—the National Archives of India and the Nehru Memorial Museum and Library; and, finally, in London—the Public Record Office and the British Library.

This English translation would not have been possible without my translator, Mrs Christel Das of Calcutta.

My most heartfelt thanks go to my parents, Herta and Hinrich Kuhlmann, for all their love and unswerving support and, not least, their reading and correcting the final draft of my manuscript.

List of Abbreviations

AA   Auswärtiges Amt (German Foreign Office)
AA-PA   Auswärtiges Amt, Politisches Archiv (Political Archive of the German Foreign Office)
Abw   Amtsgruppe Abwehr im Amt Ausland/Abwehr des OKW (German Military Intelligence)
ACS   Archivio Centrale dello Stato (Italian Central State Archive)
ADAP   Akten zur deutschen auswärtigen Politik (Documents on German Foreign Policy)
AEM   Direzione Generale degli Affari di Europa e del Mediterraneo (Italian Director General for European and Mediterranean Affairs)
AIR   All-India Radio
Amb.   Ambasciata (Italian Embassy)
AO   Auslandsorganisation der NSDAP (Foreign Organization of the NSDAP)
APA   Außenpolitisches Amt der NSDAP (NSDAP Office of Foreign Affairs)
AS-MAE   Archivio Storico—Ministereo degli Affari Esteri (Historical Archive of the Italian Foreign Ministry)
AT   Direzione Generale degli Affari Transoceani (Italian Director General for Overseas Affairs)
Ausl   Amtsgruppe Ausland im Amt Ausland/Abwehr des OKW (German Military Intelligence)
AUS-SME   Archivio dell'Ufficio Storico dello Stato Maggiore dell'Esercito (Archive of the General Staff of the Italian Army)
BA   Bundesarchiv (German Federal Archive)
BA-MA   Bundesarchiv, Militärarchiv (Military Archive of the German Federal Archive)
BBC   British Broadcasting Corporation
BfI   Beauftragter für das Informationswesen (Commissioner for Information)
Bot.   Deutsche Botschaft (German Embassy)
C   Direzione Generale del Commercio (Italian Director General for Commercial Affairs)
CID   Criminal Investigation Department

CMI	Centro Militare I (Military Centre I)
Cons.	Consolato (Italian Consulate)
CP	Central Provinces
CS	Commando Supremo (Italian Supreme Command)
CSDIC(I)	Combined Services Detailed Interrogation Centre (India)
CSDIC(UK)	Combined Services Detailed Interrogation Centre (United Kingdom)
D	Abteilung Deutschland (Division for German Affairs)
D III	Referat Information der Auslandsvertretungen (Department for Information of Foreign Missions)
D IV	Referat Herstellung und Verbreitung von Schrifttum aller Art (Department for Production and Proliferation of All Kinds of Literature)
DA	Deutsche Akademie (German Academy)
DDI	I Documenti Diplomatici Italiani (Italian Diplomatic Documents)
DGI	Director General of Information
DMI	Director of Military Intelligence
DNB	Deutsches Nachrichtenbüro (German News Office)
DOV	Deutscher Orient-Verein (German Orient Association)
EAD	External Affairs Department
ED	External Department
Ed.	Editor
EIAR	Ente italiano audizioni radiofoniche (Italian Broadcasting Corporation)
Emb.	British Embassy
EOD	Economic and Overseas Department
FHQ	Führerhauptquartier (Hitler's Headquarters)
FO	Foreign Office
FPD	Foreign and Political Department
Gab	Gabinetto (Cabinet)
GCCS	Government Code and Cypher School
GenKons.	Deutsches Generalkonsulat (German Consulate General)
Ges.	Deutsche Gesandtschaft (German Legation)
GHQ	General Headquarters
GoI	Government of India
HaPol	Handespolitische Abteilung (Economic Division)
HD	Home Department
HIF	Hitler's Indian Fith Column
i. G.	im Generalstab (in the Gerneral Staff)
IB	Intelligence Bureau
ID	Information Department
IIL	Indian Independence League
INA	Indian National Army
(Ind.)I.R.950	(Indisches) Infanterie-Regiment 950 (Indian Infantry Regiment 950)

Inf	Informationsabteilung (Information Division)
IO	India Office
IOR	India Office Records—British Library
IPI	Indian Political Intelligence
IRT	Ispettorato per la Radio e la Televisione (Inspectorate for Radio and TV)
ISMEO	Istituto Italiano per il Medio ed Estremo Oriente (Italian Institute for the Middle and Far East)
ISU	Indian Security Unit
JIF	Japanese Indian Fifth Column
Kult	Kulturpolitische Abteilung (Cultural Division)
Kult R	Referat Rundfunkangelenheiten (Department for Broadcasting Affairs)
Leg.	Legazione (Italian Legation)
MA	Ministereo dell'Aeronautica (Italian Ministry of Aviation)
MAE	Ministereo degli Affari Esteri (Italian Foreign Ministry)
MAI	Ministereo dell'Africa italiana (Italian Ministry of Italian Africa)
MC	Ministero delle Corporazioni (Italian Ministry of Corporations)
MCP	Ministereo della Cultura Populare (Italian Ministry of Popular Culture)
MD	Military Department
MG	Ministero della Guerra (Italian War Ministry)
MI	Ministero del Interno (Italian Interior Ministry)
MI2	Military Intelligence 2
MM	Ministereo della Marina (Italian Navy Ministry)
MO	Reparto Medio Oriente (Department for the Middle East)
MS	Monitoring Service
NAI	National Archives of India
NMML	Nehru Memorial Museum and Library
Nr.	Number
NSDAP	Nationalsozialistische Deutsche Arbeiterpartei (National Socialist German Workers Party)
NWFP	Northwest Frontier Province
O	Ufficio Operazioni (Operation Office)
OKH	Oberkommando des Heeres (German Army High Command)
OKW	Oberkommando der Wehrmacht (German Armed Forces High Command)
Oqu	Oberquartiermeister (Quartermaster General)
P	Nachrichten- und Presseabteilung (News and Press Division)
P III	Referat Italien (Department for Italy)
P VIII	Referat Ostasien (Department for East Asia)
P XII	Referat Nachrichtendienst (Intelligence Department)
POW	Prisoner of War
PCM	Presidenza del Consiglio dei Ministri (Italian Presidency of the Council of Ministers)

PG	Ufficio Prigionieri di Guerra (Italian Office for Prisoners of War)
Pol	Politische Abteilung (German Political Divison)
Pol IM	Referat Militärfragen (Department for Military Affairs)
Pol VII	Referat Orient (Department for the Orient)
PRO	Public Record Office
Prot	Abteilung Protokoll (Protocol Division)
PS	Direzione Generale della Pubblica Sicurezza (Italian Director General for Public Security)
PStRAM	Persönlicher Stab des Reichsaußenministers (Personal Staff of the German Foreign Minister)
PStRFSS	Persönlicher Stab des Reichsführers SS (Personal Staff of the Commander of the SS)
RAD	Reichsarbeitsdienst (German Labour Service)
RAM	Reichsaußenminister (German Foreign Minister)
RCM	Ragruppamento Centri Militari (Group of Military Centres)
RFSS	Reichsführer SS (Commander of the SS)
RK	Reichskanzlei (German Chancellery)
RM	Reichsminister (German Minister)
RMVP	Reichsministerium für Volksaufklärung und Propaganda (German Ministry of Public Enlightenment and Propaganda)
RomQ	Deutsche Botschaft Rome-Quirinal (German Embassy Rome-Quirinal)
RRG	Reichs-Rundfunk-Gesellschaft (German Broadcasting Society)
RSI	Repubblica Sociale Italiana (Italian Social Republic)
RSS	Rashtriya Swayamsevak Sangh
Ru	Rundfunkabteilung (Broadcasting Division)
SE	Direzione Generale per la Stampa Estera (Italian Gerneral Director for the Foreign Press)
SHAEF	Supreme Headquarters Allied Expeditionary Force
SIE	Servizio Informazioni Esercito (Italian Military Intelligence)
SIM	Servizio Informazioni Militari (Italian Military Intelligence)
SMG	Stato Maggiore Generale (Italian Armed Forces General Staff)
SMRE	Stato Maggiore del Regio Esercito (Italian Army General Staff)
SP	Direzione Generale per i Servizi della Propaganda (Director General for Propaganda Services)
SPD	Segretaria Particolare del Duce (Mussolini's Secretary)
SRI	Sonderreferat Indien (Special Department India)
SS	Schutzstaffel der NSDAP (Protection Squadron of the NSDAP)
SSt	Sottosecretario di Stato (Italian Secretary of State)
StS	Staatssekretär (German Secretary of State)
StS	Staatssekretär und Chef der Reichskanzlei (German Secretary of State and Head of Chancellery)
StSzbV	Staatssekretär zur besonderen Verwendung (German Secretary of State for Special Duty)
UP	United Provinces

USSt	Undersecretary of State
UStS	Unterstaatssekretär (German Undersecretary of State)
VAA	Verbindungsoffizier zum Auswärtigen Amt (Liaison Officer to the German Foreign Office)
VCO	Viceroy's Commissioned Officer
W	Wirtschaftspolitische Abteilung (Economical Division)
WD	War Department
WFSt	Wehrmacht-Führungstab (German General Staff)
WO	War Office
ZFI	Zentrale Freies Indien (Free India Centre)

Archival Sources

R60669	Indien, Volume 3
R60670	Indien, Volume 4
R60671	Indien, Volume 5
R60672	Indien, Volume 6
R60673	Indien, Volume 7
R60674	Indien, Volume 8
R60675	Indien, Volume 8a
R60676	Indien, Volume 9
R60677	Indien, Volume 10

Rundfunkpolitische Abteilung des Auswärtigen Amtes

R67482	Deutsche Auslandsrundfunkpropaganda, Volume 1
R67483	Deutsche Auslandsrundfunkpropaganda, Volume 2
R67554	Südost Propagandamaterial-Sammlung
R67599	Indien-Nachrichtenmaterialsammlung

Politische Abteilung III des Auswärtigen Amtes

R77410	Kunst und Wissenschaft im allgemeinen (Indien)
R77416	Politische Beziehungen Indiens zu Deutschland, Volume 3
R77417	Politische Beziehungen Indiens zu Deutschland, Volume 4
R77418	Politische Beziehungen Indiens zu Deutschland, Volume 5
R77419	Indisches Informations-Büro
R77442	Deutsche diplomatische und konsularische Vetretungen in Indien, Volume 2
R77462	Politische und kulturelle Propaganda (Indien)
R90656	Fremde (indische) Handelskammern in Deutschland

Abteilung Inland II des Auswärtigen Amtes

R101701	Propaganda, Volume 21

Politische Abteilung des Auswärtigen Amtes

R101836	Abwehr Afghanistan, Volume 4
R101837	Abwehr Afghanistan, Volume 5
R104777	Politische Beziehungen Indiens zu Deutschland
R104778	Indien: Innere Politik, Parlaments- und Parteiwesen
R104806	Privata Indien
	Wirtschaftspolitische Abteilung des Auswärtigen Amtes
R108647	Deutsche Handelsattachés und Handelsbeiräte im Ausland: Britisch-Indien

RomQ Botschaft Roma-Quirinal

105	Indischer Freiheitskämpfer Bose
164	Indien, Volume 1
165	Indien, Volume 2
166	Indien, Volume 3
167	Indische Legion in Deutschland und arabische Legion in Italien; indische Kriegsgefangene

497	Kriegstagebuch des Oberst Erwin Lahousen, Volume 1
498	Kriegstagebuch des Oberst Erwin Lahousen, Volume 2
RH24-88	**Generalkommando des LXXXVIII. Armeekorps**
81	Inder
RH37	**Verbände der Infanterie**
6530	Alfred Opitz: Denn wir fahren gegen Engeland. Die 'Indische Legion' im 2. Weltkrieg
RS4	**Indische Legion, (Indisches) Infanterie-Regiment 950**
1142	Bataillons-Befehle des I. Bataillons
1143	Legionszeitschrift Bhaiband, Volume 1
1144	Legionszeitschrift Bhaiband, Volume 2
1145	Legionszeitschrift Bhaiband, Volume 3
1146	Disziplinarangelegenheiten
1148	Einteilung der 2. Kompanie
MSg2	**Allgemeine Sammlungen zur Militärgeschichte**
3068	Indische Legion. Mappe I: Dokumente, Berichte und Aufzeichungen aus den Kriegsjahren
3069	Indische Legion. Mappe II: Aufzeichungen in den Fünfziger Jahren Indische Legion. Mappe III: Aufzeichnungen 1983 (und 1981)
AS-MAE	**Archivio Storico—Ministero degli Affari Esteri (Roma)**
Gab	**Gabinetto**
56	Udienze dal Duce: Bla-Bq
104	Elenchi udienze die S. E. il Capo di Governo
407	Corrispondenza relativa alla propaganda nel mondo islamico I
408	Corrispondenza relativa alla propaganda nel mondo islamico II
483	Corrispondenza relativa alla propaganda in Asia I
484	Corrispondenza relativa alla propaganda in Asia II
742	Politica musulmana dell'Italia—Ghadr Party
AC	**Affari Commerciali**
India/1930-31	India 1930-1931
India/1934	India 1934
India/1935	India 1935
India/1937	India 1937
AP	**Affari Politici 1931-1945**
India/13	India 1940-1945
Irak/18	Legione Araba
Italia/84	Dichiarazione Paesi Arabi
RG	**Raccolta generale**

80	ISMEO 1943

RSI	**Repubblica Sociale Italiana**
AT/117	Direzione Generale Affari Transoceani: India-Italia
AT/118	Direzione Generale Affari Transoceani: Giappone: Trattazione generale
AP/68	Affari Politici: India
Gab/26	Gabinetto: Società Amici dell'India[1]
Gab/36	Gabinetto: India

ACS	**Archivio Centrale dello Stato (Roma)**

SPD/CO	**Segretaria Particolare des Duce—Carteggio Ordinario**
519.319	Istituto Italiano per il Medio ed Estremo Oriente
532.797	India—Possibilità e risiche economiche

PCM	**Presidenza del Consiglio dei Ministri**
1940-1943/1.1.10	ISMEO—Mobilitazione civile

JAIA	**Joint Allied Intelligence Agency (Mikrofilme)**
30	MCP: Italian wireless propaganda for India
38	MCP: E. Bensaglio—Labh Singh—Chari Dass Bose
39	MCP: Middle East and Far East
117	MCP: Reports—Direzione Generale per i Service della Propaganda[2]

MCP	**Ministereo della Cultura Populare**
Gab/50	Rapporti ai giornalisti
Gab/58	Appunti al ministro
Gab/69	Germania—Rapporti e contatti tra il Ministero della Cultura Populare e il Ministero Propaganda del Reich
Gab/325	Propaganda e rapporti esteri

MI/PS	**Ministero dell'Interno—Direzione Generale della Publica Sicurezza**
1937/40	Movimento sovversivo antifascista—Austria

AUS-SME	**Archivio dell'Ufficio Storico dello Stato Maggiore dell'Esercito (Roma)**

M3	**Documenti (IT) forze armate italiane restituiti dagli USA[3]**
6-5	Lettera del Generale Ricciotti Garibaldi al Maresciallo Cavallero: liberazione dei prigionieri italiani in India (IT 4510)

M7	**Circolari vari uffici**
581	Circolari maggio—dicembre 1942

N	**Diari storici seconda guerra mondiale**

667	SMRE: Ufficio Prigionieri di Guerra—Segreteria
780	Commando Ragruppamento Centri Militari
1400	SIM: Allegati al diario storico 1-31 luglio 1942
1404	SIM: Novembre 1942

IsIAO	**Istituto Italiano per l'Africa e l'Oriente (Roma)**
Verbali	**Libro di verbali delle sedute del consiglio di amministrazione, della giuta eseccutiva e dell'assemblea dell'ISMEO**
1	1933-1940
2	1939-1948

NAI	**National Archives of India (New Delhi)**

EAD	**External Affairs Department**
1947/	Question in the Legislative Assembly by Maharaja Kumar Sir
31(8)-EUR-47	Vijanya Ananda regarding the demand by the memberns of the Azad Hind Sangh
1947/	Request from K. A. Bhatta (in South Germany) for an
36(36)-EUR-47	appointment in Switzerland under the Indian Foreign Service

Home-Poll	**Home Department—Political Branch**
1941/52-3-41	Effect of 'Himalaya Broadcasting Station'
1941/135-41	Disappearance of Subhas Chandra Bose
1942/18-3-42	Fortnightly reports for the month of March 1942
1942/18-4-42	Fortnightly reports for the month of April 1942
1942/18-5-42	Fortnightly reports for the month of May 1942
1942/18-8-42	Fortnightly reports for the month of August 1942
1942/18-9-42	Fortnightly reports for the month of September 1942
1942/18-10-42	Fortnightly reports for the month of October 1942
1942/18-11-42	Fortnightly reports for the month of November 1942
1942/18-12-42	Fortnightly reports for the month of December 1942
1943/18-2-43	Fortnightly reports for the month of Februrary 1943
1943/18-5-43	Fortnightly reports for the month of May 1943
1943/18-6-43	Fortnightly reports for the month of June 1943
1943/18-7-43	Fortnightly reports for the month of July 1943
1943/18-11-43	Fortnightly reports for the month of November 1943

Bose	**Subhas Chandra Bose Papers**
247	Kommerzialrat Otto Faltis Collection
312	Speeches of Subhas Chandra Bose as monitored by the Monitoring Service of All-India Radio, Simla
551	Divekar Collection

HFM	**History of Freedom Movement**
A-10-3	Statement by Swami Agehananda (formerly R. L. Fisher)

IIL	**Records of the Indian Independence League**
10	Correspondence between the German minister and Bose
35	Conversation between R. B. Bose and S. C. Bose
40	Bose's letter to the Italian minister
INA	**Indian National Army Papers**
241	POW camps, CMI, HIF
242	Brandenburg Regiment, Free Indian Legion Germany
416	Report of disciplinary investigations regarding HIFs
435	Summary of History re-disposal of JIFs/HIFs

NMML   **Nehru Memorial Museum and Library (New Delhi)**

OHT	**Oral History Transcripts**
125	Adalber Seifriz, interviewed by B. R. Nanda, Bonn, 28 October 1971
170	Emilie Schenkl, interviewed by B. R. Nanda, Vienna, 11 November 1971
285	Alexander Werth, interviewed by B. R. Nanda, Bonn, 2 October 1971
325	P. B. Sarma, interviewed by B. R. Nanda, Vienna, 15 November 1971

IOR   **India Office Records—British Library (London)**

R/3	**India: Viceroy's Private Office Papers and other Government Records**
2/21	Disappearance of Subhas Bose
R/12	Afghanistan: Kabul Legation Records
163	Information obtained from Italian Legation
L/P&S	**Political and Secret Department Records**
12/81	Activities of Gino Scarpa
12/107	Asiatic Students Congress of Rome
12/494	Radio Himalaya
12/1774	Control of foreigners or enemy agents in Afghanistan
12/1798	Afghanistan: Axis intrigues
12/1799	Afghanistan: Axis intrigues—Repatriation of members of Axis legations
12/1805	Afghanistan: Italian Legation
L/PO	**Private Office Papers**
11/20	Schacht's visit to India
L/WS	**War Staff Papers**
1/737	Military Mission to Berlin

1/1363	Subversive action against the Indian army by Germans and Italians
1/1516	POW and CSDIC

MSS EUR **European Manuscripts**
C0743   Hugh Toye: Swami: notes taken by me in Singapore, Sep/Oct 1945

PRO   Public Record Office (London)

HS1   **Special Operations Executive Far East**
200   India—General

WO208 **War Office: Directorate of Military Intelligence**
767   India—Relations with Italy
773   Internal Situation: Northwest Frontier
802   German and Italian attempts to suborn Indian POW
823   India—Relations with Germany
826   Indian civilians on the continent
831   Publicity in connection with Indian POW in German hands

WO224 **War Office: International Red Cross and Protecting Power**
14B   Stalag IV D—Annaburg
137   Italian POW camp 91

Notes

INTRODUCTION

1 Kershaw, *Hitler 1936-1945*, 61.
2 Thanks to Dr Piero Crociani of the Historical Archive of the Italian Army for pointing me to this book.

SUBHAS CHANDRA BOSE

1 Bose, *The Indian Struggle 1920-1940*, 329-33; the first edition of this book appeared as *The Indian Struggle 1920-1934*.
2 Ibid. 351.
3 Palme Dutt, Interview with Bose, in *Daily Worker*, dated 24 January 1938. See Bose, *Congress President*, 1-3.
4 Bose, 'The Role of Forward Bloc', dated 12 August 1939; Bose, *The Alternative Leadership*, 4-7.
5 Misra, *The Indian Political Parties*, 473.
6 Frank, 'Revolution oder Reform', in Werth, *Der Tiger Indiens*, 59-80; see 59-60 and 67-80.
7 Bose to Divekar, Letter from 18 May 1935, NAI/Bose/551.
8 Frank, 'Revolution oder Reform', in Werth, *Der Tiger Indiens*, 61-3.
9 AA/Pol VII (Hentig): Memorandum dated 17 December 1937, AA-PA/R104777.
10 AA/Pol III (Prüfer) to AA/Pol III (Dieckhoff): Memorandum dated 25 July 1933, AA-PA/R77416.
11 AA/Pol III (Dieckhoff) to AA (Schmidt-Rolke): Memorandum dated 28 March 1934, AA-PA/R77417.
12 Bose to AA (Dieckhoff): Letter dated 05.04.34, in Bose, *Letters, Articles, Speeches and Statements 1933-1937*, 61-4.
13 DA/Indischer Ausschuss (Thierfelder) to AA: Letter dated 27 March 1934, AAPA/R77416.
14 Bose to Thierfelder: Letter dated 7 November 1935, in Bose, *Letters, Articles, Speeches and Statements 1933-1937*, 111-5.

15   Faltis to AA (Aschmann): Letter dated 22 November 1938, AA-PA/R104777.
16   Faltis to AA/SRI (Trott): Letter dated 4 July 1944, AA-PA/R27504.
17   Bose to AA (Prüfer): Letter dated 7 May 1935, AA-PA/R77417.
18   Thierfelder, *Deutsch-indische Begegnungen 1926-56*, 154-5.
19   AA/Pol III (Dieckhoff): Memorandum dated 14 January 1936, AA-PA/ R774167.
20   Bose: Notes dated 9 December 1937, AA-PA/R104777.
21   Urchs to Leitung der AO: Report dated 24 December 1938, AA-PA/104777.
22   Hentig: Memorandum dated 17 December 1937, AA-PA/R104777.
23   Bose to Thierfelder: Letter from 25 March 1936, in Bose, *Letters, Articles, Speeches and Statements 1933-37*, 165-8. Also see Thierfelder, *Deutsch-indische Begegnungen*, 154.
24   Urchs to die Leitung der AO: Report dated 24 December 1938, AA-PA/104777.
25   Bose, 'A Word About Germany' [Forward dated 13 March 1940], in *The Alternative Leadership*, 81-2.
26   Prefect of Venice (Bianchetti) to MAE: Letter dated 4 March 1931, AS-MAE/ AP/India/3.
27   Bose to Divekar: Letter dated 15 March 1933, NAI/Bose/551.
28   ConsGen.Calcutta (Scarpa) to MAE: Telex dated 25 March 1933.
29   Amb.Berlino to MAE: Fernschreiben dated 11 September 1933, AS-MAE/ AP/India/3.
30   Bose to Naomi C. Vetter: Letter dated 21 December 1933, in Bose, *Letters, Articles, Speeches and Statements 1933-37*, 44.
31   Bose to Naomi C. Vetter: Letter dated 12 January 1934, in Bose, *Letters, Articles, Speeches and Statements 1933-37*, 45-7.
32   MAE: Memorandum dated 29 December 1933, AS-MAE/Gab/56.
33   Register of Audiences, AS-MAE/Gab/104.
34   Bose, *The Indian Struggle 1920-42*, 364.
35   *Il Giornale d'Italia*, 29 December 1933.
36   MAE/SSt (Survich): Note dated 16 January 1934, AS-MAE/Gab/56.
37   MAE/Gab to Mussolini: Note dated 25 January 1934, AS-MAE/Gab/56.
38   Register of Audiences, AS-MAE/Gab/104.
39   Bose to Mussolini: Letter dated 29 November 1934, AS-MAE/Gab/56.
40   Register of Audiences, AS-MAE/Gab/104.
41   MAE/Gab to Mussolini: Memorandum dated 23 January 1935, AS-MAE/ Gab/56.
42   MAE: Memorandum dated 11 January 1935, AS-MAE/AP/India/3.
43   Emb.Rome (Drummund) to MAE/SSt (Suvich): Letter dated 28 January 1935, AS-MAE/Gab/56.
44   MAE/Gab to Mussolini: Memorandum dated 19 June 1935, AS-MAE/ Gab/53.
45   MAE/Gab: Note dated 23 August 1935, AS-MAE/Gab/56.
46   MAE: Note dated 28.September 1934, AS-MAE/Gab/56.

47 MAE to ConsGens.Dublino: Telegram dated 6 February 1936, AS-MAE/Gab/56.

48 MAE/Gab to MAE/Ufficio del Cerimoniale: Memorandum dated 2 April 1936, AS-MAE/Gab/56.

49 MAE/Gab to Mussolini: Memorandum dated 15 February 1936, AS-MAE/Gab/56.

50 MAE/Gab to Bose: Letter dated 27 March 1936, AS-MAE/Gab/56.

51 Bose to Schenkl: Letter dated 29 March 1936, in Bose, *Letters to Emilie Schenkl 1934-42*, 49-53.

52 Bose to Rapicavoli: Letter dated 21 November 1937, AS-MAE/Gab/56.

53 Bose to MAE: Letter dated 10 December 1937, AS-MAE/Gab/56.

54 MI/PS: Memorandum dated 18 December 1937, ACS/MI/PS/1937/40.

55 MAE/Gab to Mussolini: Memorandum dated 5 January 1938, AS-MAE/Gab/56.

56 MAE/Gab to Mussolini: Memorandum dated 26 January 1938, AS-MAE/Gab/56.

57 Bose, *Letters to Emilie Schenkl*, 177-9.

BOSE'S ESCAPE TO EUROPE

1 *Netaji Collected Works* ii, 379.

2 Bose, *The Indian Struggle*, 378-81.

3 Ibid. 382.

4 Ibid. 383.

5 Ibid. 384.

6 Mukherjee, *Two Great Indian Revolutionaries*, 159. Mukherjee quotes a Marathi book titled *Veer Savarkaranchi Abhinav Bharat Sangata Amayinchi Utkrishta Bhashane* (Veer Savarkar's Best Speeches about Abhinav Bharat), 72-6. He also refers to a letter from Savarkar's private secretary Bal Savakar to Khitis Chandra Das, the secretary of the Rash Behari Basu Smarak Samity, dated 2 June 1954. There it says: 'It may be mentioned here that it was a private and personal meeting between Netaji Subhas Babu and Savarkarji at Savarkar Sadan, Bombay, that a definite suggestion was made to Subhas Babu by Savarkarji that he should try to leave India and undertake the risk of going over to Germany to organize the Indian forces there fallen into German hands as captives and then with German help should proceed to Japan to join hands with Sri Rash Behari Bose.'

7 Marzia Casolari, Nazionalismo indiano, Italia e fascismo, 357-8.

8 Gandhi to Hitler: Letter dated 23 July 1939, *Collected Works* 70/26.

9 Gandhi, 'Source of my Sympathy', *Harijan*, 16 September 1934; *Collected Works* 70/199.

10 Gandhi to Linlithgow: Letter dated 26 May 1940, *Collected Works* 72/128.

11 Gandhi, 'To Every Briton', *Harijan*, 6 July 1940; *Collected Works* 72/229.

12 Gandhi, 'Two Thought-Provoking Letters', *Harijan*, 13 October 1940; *Collected Works* 73/67.

13 Gandhi, 'Letter to Adolf Hitler' dated 24 December 1940, *Collected Works* 73/307.

14 Gordon, *Brothers Against the Raj*, 412.

15 Bose, *The Indian Struggle*, 386

16 Ibid. 387.

17 Cons.Calcutta (Milesi) to MAE/AT: Telegram No. 40 dated 6 November 1939, AS-MAE/Gab/56.

18 MAE/Gab (Anfuso) to Cons.Calcutta: Telegram dated 17 November 1939, AS-MAE/Gab/56.

19 Gordon, *Brothers Against the Raj*, 416-7. Gordon quotes the interview with Dwijen Bose on 22 August 1977.

20 Talwar, *Talwars of Pathan Land*, 55.

21 Ibid. 57.

22 Ibid. 59-60.

23 Ibid. 256.

24 Ibid. 257.

25 Weidemann, *Bose's Passage*, 447-9.

26 Chand, *When Bose Was Ziauddin*, 40.

27 Bose, *The Great Escape*, 51.

28 Ibid. 12.

29 Ibid. 23-4.

30 Ibid. 37-40.

31 Ibid. 47-50.

32 Talwar, *Talwars of Pathan Land*, 64-5.

33 Ibid. 65-84. Talwar gives details of the journey.

34 HD/IB to HD (Simms): Report dated 29 January 1941, NAI/Home-Poll/1941/135-41.

35 Bose, *The Great Escape*, 52-4.

36 Gandhi to Sarat Chandra Bose: Telegram dated 28 January 1941, *Collected Works* 73/383.

37 Calcutta Police (Janvrin): Memorandum dated 1 February 1941, IOR/R/3/2/21.

38 Calcutta Police (Janvrin) to HD/IB (Puckle): Letter dated 28 January 1941, IOR/R/3/2/21.

39 Talwar, *Talwars of Pathan Land*, 81-8.

40 Ges.Kabul (Pilger) to AA: Telegram No. 39 dated 4 February 1941, AA-PA/R29615.

41 Ges.Kabul (Pilger) to AA: Telegram N0. 32 dated 1 February 1941, AA-PA/R29534.

42 Talwar, *Talwars of Pathan Land*, 90. Talwar gives the date 2 February 1941, which is not correct.

43 Ges.Kabul (Pilger) to AA: Telegram No. 32 dated 1 February 1941, AA-PA/R29534.

44 Talwar, *Talwars of Pathan Land*, 92.
45 Ibid. 89.
46 Unsigned memorandum dated 2 February 1941, AA-PA/R29534.
47 Ges.Kabul (Pilger) to AA: Telegram No. 46 dated 12 February 1941, AA-PA/R29572.
48 Wassiltschikow: Diary entry dated 23 December 1940. *Wassiltschikow-Tagebuch.*
49 HaPol II (Rüter) to HaPol (Wiehl): Memorandum dated 24 January 1941, AA-PA/R108647.
50 Ges.Kabul (Pilger) to AA: Telegram No. 39 dated 4 February 1941, AA-PA/R29615.
51 Talwar, *Talwars of Pathan Land*, 93-4.
52 AA/UStS Pol (Woermann) to AA/StS (Weizsäcker): Memorandum dated 8 February 1941, AA-PA/R29615.
53 AA/UStS Pol (Woermann) to Bot.Moskau: Telegram No. 245 dated 8 February 1941, ADAP-D-XII/36.
54 Talwar, *Talwars of Pathan Land*, 96-109.
55 Ibid. 110.
56 AA/UStS Pol (Woermann) to Bot.RomQ: Telegram No. 504 dated 7 March 1941, AA-PA/RomQ/105.
57 MAE/Gab (Anfuso) to Leg.Kabul (Quaroni): Telegram No. 28 dated 28 February 1941, DDI-9-VI/647.
58 Ges.Kabul (Pilger) to AA: Telegram No. 71 dated 25 February 1941, AA-PA/R29615.
59 Talwar, *Talwars of Pathan Land*, 114-6. Leg.Kabul (Quaroni) to MAE: Telegram No. 47 dated 24 February 1941, DDI-9-VI/657.
60 Ges.Kabul (Pilger) to AA: Telegram No. 71 dated 25 February 1941, AA-PA/R29615.
61 Bot.Moskau (Schulenburg) to AA: Telegram No. 470 dated 3 March 1941, AA-PA/R29615.
62 AA/UStS Pol (Woermann) to AA/StS (Weizsäcker): Memorandum dated 4 March 1941, AA-PA/R29615.
63 AA/UStS Pol (Woermann) to AA/StS (Weizsäcker): Memorandum dated 13 March 1941, AA-PA/R29615.
64 Ges.Kabul (Pilger) to AA: Telegram No. 103 dated 17 March 1941, AA-PA/R29615.
65 Leg.Kabul (Quaroni) to MAE: Telegram No. 121, DDI-9-VI/781.
66 Ges.Kabul (Pilger) to AA: Telegram No. 46 dated 12 February 1941, AA-PA/R29572.
67 Ges.Kabul (Pilger) to AA: Telegram No. 108 dated 24 March 1941, AA-PA/R29615.
68 Bot.Moskau (Schulenburg) to AA: Telegram No. 31 March 1941, AA-PA/R29615.
69 Bose, *The Great Escape*, 55-7; Talwar, *Talwars of Pathan Land*, 127.

THE BEGINNING OF INDIA-POLITICS WITH BOSE'S ARRIVAL IN BERLIN

1   Weidemann, *Bose's Passage*, 456.
2   AA/USts Pol (Woermann): Memorandum dated 3 April 1941, ADAP-D-XII/257.
3   Bose to Schenkl: Letter dated 3 April 1941, in Bose, *Letters to Emilie Schenkl.*
4   GoI/HD/IB: 'Notes on Suspect Civilian Indians on the Continent of Europe', July 1944, IOR/L/WS/1/1363.
5   Vyas, *Passage Through A Turbulent Era*, 260-6.
6   Bose: Memorandum dated 9 April 1941, ADAP-D-XII/300.
7   AA/USts Pol (Woermann): Memorandum dated 12 April 1941, ADAP-D-XII/323.
8   AA/USts Pol (Woermann) to RAM (Ribbentrop): Memorandum dated 11 April 1941, AA-PA/R29615.
9   AA/USts Pol (Woermann): Memorandum dated 12 April 1941, ADAP-D-XII/323.
10 Bose to AA/USts Pol (Woermann): Letter dated 15 April 1941, AA-PA/R29572.
11 BRAM (Schmidt): Memorandum dated 1 May 1941, ADAP-D-XII/425.
12 Bose: 'Supplementary Memorandum' dated 3 May 1941, AA-PA/R29615.
13 AA/USts Pol (Woermann) to RAM (Ribbentrop): Memorandum dated 4 May 1941, AA-PA/R29615.
14 Ges.Kabul (Pilger) to AA/StS (Weizsäcker): Telegram No. 248 dated 26 June 1940, ADAP-D-X/30.
15 AA/Kult R (Rühle) to RAM (Ribbentrop): Note dated 3 May 1941, AA-PA/R67483.
16 AA/Kult R (Rühle) to RAM (Ribbentrop): Note from 3 May 1941, AA-PA/R67483.
17 Schedai to MAE/Gab (Lanza d'Ajeta): Letter dated 24 October 1942, AS-MAI/Gab/408.
18 *The Ghadr Directory*, 196-8; GoI/HD/IB: 'Notes on Suspect Civilian Indians on the Continent of Europe', July 1944, IOR/L/WS/1/1363.
19 AS-MAE/Gab/407.
20 Enderle to MAE: Letter dated 29 March 1937, AS-MAE/Gab/742.
21 MAE/Gab: Memorandum dated 19 October 1940, AS-MAE/Gab/407.
22 GoI/HD (Puckle) to IO (Joyce): Telegram dated 26 March 1941, IOR/L/P&S/12/494.
23 Schedai to MAE/AT (Alessandrini): Letter dated 15 March 1941, AS-MAE/Gab/408.
24 Schedai to MAE/AT (Alessandrini): Letter dated 5 April 1941, AS-MAE/Gab/407.
25 GoI/HD/IB (Johnston) to GoI/HD/DGI: Report dated 27 May 1941, NAI/Home-Poll/1941/52-3-41.

26 MAE: Memorandum undated, probably April 1941, AS-MAE/Gab/408.

27 MCP/SP (Koch) to MCP (Pavolini): Report dated 10 May 1941, ACS/JAIA/117.

28 MAE/AT/II (Prunas) to MG, MM, MA, MAI, MCP: Telex dated 2 May 1941, AS-MAE/Gab/408.

29 MAE: Memorandum undated, probably April 1941, AS-MAE/Gab/408.

30 BRAM (Schmidt): Memorandum dated 14 May 1941, ADAP-D-XII/511.

31 Bensaglio: Report dated 16 November 1943, ACS/JAIA/38.

32 Schedai to MAE/AT (Prunas): Letter dated 7 May 1941, AS-MAE/Gab/408.

33 Leg.Kabul (Squire) to GoI/EAD (Weightman): Report dated 3 December 1943, IOR/R/12/163.

34 Leg.Kabul (Quaroni) to MAE: Telegram dated 17 December 1940, intercepted by GCCS, PRO/WO208/767.

35 Leg.Kabul (Quaroni) to MAE: Telegram dated 27 January 1942, intercepted by GCCS, PRO/WO208/767.

36 Ges.Kabul (Rasmuss) to AA: Telegram No. 224 dated 14 September 1941, ADAP-D-XIII/107.

37 Ges.Kabul (Witzel) to OKW/AbwII: Telegram No. 165 dated 24 May 1941, AA-PA/R29615.

38 British Legation Kabul (Squire) to GoI/EAD (Weightman): Report dated 3 December 1943, IOR/R/12/163.

39 Talwar, *Talwars of Pathan Land*, 135-7; Leg.Kabul (Quaroni) to MAE: Telegram dated 7 May 1941, DDI-9-VII/69.

40 Talwar: *Talwars of Pathan Land*, 138-9.

41 IO/IPI: 'Statement of Bhagat Ram Talwar', undated, PRO/WO208/773.

42 Talwar: *Talwars of Pathan Land*, 160.

43 AA/Inf (Stahlecker) to RAM (Ribbentrop): Memorandum dated 6 May 1941, AA-PA/R60667.

44 Indians in the Indian army could only, in exceptional cases, join the higher ranks of officers. The commission of the king was required for this, but Indians as a rule received only the commission of the viceroy. The Viceroy's Commissioned Officers (VCO) were ranked between officers and non-commissioned officers and were engaged as platoon leaders. To be put on a par with the KCOs in the prisoner-of-war camp must have meant a revalorization for them.

45 Mangat, *Indian National Army*, 33.

46 Vyas, *Passage Through A Turbulent Era*, 284.

47 Mangat, *The Tiger Strikes*, 36-7.

48 Ibid. 44.

49 Schedai to MAE/AT (Alessandrini): Letter dated 28 April 1941, AS-MAE/Gab/408.

50 MAE: Memorandum undated, probably April 1941, AS-MAE/Gab/408.

51 Schedai to MAE/Gab (Lanza d'Ajeta): Letter dated 4 June 1941, AS-MAE/Gab/408.

52 AA/UStS Pol (Woermann): Circular dated 10 May 1941, AA-PA/R29615

53 BRAM (Schmidt): Memorandum dated 14 May 1941, ADAP-D-XII/511.

54 AA/UStS Pol (Woermann): Memorandum dated 20 May 1941, AA-PA/R67483.

55 Attachment 1a and 1b to Woermann's memorandum dated 20 May 1941, AA-PA/R67483.

56 Attachment 4 to Woermann's memorandum dated 20 May 1941, AA-PA/R67483.

57 AA/UStS Pol (Woermann) to AA/Pers: Memorandum dated 23 May 1941, AA-PA/R60667.

58 AA/Kult R (Timmler): Memorandum dated 22 May 1941, AA-PA/R67482.

59 AA/Kult R (Mair) to AA/Kult R (Schirmer): Memorandum dated 20 May 1941, AA-PA/R67482.

60 Vyas, *Passage Through A Turbulent Era*, 285.

61 MCP: Memorandum dated 23 June 1941, ACS/MCP/Gab/69.

62 AA/UStS Pol (Woermann) to RAM (Ribbentrop): Telex dated 25 May 1941, ADAP-D-XII/553.

63 Katpitia, *Boses Verhandlungen*, 138-9.

64 Hillgruber, *Hitlers Strategie,* 483.

65 Hauner, *India in Axis Strategy*, 256.

66 BRAM (Loesch): Memorandum dated 29 November 1941, ADAP-D-XIII/521.

67 Vyas, *Passage Through A Turbulent Era*, 322.

68 MAE (Ciano) to Amb.Berlino (Zamboni): Telegram No. 819 dated 23 May 1941, DDI-9-VII/159.

69 AA/UStS Pol (Woermann) to RAM (Ribbentrop): Telex dated 25 May 1941, ADAP-D-XII/553.

70 BRAM (Sonnleithner) to AA/UStS Pol (Woermann): Telegram No. 443 dated 26 May 1941, AA-PA/R29615.

71 AA/UStS Pol (Woermann) to BRAM: Telex dated 27 May 1941, AA-PA/R29615.

72 BRAM (Sonnleithner) to AA/UStS Pol (Woermann): Telegram No. 458 dated 27 May 1941, AA-PA/R29615.

73 AA/UStS Pol (Woermann) to Bot.RomQ: Telegram No. 1264 dated 28 May 1941, ADAP-D-XII/561.

74 Amb.Berlino (Zamboni) to MAE (Ciano): Telegram No. 886 dated 28 May 1941, DDI-9-VII/172.

75 AA/UStS Pol (Woermann) to Bot.RomQ: Telegram No. 1264 dated 28 May 1941, ADAP-D-XII/561.

76 It seems Hauner did not have access to this file, else he could not have come to the conclusion on page 358 in his book *India in Axis Strategy* that Bose 'was clearly regarded as a nuisance by the political department.'

77 Bot.RomQ (Bismarck) to AA: Telegram No. 1296 dated 6 June 1941, AA-PA/R29615.

78 Bot.RomQ (Bismarck) to AA: Telegram No. 1299 dated 6 June 1941, AA-PA/R29615.

79 AA/UStS Pol (Woermann) to Bot.RomQ: Telegram No. 1406 dated 14 June 1941, AA-PA/R29615.

80 Bot.RomQ (Bismarck) to AA: Telegram No. 1331 dated 11 June 1941, AA-PA/R29615.

81 AA/UStS Pol (Woermann) to RAM (Ribbentrop): Memorandum dated 16 June 1941, AA-PA/R29615.

82 Bot.RomQ (Bismarck) to AA: Telegram No. 1380 dated 19 June 1941, AA-PA/R29615.

83 Bot.RomQ (Bismarck) to AA: Telegram No. 1455 dated 27 June 1941, AA-PA/R29615.

84 Bot.RomQ (Doertenbach) to AA: Letter dated 13 September 1941, AA-PA/RomQ/105.

85 Ciano, Diary entry dated 6 June 1941, *Diario*, ii.

86 Vyas, *Passage Through A Turbulent Era*, 290.

87 Protocol dated 15 June 1941. DDI-9-VII/260.

88 Bot.RomQ (Doertenbach) to AA: Letter dated 13 September 1941, AA-PA/RomQ/105.

89 AA/UStS Pol (Woermann): Memorandum dated 17 September 1941, ADAP-D-XIII/120.

90 Schedai to MAE/Gab (Lanza d'Ajeta): Letter from 4 June 1941, AS-MAE/Gab/408.

91 Bot.RomQ (Doertenbach) to AA: Letter dated 13 September 1941, AA-PA/RomQ/105.

92 Bensaglio: Report dated 16 November 1943, ACS/JAIA/38.

93 Attachment 4 to Woermann's memorandum dated 20 May 1941, AA-PA/R67483.

94 Bose to AA/UStS Pol (Woermann): Letter dated 5 July 1941, AA-PA/R29615.

95 AA/UStS Pol (Woermann) to RAM (Ribbentrop): Memorandum dated 17 July 1941.

96 Vyas, *Passage Through A Turbulent Era*, 306-7.

THE PROGRESS OF INDIA-POLITICS DURING BOSE'S INCOGNITO

1 Werth, *Der Tiger Indiens*, 128-9.

2 Alsdorf, *Indien*.

3 Wirsing, *Indien*, 8.

4 Wüster: 'Gutachten über Trott' dated 16 October 1941, AA-PA/Personalakte 279.

5 Wassiltschikow: Diary entry dated 23 December 1940, *Wassiltschikow-Tagebuch*.

6 AA/UStS Pol (Woermann) to BRAM: Telex dated 27 May 1941, AA-PA/R29615.

7 Trott, *Lebensbeschreibung*, 181-7.

8 Sykes, *Adam von Trott*, 292-3.

9   Vyas, *Passage Through a Turbulent Era*, 477-8.

10   Van Roon, *Neuordnung im Widerstand*, 466.

11   Moltke, Letter to his wife dated 12 June 1941, *Briefe an Freya 1939-45*.

12   Döscher, *Das Auswärtige Amt im Dritten Reich*, 181.

13   Summary of documents, AAPA/ R27504.

14   Vyas, *Passage Through A Turbulent Era*, 281-2.

15   AA/StSzbV (Keppler) to RAM (Ribbentrop): Letter dated 17 October 1942 and AA/StSzbV (Keppler) to Schroeder: Letter dated 8 May 1942, AA-PA/ Personalakte 279.

16   'Arbeitsplan für die Indienpropaganda', undated, probably March 1942, AA-PA/R60671.

17   Kruse to AA/Inf: Letter dated 15 May 1941, AA-PA/R60667.

18   AA/SRI (Trott) to RMVP (Todenhöfer): Memorandum dated 23 January 1942, AA-PA/R60670.

19   AA/Inf (Stahlecker): Telegram dated 28 May 1941, AA-PA/R60667.

20   AA/SRI (Trott) to Bot.Washington (Strempel): Telegram No. 1510 dated 5 August 1941, AA-PA/R60667. Also Bot.Washington (Thomsen) to AA: Telegram No. 3628 dated 20 October 1941, BA/R9.01/69566.

21   Bot.Washington (Thomsen) to AA: Telegram No. 3927 dated 11 November 1941, BA/R9.01/69566.

22   Büro Reichsführer SS and Chef der Deutschen Polizei (Krönig) to AA/SRI (Trott): Letter dated 5 November 1941, AA-PA/R60668.

23   Bose to AA/SRI (Trott): Letter dated 21 November 1941, AA-PA/R60668.

24   AA/SRI (Trott) to Ges.Kabul (Rasmuss): Letter dated 6 June 1941, AA-PA/60667.

25   Glasneck and Kircheisen, *Türkei und Afghanistan*, 251.

26   AA/SRI (Trott) to AA/UStS Pol (Woermann) and RAM (Ribbentrop): Memorandum dated 28 July 1942, BA/R9.01/61122.

27   AA/StSzbV (Keppler) to Ges.Bangkok: Telegram No. 210 dated 19 September 1941, BA/R9.01/69565.

28   Ges.Bangkok (Thomas) to AA/StSzbV (Keppler): Telegram No. 313 dated 26 September 1941, BA/R9.01/69565.

29   AA/SRI (Trott) to Ges.Lissabon: Telegram No. 1840 dated 27 October 1941, BA/R9.01/69565.

30   AA/SRI (Trott) to AA/StSzbV (Keppler) and AA/UStS Pol (Woermann): Memorandum dated 1 October 1941, BA/R9.01/69565.

31   AA/StS (Weizsäcker) to AA/StSzbV (Keppler), AA/UStS Pol (Woermann) and BRAM (Schmieden): Memorandum dated 17 Novermber 1941, AA-PA/R29615.

32   BRAM to AA/StS (Weizsäcker): Memorandum dated 17 Novermber 1941, AA-PA/R29615.

33   BRAM (Schmieden) to AA/StS (Weizsäcker): Memorandum dated 27 November 1941, AA-PA/R29615.

34   FHQ (Heim): Memorandum dated 22 August 1942, *Hitler-Monologe*/181.

35 'Arbeitsplan für die Indienpropaganda', undated, probably March 1942, AA-PA/R60671.

36 AA/UStS Pol (Woermann): Memorandum dated 20 May 1941, AA-PA/R67483.

37 AA/UStS Pol (Woermann) to RAM (Ribbentrop): Telex dated 25 May 1941, ADAP-D-XII/553.

38 AA/UStS Pol (Woermann) to Ges.Bern: Telegram No. 494 dated 24 May 1941, AA-PA/R29615.

39 UStS Pol (Woermann): Circular dated 4 June 1941, AA-PA/R101701.

40 Design for an organization-plan for the 'Zentralstelle Freies Indien' (ZFI). Enclosed in: AA/D III (Rademacher) to AA/UStS D (Luther): Memorandum dated 7 June 1941, AA-PA/R100701.

41 Enclosure 4 in Woermann's memorandum dated 20 May 1941, AA-PA/R67483.

42 AA/StSzbV (Keppler) to RAM (Ribbentrop): Memorandum dated 13 October 1942, BA/R9.01/69567.

43 Vyas, *Passage Through A Turbulent Era*, 318.

44 Ibid. 319-20.

45 GoI/HD/IB: 'Notes on Suspect Civilian Indians on the Continent of Europe', July 1944, IOR/L/WS/1/1363.

46 Vyas, *Passage Through A Turbulent Era*, 264.

47 GoI/HD/IB: 'Notes on Suspect Civilian Indians on the Continent of Europe', July 1944, IOR/L/WS/1/1363.

48 Toye, Interview with Swami dated September/October 1945, IOR/MSS EUR/C0743.

49 GoI/HD/IB: 'Notes on Suspect Civilian Indians on the Continent of Europe', July 1944, IOR/L/WS/1/1363.

50 Ibid.

51 Bot.Paris (Schleier) to AA/SRI (Trott): Telegram No. 110 dated 11 August 1941, AA-PA/R60667.

52 AA/SRI (Werth): Memorandum dated 2 September 1941, AA-PA/R60668.

53 GoI/HD/IB: 'Notes on Suspect Civilian Indians on the Continent of Europe', July 1944, IOR/L/WS/1/1363.

54 Ibid. Also Bhatta to Nehru: Letter from May 1947, NAI/EAD/1947/36(36)-EUR-47.

55 GoI/HD/IB: 'Notes on Suspect Civilian Indians on the Continent of Europe', July 1944, IOR/L/WS/1/1363.

56 Mookerjee, *Labyrinth Europa*, 94.

57 Ibid. 112-4.

58 GoI/HD/IB: 'Notes on Suspect Civilian Indians on the Continent of Europe', July 1944, IOR/L/WS/1/1363.

59 Weidemann, *Indische Emigranten*, 247. Also ibid.

60 GoI/HD/IB: 'Notes on Suspect Civilian Indians on the Continent of Europe', July 1944, IOR/L/WS/1/1363.

61 Ibid.
62 Günther and Rehmer, *Inder, Indien und Berlin*, 217.
63 GoI/HD/IB: 'Notes on Suspect Civilian Indians on the Continent of Europe', July 1944, IOR/L/WS/1/1363
64 Günther and Rehmer, *Inder, Indien und Berlin*, 175.
65 AA/SRI (Trott): Memorandum dated 13 March 1942, AA-PA/R27505. Hassan and Swami are not on the list.
66 Günther and Rehmer, *Inder, Indien und Berlin*, 172-4.
67 NMML (Nanda): Interview with Sarma dated 15 November 1971, NMML/OHT/325.
68 Mookerjee, *Labyrinth Europa*, 115-7.
69 Ibid. 118-9.
70 Werth, *Der Tiger Indiens*, 133-4.
71 Ibid. 131.
72 Mookerjee, *Labyrinth Europa*, 125.
73 Ganpuley, *Netaji in Germany*, 41-3; Vyas, *Passage Through A Turbulent Era*, 324.
74 Ganpuley, *Netaji in Germany*, 43-4; Vyas, *Passage Through A Turbulent Era*, 325.
75 Ganpuley, *Netaji in Germany*, 45-6.
76 Vyas, *Passage Through A Turbulent Era*, 325.
77 NMML (Nanda): Interview with Sarma dated 15 Novermber 1971, NMML/OHT/325.
78 RMVP/LeiterRundfunk (Schaudinn) to RMVP (Goebbels): Memorandum dated 24 December 1941, BA/R55/20822.
79 Boelcke, *Die Macht des Radios*, 94-9.
80 RMVP/AbtRundfunk (Bock): Memorandum dated 5 January 1942, BA/R55/20822.
81 RMVP/AbtRundfunk (Bock): Memorandum dated 31 December 1941, BA/R55/20822.
82 Vyas, *Passage Through A Turbulent Era*, 344.
83 RMVP/AbtRundfunk (Knochenhauer) to RMVP/LeiterRundfunk: Memorandum dated 11 March 1942, BA/R55/20822.
84 Boelcke, *Die Macht des Radios*, 206-97.
85 RMVP/AbtRundfunk/ReferatErkundung: Intelligence dated 14 March 1942, BA/R55/20822.
86 'Arbeitsplan für die Indienpropaganda', undated, probably March 1942, AA-PA/R60671.
87 Furtwängler, *Männer, die ich sah und kannte*, 200.
88 RRG/BüroConcordia (Hetzler) to RMVP/AbtRundfunk (Dominik): Memorandum dated 11 July 1942, BA/R55/20851.
89 Vyas, *Passage Through A Turbulent Era*, 343.
90 NMML (Nanda): Interview with Sarma dated 15 November 1971, NMML/OHT/325.
91 OKW/AbwII (Lahousen): War diary, entry dated 22 March 1941, BA-MA/RW5/497.

92 OKW/AbwII (Lahousen): War diary, entry dated 20 July 1941, BAMA/ RW5/498.

93 OKW/AbwII (Brandt): Memorandum dated 7 February 1942, BA/ R9.01/69566.

94 British Legation Kabul: 'Intelligence Summary' dated 25 July 1941, IOR/L/ P&S/12/1774.

95 British Legation Kabul: 'Intelligence Summary' dated 1 August 1941, IOR/L/ P&S/12/1774.

96 Ges.Kabul (Pilger) to RAM (Ribbentrop): Telegram No. 256 dated 30 July 1941, ADAP-D-XIII/169.

97 AA/UStS Pol (Woermann) to Ges.Kabul: Draft telegram dated 4 August 1941, AA-AP/R60667.

98 RAM (Ribbentrop) to Ges.Kabul: Telegram No. 223 dated 9 August 1941, ADAP-D-XIII/190.

99 British Legation Kabul (Squire) to GoI/EAD (Weightman): Report on interrogation of Quaroni dated 11 December 1943, IOR/R/12/163.

100 Ges.Kabul (Rasmuss) to AA/Pol VII and OKW/AbwI: Telegram No. 263 dated 14 April 1942, BA/R9.01/61122.

101 GHQ India: 'Weekly Intelligence Summary of the North West Frontier and Afghanistan' 13, dated 4 April 1942, PRO/WO208/773.

102 Schedai to MAE/Gab (Lanza d'Ajeta): Letter dated 18 July 1941, AS-MAE/ Gab/408.

103 AA/StSzbV (Keppler) to Bot.RomQ: Letter dated 24 July 1941, AA-PA/ RomQ/105.

104 Amb.Berlino (Alfieri) to MAE/Gab: Telegram No. 123 dated 16 March 1941, AS-MAE/Gab/408.

105 Schedai to MAE/AT (Prunas): Letter dated 4 September 1941, AS-MAE/ Gab/408.

106 Schedai to Bot.RomQ (Doertenbach): Letter dated 21 September 1941, AA-PA/RomQ/105.

107 Ges.Kabul (Pilger) to AA: Telegram No. 259 dated 30 July 1941, ADAP-D-XIII/169.

108 Amb.Berlino (Alfieri) to MAE/Gab: Telegram No. 123 dated 16 August 1941. AS-MAE/Gab/408.

109 Schedai to MAE/AT (Prunas): Letter dated 4 September 1941, AS-MAE/ Gab/408.

110 Bot.RomQ (Doertenbach): Memorandum dated 10 October 1941, AA-PA/ RomQ/105; Schedai to MAE/Gab (Alessandrini): Letter dated 4 October 1941, AS-MAE/Gab/408.

111 AA/Inf to Bot.RomQ: Letter dated 24 September 1941, BA/R9.01/69565.

112 AA/SRI (Werth) to AA/StSzbV (Keppler): Memorandum dated 16 September 1941, BA/R9.01/69565.

113 AA/SRI (Trott) to Bot.RomQ (Doertenbach): Letter dated 29 October 1941, AA-PA/R9.01/695966.

114 Bot.RomQ (Mackensen) to AA: Telegram No. 2413 dated 4 October 1941, ADAP-D-XIII/379.

115 Bot.RomQ (Bismarck) to AA: Telegram No. 2507 dated 11 October 1941, AA-PA/RomQ/105.

116 Sita Devi, born in 1900, was a Christian from Bombay. She lived in Europe from 1923 onwards and studied music in Rome since the beginning of the 1930s. She was a governing body member of the Hindustan Association Italiens in 1935. Italian newspapers published her critical articles on England. The Indian police suspected her to be in the pay of the Fascists (GoI/HD/IB: 'Notes on Suspect Civilian Indians on the Continent of Europe', July 1944, IOR/L/WS/1/1363).

117 MCP/IRT/MO (Lucidi): Report dated 30 March 1942, ACS/JAIA/39.

118 MAE/AT (Alessandrini) to MAE (Ciano): Memorandum dated 31 December 1941, DDI-9-VIII/88.

119 MAE/AT (Alessandrini) to MAE (Ciano): Memorandum dated 31 December 1941, DDI-9-VIII/88.

120 AA/SRI (Trott) to AA/StSzbV (Keppler) and AA/Inf (Wüster): Memorandum dated 25 October 1941, AA-PA/R60668.

121 Schedai to AA/SRI (Trott): Letter dated 23 October 1941, BA/R9.01/69566.

122 AA/SRI (Werth) to AA/Inf (Wüster): Memorandum dated 11 December 1941, AA-PA/R60669.

123 Schedai to MAE/Gab (Lanza d'Ajeta): Letter dated 21 December 1941, AS-MAE/Gab/408.

124 AA/SRI (Trott) to Bot.RomQ: Telegram No. 37 dated 5 January 1942, AA-PA/R60669.

125 AA/StSzbV (Keppler) to Bot.RomQ: Telegram No. 1029 dated 7 March 1942, AA-PA/RomQ/Q164.

126 AA/SRI (Assmann) to AA/SRI (Trott): Memorandum dated 20 February 42, AA-PA/R6070.

127 AA/UStS Pol (Woermann): Memorandum dated 17 July 1941, ADAP-D-XIII/120.

128 AA/Ru (Timmler) to AA/Ru (Rühle): Notes dated 28 July 1941, AA-PA/R67483.

129 Katpitia, *Boses Verhandlungen*, 155-6.

130 Bose to RAM (Ribbentrop): Letter from 15 August 1941, ADAP-D-XIII/213.

131 AA/UStS Pol (Woermann) to RAM (Ribbentrop): Memorandum dated 18 August 1941, ADAP-D-XIII/213.

132 FHQ (Heim): Memorandum dated 17 and 18 September 1941, *Hitler-Monologe*/19.

133 Voigt, *Indien im Zweiten Weltkrieg*, 112.

134 AA/StS (Weizsäcker) to BRAM: Memorandum dated 25 August 1941, AA-PA/R29615.

135 Bose to AA/UStS Pol (Woermann): Letter dated 25 September 1941, AA-PA/R29615.

136 Weizsäcker, Note dated 30 September 1941, *Die Weizsäcker-Papiere 1933-50*.

137 AA/UStS Pol (Woermann) to RAM (Ribbentrop): Memorandum dated 6 September 1941, AA-PA/R28876.

138 AA/StSzbV (Keppler) to RAM (Ribbentrop): Memorandum dated 13 September 1941, AA-PA/R28876.

139 Vidkun Quisling was the leader of the Norwegian Fascist movement. During the German occupation of Norway, Quisling was appointed head of government. His name later became synonymous with a traitor who collaborates with enemies in many European languages.

140 AA/StSzbV (Keppler) to RAM (Ribbentrop): Memorandum dated 13 September 1941.

141 AA/UStS Pol (Woermann) to Hitler: Note dated 6 November 1941, AA-PA/R28876. Also see RAM (Ribbentrop) to Hitler: Note dated 13 November 1941, ADAP-D-XIII/468.

142 Katpitia, *Boses Verhandlungen*, 170.

143 AA/UStS Pol (Woermann) to AA/Prot: Memorandum dated 22 November 1941, AA-PA/R29615.

144 BRAM (Loesch): Memorandum dated 29 November 1941, ADAP-D-XIII/521.

145 AA/StSzbV (Keppler) to RAM (Ribbentrop): Memorandum dated 3 December 1941, AA-PA/R27501.

THE HEIGHT OF INDIA-POLITICS AFTER BOSE'S INTERVENTION

1   Voigt, *Indien im Zweiten Weltkrieg*, 97-8.

2   Ibid. 99.

3   Schedai to the Japanese embassy in Rome (Ando): Letter dated 22 November 1941, AA-PA/RomQ/105.

4   Bot.RomQ (Mackensen) to AA: Telegram No. 3135 dated 1 December 1941, ADAP-D-XIII/526.

5   Bot.Tokio (Ott) to AA: Telegram No. 2609 dated 2 December 1941, AA-PA/R29615.

6   Bot.RomQ (Mackensen) to AA: Telegram No. 3135 dated 1 December 41, AA-PA/RomQ/105.

7   AA/UStS Pol (Woermann) to Bot.Tokio: Telegram No. 2293 dated 8 December 41, BA-PA/R9.01/69566.

8   Bot.Tokio (Ott) to AA: Telegram No. 2749 dated 12 December 1941, BA/69566.

9   AA/SRI (Werth): Memorandum dated 8 December 1941, AA-PA/R60669.

10 AA/StSzbV (Keppler) to GenKons.Schanghai (Puttkamer): Telegram No. 270 dated 11 November 1941, BA/R9.01/69566.

11 RMVP/Leiter A to RAM (Ribbentrop): Memorandum dated 24 December 1941, BA/R55/20822.

12   AA/UStS Pol (Woermann) to BRAM (Rintelen): Memorandum dated 13 December 1941, AA-PA/R29615.

13   AA/UStS Pol (Woermann): Memorandum dated 18 December 1941, ADAP-E-I/31.

14   Ges.Bangkok (Thomas) to AA/Inf: Telegram No. 473 dated 18 December 1941, BA/R9.01/69566.

15   MAE/AT (Alessandrini) to MAE (Ciano): Memorandum dated 31 December 1941, DDI-9-VIII/88.

16   AA/SRI (Trott) to Roma: Telex dated 2 January 1942, AA-PA/R60669.

17   RAM (Ribbentrop) to Bot.Tokio: Telegram No. 47 dated 4 January 1942, AA-PA/R29615

18   Amb.Berlino (Cossato) to MAE/AEM: Telegram No. 12 dated 3 January 1942, AS-MAE/AP/Italia/84.

19   Memorandum dated 2 January 1941, ADAP-E-I/84.

20   FHQ (Hewel): Memorandum dated 3 January 1942, ADAP-E-I/87.

21   AA/UStS Pol (Woermann) to RAM (Ribbentrop): Memorandum dated 14 January 1942, AA-PA/R29615.

22   AA/UStS Pol (Woermann): Memorandum dated 10 January 1942, ADAP-E-I/110.

23   AA/UStS Pol (Woermann) to RAM (Ribbentrop): Memorandum dated 14 January 1942, AA-PA/R29615.

24   AA (Gottfriedsen) to BRAM (Weber): Memorandum dated 27 January 1941, ADAP-E-I/176.

25   Amb.Berlino (Alfieri) to MAE/AEM: Telegram No. 53 dated 12 January 1942, AS-MAE/AP/Italia/84.

26   MAE/AEM: Memorandum dated 3 March 1942, AS-MAE/AP/Irak/18; AA/UStS Pol (Woermann): Memorandum dated 6 November 1941, AA-PA/R28876.

27   Amb.Berlino (Alfieri) to MAE/AT: Telegram No. 71 dated 15 January 1942, AS-MAE/AP/Italia/84.

28   Amb.Berlino (Alfieri) to MAE/AEM: Telegram No. 176 dated 2 February 1942, AS-MAE/AP/Italia/84.

29   FHQ (Heim): Memorandum dated 5 January 1942, *Hitler-Monologe*/83.

30   FHQ (Heim): Memorandum dated 10 January 1942, *Hitler-Monologe*/91.

31   FHQ (Heim): Memorandum dated 12 and 13 January 1942, *Hitler-Monologe*/92.

32   Martin, *Deutschland und Japan*, 46-54.

33   AA/UStS Pol (Woermann) to BRAM (Rintelen): Telex dated 17 January 1942, AA-PA/R29615.

34   Ibid.

35   AA/UStS Pol (Woermann): Memorandum dated 18 January 1942, AA-PA/R29615.

36   Amb.Berlino (Alfieri) to MAE (Ciano): Telex dated 15 January 1942, AS-

MAE/AP/Italia/84. Memorandum on Ribbentrop's conversation with Oshima dated 2 January 1941, ADAP-E-I/84.

37 Amb.Berlino (Alfieri) to MAE (Ciano): Telex dated 16 January 1942, AS-MAE/AP/Italia/84.

38 MAE/AEM to Amb.Berlino: Telex dated 26 January 1942, AS-MAE/AP/Italia/84.

39 Adjutantur RAM (Gottfriedsen) to BRAM (Weber): Memorandum dated 27 January 1942, ADAP-E-I/176.

40 Ibid.

41 OKW/AbwII: Memorandum dated 28 January 1942, BA/R9.01/69566.

42 OKW/AbwII: Memorandum dated 6 February 1942, BA/R9.01/69566.

43 For Mussolini's policy on Arabia, see De Felice, *Il fascismo e l'Oriente*, 15-124.

44 AA/UStS Pol (Woermann) to RAM: Memorandum dated 2 February 1942, AA-PA/R29615.

45 Amb.Berlino (Alfieri) to MAE/AEM: Telegram No. 222 dated 12 February 1942, AS-MAE/AP/Italia/84.

46 Ges.Kabul (Pilger) to AA: Telegram No. 69 dated 4 February 42, AA-PA/R29615.

47 Schedai to Japanese Embassy Rome (Ando): Letter undated (probably February 1942), AS-MAE/Gab/408.

48 Ges.Bangkok (Thomas) to AA: Telegram No. 82 dated 11 February 1942, AA-PA/R29615.

49 AA/StS (Weizsäcker) to AA/StSzbV (Keppler): Memorandum dated 11 February 1942, AA-PA/R29615.

50 Martin, *Deutschland und Japan*, 70.

51 Bose to AA/UStS Pol (Woermann): Letter dated 17 February 1942, AA-PA/R29615.

52 Voigt, *Indien im Zweiten Weltkrieg*, 117.

53 RAM (Ribbentrop) to Bot.Tokio: Telegram No. 512 dated 21 February 1942, ADAP-E-I/266.

54 Ibid.

55 Attachment from BRAM (Schmieden) to AA/StS (Weizsäcker): Note dated 23 February 1942, AA-PA/R29615.

56 Bot.Tokio (Ott) to AA: Telegram No. 577 dated 25 February 1942, AA-PA/R29615.

57 Bot.RomQ (Mackensen) to AA: Telegram No. 661 dated 25 February 1942, AA-PA/R29615.

58 Bot.RomQ (Mackensen) to AA: Telegram No. 661 dated 25 February 42, AA-PA/R29615.

59 AA/Pol VIII to AA/UStS Pol (Woermann): Memorandum dated 31 January 1942, AA-PA/R30005.

60 AA/P XII/Chef dated Dienst: Memorandum dated 20 February 1942, BA/R9.01/60423.

61 MCP/IRT/MO (Lucidi) to MCP/Gab: Memorandum dated 28 February 1942, ACS/JAIA/39.

62 MCP: Protocol of Press Conference dated 26 February 1942, ACS/MCP/Gab/50.

63 Goebbels, Diary entry dated 1 March 1942, *Goebbels-Tagebücher* ii:3.

64 Bose, 'Statement', *Azad Hind*, 2 (1942), 13-14.

65 Government of Bihar to GoI/HD: 'Fortnightly Report', 1 March 1942, NAI/Home-Poll/1942/18-3-42.

66 Government of NWFP to GoI/HD: 'Fortnightly Report', 1 March 1942, NAI/Home-Poll/1942/18-3-42.

67 Government of Punjab to GoI/HD: 'Fortnightly Report', 1 March 1942, NAI/Home-Poll/1942/18-3-42.

68 IO (Amery) to GoI (Linlithgow): Letter dated 3 November 1942, ToP-III/138.

69 Government of Bengal to GoI/HD: 'Fortnightly Report', 1 and 2 March 1942, NAI/Home-Poll/1942/18-3-42.

70 Government of UP to GoI/HD: 'Fortnightly Report', 1 March 1942, NAI/Home-Poll/1942/18-5-42.

71 Ges.Bangkok (Thomas) to AA: Telegram No. 129 dated 3 March 1942, AA-PA/R29615.

72 Ges.Bangkok (Thomas) to AA: Telegram No. 147 dated 16 March 1942, AA-PA/R29615.

73 DNB-Presseschreibfunk: Meldung dated 28 February 1942, BA/R9.01/59887.

74 Reports of varions diplomatic missions, dated 2 and 3 March 1942, AA-PA/R60670.

75 Ges.Bangkok (Thomas) to AA: Telegram No. 127 dated 3 March 1942, AA-PA/R60670.

76 Bot.Tokio (Ott) to AA: Telegram. 667 dated 4 March 1942, AA-PA/R60670.

77 Ges.Bangkok (Thomas) to AA: Telegram No. 149 dated 11 March 1942, AA-PA/R29615.

78 AA/StSzbV (Keppler) to Ges.Bangkok: Telegram No. 170 dated 13 March 1942, BA/R9.01/69567.

79 RAM (Ribbentrop): Excerpt from a memorandum dated 2 March 1942, AA-PA/R60670.

80 Goebbels: Diary entry dated 2 March 1942, *Goebbels-Tagebücher* ii:3.

81 Ibid.

82 Ibid.

83 Bose, 'The Second Statement', *Azad Hind*, 2 (1942), 46-50.

84 RMVP/AbtRundfunk (Knochenhauer) to RMVP/LeiterRundfunk: Memorandum dated 11 March 1942, BA/R55/20822.

85 AA/Ru (Rühle) to RAM (Ribbentrop): Memorandum dated 23 March 1942, AA-PA/R60671.

86 AA/SRI (Trott) to AA/P (Studnitz): Memorandum dated 12 March 1942, BA/R9.01/60423.

87 BA/R9.01/59887.

88 AA/Pol IM (Grotte) to AA/StSzbV (Keppler): Memorandum dated 18 March 1942, AA-PA/R60671.

89 AA/P III (Urach) to BRAM (Schmidt): Memorandum dated 16 March 1942, BA/R9.01/60423.

90 Amb.Berlino (Alfieri) to MAE/AT: Telegram No. 391 dated 10 March 1942, AS-MAE/AP/Italia/84.

91 Goebbels, Diary entry dated 2 March 1942, *Goebbels-Tagebücher* ii:3.

92 FHQ (Heim): Memorandum dated 3 March 1942, *Hitler-Monologe*/155.

93 Voigt, *Indien im Zweiten Weltkrieg*, 135-7.

94 Ibid. 137-8.

95 Trott, *Lebensbeschreibung*, 157.

96 AA/SRI (Trott) to BRAM (Megerle): Telex dated 14 March 1942, AA-PA/R60671.

97 BRAM (Megerle) to AA/StSzbV (Keppler): Telegram No. 312 dated 27 March 1942, ADAP-E-II/87.

98 Goebbels, Diary entry dated 26 March 1942, *Goebbels-Tagebücher* ii:3.

99 BRAM (Megerle) to AA/StSzbV (Keppler): Telegram No. 304 dated 27 March 1942, AA-PA/R29615.

100 RMVP/AbtRundfunk   (Dominik)   to   RMVP/LeiterRundfunk (Knochenhauer): Memorandum dated 30 March 1942, BA/R55/20822.

101 Collection of articles from varous newspapers, BA/59888.

102 RMVP/AbtRundfunk   (Dominik)   to   RMVP/LeiterRundfunk (Knochenhauer): Memorandum dated 30 March 1942, BA/R55/20822.

103 RMVP: Protocol of Press Conference dated 24 March 1942, BA/R55/20898.

104 Ibid.

105 RMVP: Protocol of Press Conference dated 27 March 1942, BA/R55/20898.

106 MAE/AT (Lanza d'Ajeta) to MCP/Gab: Telegram dated 30 March 1942, ACS/JAIA/39.

107 MCP: Protocol of Press Conference dated 1 April 1942, ACS/MCP/Gab/50.

108 Gandhi to Prabhavatidevi Bose: Telegram (*Bombay Chronicle* dated 30 March 1942), *Collected Works* 75/538; GenKons.Schanghai (Randow) to AA: Telegram No. 359 dated 30 March 1942, AA-PA/R29615.

109 Government of UP to GoI/HD: 'Fortnightly Report', 1 April 1942, NAI/Home-Poll/1942/18-4-42.

110 Goebbels, Diary entry dated 31 March 1942, *Goebbels-Tagebücher* ii:3.

111 Ges.Bangkok (Wendler) to AA: Telegram No. 223 dated 4 April 1942, BA/R9.01/69567.

112 IO (Amery) to GoI (Linlithgow): Telegram dated 8 March 1942, ToP-I/280.

113 GoI (Linlithgow) to Emb.Washington (Halifax): Telegram dated 27 March 1942.

114 West, *Orwell: The Lost Writings*, 33.

115 AA/StSzbV (Keppler) to AA/StS (Weizsäcker): Telex dated 1 April 1942, AA-PA/R29616.

116 RMVP: Protocol of Press Conference dated 30 March 1942, BA/R55/20898.

117 RMVP: Protocol of Press Conference dated 31 March 1942, BA/R55/20898.
118 Bot.Tokio (Ott) to AA: Telegram No. 1048 dated 7 March 1942, AA-PA/ R29616.
119 Wolpert, *A New History of India*, 334.
120 BRAM (Megerle) to AA/StSzbV (Keppler): Telegram No. 419 dated 12 April 1942, AA-PA/R29616.
121 Chandra, *India's Struggle for Independence*, 456.
122 Gandhi, 'Question Box', *Harijan*, 21 June 1942; *Collected Works* 76/253.
123 Azad, *India Wins Freedom*, 41.
124 Ibid. 50.
125 Voigt, *Indien im Zweiten Weltkrieg*, 140.
126 Hauner, *India in Axis Strategy*, 562
127 BRAM (Schmieden) to AA/StSzbV (Keppler): Telegram No. 430 dated 13 April 1942, AA-PA/R29616.
128 Goebbels, Diary entry dated 5 April 1942, *Goebbels-Tagebücher* ii:4.
129 Vyas, *Passage through a Turbulent Era*, 358.
130 Orwell, Diary entry dated 15 May 1942, 'War-Time Diary', in *The Collected Essays* ii, 339-450.
131 AA/UStS Pol (Woermann) to RAM (Ribbentrop): Memorandum dated 13 April 1942, AA-PA/R29616. Also see Amb.Tokio (Indelli) to MAE (Ciano): Telegram dated 14 April 1942, DDI-9-VII/450.
132 AA/UStS Pol (Woermann) to Bot.RomQ: Telegram No. 1543 dated 21 April 1942, AA-PA/RomQ/169.
133 Bot.Tokio (Ott) to RAM (Ribbentrop): Telegram No. 1261 dated 23 April 1942, AA-PA/R29616.
134 Ciano, Diary entry dated 14 April 1942, *Diario* ii.
135 Bot.RomQ (Mackensen) to AA: Telegram No. 1219 dated 15 April 1942, AA-PA/R29616.
136 AA/UStS Pol (Woermann) to RAM (Ribbentrop): Memorandum dated 15 April 1942, AA-PA/R29616.
137 RAM (Ribbentrop) to Hitler: Note dated 16 April 1942, ADAP-E-II/144.
138 FHQ (Hewel) to RAM (Ribbentrop): Note dated 17 April 1942, ADAP-E-II/144 (footnote 10).
139 Bot.Tokio (Ott) to RAM (Ribbentrop): Telegram No. 1261 dated 23 April 1942, AA-PA/R29616.
140 BRAM (Schmidt): Memorandum dated 2 May 1942, ADAP-E-II/182.
141 Mussolini, Memorandum dated 2 May 1942, *Opera Omnia* xxxi, 54-7.
142 AA/UStS Pol (Woermann): Memorandum dated 4 May 1942, ADAP-E-II/185.
143 BRAM (Rintelen) to RAM (Ribbentrop): Note dated 3 May 1942, AA-PA/ R28876.
144 Ciano, Diary entry dated 5 May 1942, *Diario* ii.
145 RAM (Ribbentrop) to Hitler: Memorandum dated 14 May 1942, ADAP-E-II/206.

146 Amb.Berlino (Alfieri) to MAE (Ciano): Telegram dated 13 May 1942, DDI-9-VIII/538. Also see AA/StS (Weizsäcker) to AA/StSzbV (Keppler): Memorandum dated 21 May 1942, AA-PA/R29836.

147 Ges.Kabul (Pilger) to AA: Telegram No. 493 dated 20 June 1942, AA-PA/ R60673.

148 BRAM (Sonnleithner) to AA/UStS Pol (Woermann): Memorandum dated 23 June 1942, AA-PA/R60673.

149 Hauner, *India in Axis Strategy*, 620-5.

150 AA/StSzbV (Keppler) to BRAM: Note dated 7 May 1942, AA-PA/R29616.

151 RAM (Ribbentrop) to RK (Lammers): Letter dated 10 May 1942, BA/ R43II/1422.

152 Ges.Bangkok (Wendler) to AA: Telegram No. 291 dated 13 May 1942, AA-PA/R29616.

153 BRAM (Schmidt): Memorandum dated 28 May 1942, ADAP-E-II/247.

154 Nothing speaks against the fact that Hitler really meant what he said at the given time, because a few weeks after the talk with Bose, the Axis Powers issued a declaration of independence for Egypt on 2 July 1942 after they had marched into the country (ADAP-E-III/56).

155 Vyas, *Passage through a Turbulent Era*, 375.

156 BRAM (Schmidt): Memorandum dated 30 May 1942, ADAP-E-II/254.

157 Vyas, *Passage through a Turbulent Era*, 376.

158 Mookerjee, *Labyrinth Europa*, 137.

159 Vyas, *Passage through a Turbulent Era*, 379-80.

160 AA/UStS Pol (Woermann) to BRAM: Memorandum dated 29 May 1942, AA-PA/R29616.

161 MCP/SE to MCP (Tavolini): Memorandum dated 20 April 1942, ACS/MCP/ Gab/58.

162 Inaugurazione della 'Società Amici dell'India', *Asiatica* (1942), 97-8.

163 AA/SRI (Trott) to Bot.RomQ: Telegram No. 1760, AA-PA/RomQ/164.

164 Bot.RomQ (Plessen) to AA: Telegram No. 615 dated 2 May 1942, AA-PA/ RomQ/164.

165 Inaugurazione della 'Società Amici dell'India', *Asiatica* (1942), 90.

166 Ibid. 90-4.

167 Ibid.

168 Leg.Bangkok (Crolla) to MCP: Telegram dated 2 May 1942, ACS/MCP/ Gab/325.

169 Ganpuley, *Netaji in Germany*, 95-7.

170 BRAM (Schmidt): Memorandum dated 1 May 1941, ADAP-D-XII/425.

171 Vyas, *Passage through a Turbulent Era*, 306.

172 Neulen, *An deutscher Seite*, 18.

173 Gandhi, 'Suppose Germany Wins', *Harijan*, 15 February 1942; *Collected Works* 75/367.

174 Werth, *Der Tiger Indiens*, 137-8.

175 Harbich, 'A Report on the Organisation and Training of the Free India Army

in Europe 1941-1942', in Harbich and Werth, *Netaji in Germany*, 47-8.

176 AA/Pol (Rintelen): Memorandum dated 16 October 1941, ADAP-D-XIII/404.

177 Ganpuley, *Netaji in Germany*, 70-1.

178 MAE/AT (Alessandrini) to MAE (Ciano): Memorandum dated 31 October 1941, DDI-9-VIII/88.

179 AA/SRI (Werth) to AA/Inf (Wüster): Memorandum dated 11 October 1941, AA-PA/R60669.

180 Mangat, *The Tiger Strikes*, 56.

181 Ibid. 73.

182 Ibid. 75-9.

183 Ibid. 88-90.

184 Kritter: Diary entry dated 11 February 1943, BA-MA/MSg2/3068.

185 VAA Panzerarmee Afrika: Report dated 11 June 1942, AA-PA/RomQ/164.

186 Kritter: Diary entry dated 11 February 1943, BA-MA/MSg2/3068.

187 AA/SRI (Trott) to Bot.RomQ (Doertenbach): Letter dated 29 January 1942, AA-PA/R60669.

188 Toye: Interview with Swami dated September/October 1945, IOR/MSS EUR/C0743.

189 Mangat, *The Tiger Strikes*, 100-1.

190 Kritter: Diary entry dated 20 November 1942, BA-MA/MSg2/3068.

191 Kritter: Diary entry dated 11 February 1943, BA-MA/MSg2/3068.

192 Kritter: Diary entry dated 8 March 1942, BA-MA/MSg2/3068.

193 Schweizer Gesandtschaft Berlin (Ankenthaler/Burckhardt): Report dated 22 September 1942, PRO/WO224/14B. The report does not lead to the assumption that the German camp leader encouraged such violence, for the final verdict of the inspectors after talks with representatives of the prisoners reads: 'This camp is not bad at all. The camp leader is doing all he can to help the Indians, who seem to like him very much.'

194 Schweizer Gesandtschaft Berlin (Naville): Report dated 23 July 1943, PRO/WO224/14B.

195 CSDIC (UK): Report dated 12 January 1945, NAI/INA/242.

196 Bot.RomQ (Doertenbach) to OquRom(Heer)/Abteilung O1: Letter dated 15 April 1942, AA-PA/RomQ/167.

197 Bot.RomQ (Mackensen) to AA: Telegram No. 1377 dated 24 April 1942, AA-PA/RomQ/167.

198 Kritter: Diary entry dated 12 February 1943, BA-MA/MSg2/3068. Bot.RomQ (Mackensen) to AA: Telegram No. 45540 dated 16 November 1942, AA-PA/RomQ/167.

199 AA/SRI (Werth) to AA/Inf (Wüster): Memorandum dated 11 November 1941, AA-PA/R60669.

200 Bot.RomQ (Mackensen) to AA: Telegram No. 2895 dated 32 July 1942, AA-PA/RomQ/167.

201 Bot.RomQ (Mackensen) to AA: Telegram No. 1732 dated 19 May 1942, AA-PA/R29616.

202 MAE (Ciano) to CS/SIM: Telegram dated 24 April 1942, AS-MAE/AP/Irak/18.

203 AA/StSzbV (Keppler) to Bot.RomQ: Telegram No. 1788 dated 28 April 1942, AA-PA/RomQ/167.

204 Bot.RomQ (Plessen) to AA: Telegram No. 1510 dated 1 May 1942, AA-PA/RomQ/167.

205 AA/StSzbV (Keppler) to Bot.RomQ: Telegram No. 2699, AA-PA/RomQ/167. MAE to CS: Note dated 16 July 1942, AS-MAE/AP/Irak/18.

206 Bot.RomQ (Mackensen) to AA: Telegram No. 2671 dated 15 July 1942, AA-PA/RomQ/167. CS to MAE: Note dated 31 July 1942, AS-MAE/AP/Irak/18.

207 AA/SRI (Trott) to Bot.RomQ (Doertenbach): Letter dated 18 August 1942, AA-PA/RomQ/167.

208 Vyas, *Passage through a Turbulent Era*, 332-4.

209 MAE/AT (Prunas) to CS: Telegram dated 11 September 1942, AS-MAE/AP/India/13.

210 Werth, *Der Tiger Indiens*, 137-8.

211 Toye: Interview with Swami dated September/October 1945, IOR/MSS EUR/C0743.

212 Harbich, 'A Report on the Organisation and Training of the Free India Army in Europe 1941-1942', in Harbich and Werth, *Netaji in Germany*, 47-8.

213 OKW/AbwII (Lahousen): War diary, entry dated 29 June 1942, BA-MA/RW5/497.

214 Harbich, 'A Report on the Organisation and Training of the Free India Army in Europe 1941-1942', in Harbich and Werth, *Netaji in Germany*, 53-4.

215 Toye: Interview with Swami dated September/October 1945. IOR/MSS EUR/C0743.

216 Ibid.

217 Harbich, 'A Report on the Organisation and Training of the Free India Army in Europe 1941-1942', in Harbich and Werth, *Netaji in Germany*, 56.

218 Vyas, *Passage through a Turbulent Era*, 395.

219 Ges.Kabul (Pilger) to AA: Telegram No. 265 dated 2 August 1941, BA/R9.01/69565.

220 Ges.Kabul (Rasmuss) to AA/Inf: Telegram No. 352 dated 20 September 1941, BA/R9.01/69565.

221 Talwar, *Talwars of Pathan Land*, 141.

222 AA/SRI (Zitzewitz): Note dated 12 August 1941, AA-PA/R60669.

223 OKW/AbwII (Lahousen): War diary, entry dated 23 October 1941, BA-MA/RW5/498.

224 OKW/AbwII to AA/Inf: Letter dated 30 August 1941, BA/R9.01/69565.

225 AA/SRI (Werth) to Ges.Kabul (Rasmuss): Telegram No. 270 dated 5 September 1941, BA/R9.01/69565.

226 Ges.Kabul (Rasmuss) to AA: Telegram No. 312 dated 30 August 1941, BA/R9.01/69565.

227 OKW/AbwII (Lahousen): War diary, entry dated 1 March 1942, BA-MA/RW5/498.

228 Ges.Kabul (Witzel) to AA/Inf: Telegram No. 409 dated 8 December 1941, BA/R9.01/69566.

229 Talwar, *Talwars of Pathan Land*, 144-5.

230 Ges.Kabul (Witzel) to AA/Pol I: Telegram No. 39 dated 23 January 1942, BA/R9.01/69566.

231 AA/StSzbV (Keppler) to Ges.Kabul: Telegram No. 139 dated 20 April 1942, BA/R9.01/69567; Talwar, *Talwars of Pathan Land*, 151.

232 Ges.Kabul (Pilger) to AA: Telegram No. 377 dated 30 May 1942, BA/R9.01/61122.

233 AA/SRI (Trott) to AA/UStS Pol (Woermann): Memorandum dated 28 July 1942, BA/R9.01/61122.

234 Talwar, *Talwars of Pathan Land*, 163.

235 Ibid. 165-6.

236 IO/IPI: 'Statement of Bhagat Ram Talwar', undated, PRO/WO208/773.

237 Talwar, *Talwars of Pathan Land*, 172-3.

238 Ibid. 143.

239 Leg.Kabul (Squire) to GoI/EAD (Weightman): Reports dated 11 and 18 December 1943, IOR/R/12/163.

THE CONTINUATION OF INDIA-POLITICS UNTIL BOSE'S DEPARTURE

1   NMML (Nanda): Interview with Sarma dated 15 November 1971, NMML/OHT/325.

2   AA/SRI (Trott): Memorandum dated 26 February 1942, ADAP-E-I/292.

3   BRAM (Megerle) to AA/StSzbV (Keppler): Telegram No. 312 dated 27 March 1942, ADAP-E-II/87.

4   Ges.Bangkok (Wendler) to AA: Telegram No. 276 dated 30 April 1942, AA-PA/R29616.

5   Ges.Bangkok (Wendler) to AA: Telegram No. 283 dated 6 May 1942, AA-PA/R29616.

6   Ges.Bangkok (Wendler) to AA: Telegram No. 293 dated 15 May 1942, AA-PA/R29616.

7   RAM (Ribbentrop) to Ges.Bangkok: Telegram No. 542 dated 18 May 1942, AA-PA/R29616.

8   Bose to RAM (Ribbentrop): Letter dated 22 May 1942, AA-PA/R29616.

9   AA/UStS Pol (Woermann) to RAM (Ribbentrop): Memorandum dated 22 May 1942, AA-PA/R29616.

10 AA/UStS Pol (Woermann): Memorandum dated 23 May 1942, ADAP-E-II/240.

11 AA/StSzbV (Keppler) to BRAM: Telex dated 23 May 1942, AA-PA/R29616.

12 AA/UStS Pol (Woermann) to RAM (Ribbentrop): Memorandum dated 27 May 1942, AA-PA/R29616.

13 BRAM (Schmidt): Memorandum dated 28 May 1942, ADAP-E-II/247.

14 BRAM (Schmidt): Memorandum dated 30 May 1942, ADAP-E-II/254.

15 Herde, *Japanflug*, 147-89.

16 Goebbels, Diary entry dated 16 July 1942, *Goebbels-Tagebücher* ii:5.

17 Ges.Bangkok (Wendler) to AA: Telegram No. 352, BA/R9.01/69567.

18 Leg.Bangkok (Crolla) to MAE/AT: Telegram No. 78, AS-MAE/AP/India/13.

19 IIL (R.B.Bose) to Ges.Bankok: Letter dated 5 July 1942, NAI/IIL/10; IIL (R.B.Bose) to Leg.Bangkok: Letter dated 5 July 1942, NAI/IIL/40.

20 Bot.Bangkok (Wendler) to AA: Telegram No. 425 dated 15 July 1942, BA/R9.01/69567.

21 Voigt, *Indien im Zweiten Weltkrieg*, 206.

22 IIL: Note dated 3 July 1942, NAI/IIL/35.

23 Leg.Bangkok (Crolla) to MCP: Telegram No. 97 dated 16 July 1942, ACS/MCP/Gab/325.

24 AA/UStS Pol (Woermann) to RAM (Ribbentrop): Memorandum dated 14 January 1943, ADAP-E-V/41.

25 AA/SRI (Trott) to BRAM (Schmieden): Letter dated 16 July 1942, AA-PA/R60673.

26 AA/StSzbV (Keppler): Memorandum dated 10 July 1942, AA-PA/R60673.

27 AA/StS (Weizsäcker): Memorandum dated 27 June 1942, AA-PA/R29616.

28 Special Operations Executive to GoI: Telegram dated 8 August 1942, PRO/HS1/200.

29 MAE (Ciano) to Amb.Berlino (Alfieri): Telegram dated 21 May 1942, DDI-9-VIII/554.

30 MAE (Ciano) to Amb.Berlino (Alfieri): Telegram dated 16 June 1942, DDI-9-VII/624.

31 Herde, *Japanflug*, 190-214.

32 RAM (Ribbentrop) to Bot.RomQ: Telegram No. 2623 dated 26 June 1942, AA-PA/R29616; also see Amb.Berlino (Alfieri) to MAE (Ciano): Telegram dated 27 June 1942, DDI-9-VIII/662.

33 MAE (Ciano) to Amb.Berlino: Telegram dated 27 June 1942, DDI-9-VIII/660.

34 BRAM (Schmieden) to AA/StSzbV (Keppler): Note dated 23 July 1942, AA-PA/R60673.

35 Bose to RAM (Ribbentrop): Letter dated 23 July 1942, BA/R9.01/69567.

36 RAM (Ribbentrop) to Bose: Letter dated 2 August 1942, AA-PA/R29616.

37 PStRAM (Gottfriedsen) to BRAM: Telex dated 17 August 1942, ADAP-E-III/198.

38 Bot.RomQ (Mackensen) to AA: Telegram No. 3638 dated 24 September 1942, BA/R9.01/69567.

39 MAE (Ciano) to Amb.Berlino (Alfieri): Telegram dated 9 October 1942, DDI-9-IX/201.

40 Amb.Berlino (Alfieri) to MAE (Ciano): Telegram dated 10 October 1942, DDI-9-IX/203.

41 MAE/Gab. (Lanza d'Ajeta) to Amb.Berlino (Alfieri): Telegram dated 10 October 1942, DDI-9-IX/205.

42 AA/SRI (Trott) to RAM (Ribbentrop): Memorandum dated 14 October 1942, ADAP-E-IV/50.

43 AA/UStS Pol (Woermann): Memorandum dated 15 October 1942, AA-PA/R29617.

44 Bot.RomQ (Mackensen) to AA: Telegram No. 4553, AA-PA/RomQ/165.

45 Herde, *Japanflug*, 214-52.

46 Amb.Berlino (Alfieri) to MAE (Ciano): Telegram dated 20 October 1942, DDI-9-IX/243.

47 Bose to RAM (Ribbentrop): Letter dated 5 December 1942, ADAP-E-IV/262.

48 AA/StS (Weizsäcker) to RAM (Ribbentrop): Memorandum dated 2 February 1943, AA-PA/R29617.

49 Wert, *Der Tiger Indiens*, 149.

50 AA/StS (Weizsäcker) to Bot.RomQ (Mackensen): Telegram dated 8 February 1943, ADAP-E-V/107.

51 Vyas, *Passage through a Turbulent Era*, 428.

52 Werth, *Der Tiger Indiens*, 150.

53 Bose had written in a letter dated 8 February 1943 to his brother Sarat Chandra, that he was married and had a daughter (Bose, *Letters to Emilie Schenkl*, 228). The Boses welcomed them to the family after the war (Gordon, *Brothers Against the Raj*, 604).

54 Voigt, *Indien im Zweiten Weltkrieg*, 210.

55 Abid Hasan, 'A Soldier Remembers', *The Oracle*, 6/1 (1984), 24-65

56 Ibid. 58-9.

57 Voigt, *Indien im Zweiten Weltkrieg*, 210.

58 OKM to AA (Ritter): Telegram dated 28 April 1943, AA-PA/R29617. Bose's and Hasan's changing over to the Japanese vessel in rough weather and a sea watched by the enemy was a dangerous undertaking lasting nearly for two days. It was the only time during the Second World War that two persons changed over from one submarine to another.

59 Toye: Interview with Swami dated September/October 1945, IOR/MSS EUR/C0743.

60 *Michel-Briefmarken-Katalog Deutschland 1996/97*, 295.

61 Attachment 4 to Woermann's memorandum dated 20 May 1941, AA-PA/R67483.

62 Bose to MAE/AT (Prunas): Letter dated 4 June 1942, AA-PA/RomQ/164.

63 AA/SRI (Werth) to AA/StSzbV (Keppler): 1. Memorandum dated 14 July 1942, AA-PA/R60673.

64 MCP/IRT/MO (Lucidi): Memorandum dated 15 September 1942, ACS/JAIA/39.

65 AA/SRI (Werth) to AA/StSzbV (Keppler): 2. Memorandum dated 14 July 1942, AA-PA/R60673.

66 AA/StSzbV (Keppler) to Bot.Paris: Telegram No. 37 dated 5 January 1942, AA-PA/R27504.

67 Bose to AA: Memorandum dated 11 June 1942, AA-PA/R27504.

260 • *Netaji in Europe*

68 AA/StSzbV (Keppler) to Bot.Paris: Letter dated 20 August 1942, AA-PA/ R27504.
69 AA/StSzbV (Keppler) to Bot.Paris: Letter dated 15 February 1943, AA-PA/ R27504.
70 Bot.Paris (Schleier) to AA: Telegram No. 564 dated 26 January 1943, AA-PA/ R27504.
71 Bot.Paris (Schleier) to AA: Telegram No. 2367 dated 14 April 1943, AA-PA/ R27504.
72 ZFI (Nambiar) to AA/SRI (Trott): Letter dated 21 September 1943, AA-PA/ R27504.
73 Bot.Paris to AA: Letter dated 31 January 1944, AA-PA/R27504.
74 Bot.Paris (Abetz) to AA: Telegram No. 3872 dated 11 August 1944, AA-PA/ R27504.
75 RAD/LeiterAuswärtiges to AA/StSzbV (Keppler): Note dated 27 June 1942, AA-PA/R60673.
76 AA/SRI (Trott) to AA/D ReferatPartei: Memorandum dated 12 May 1942, AA-PA/R60672.
77 AA/SRI (Trott) to RAM (Ribbentrop): Memorandum dated 14 October 1942, ADAP-E-IV/50.
78 AA/SRI (Trott) to PStRFSS (Grothmann): Letter dated 21 August 1942, BA/ NS19/103; AA/SRI (Trott) to BRAM (Schmieden): Letter dated 16 July 1942, AA-PA/R60673.
79 AA/StSzbV (Keppler) to RFSS (Himmler): Letter dated 16 February 1943, BA/NS19/3769.
80 Kritter: Diary entry dated 3 June 1943, BA-MA/MSg2/3068.
81 RFSS (Himmler) to AA/StSzbV (Keppler): Letter dated 24 February 1943, BA/NS19/3769.
82 AA/SRI (Trott) to BRAM (Megerle): Telex dated 11 August 1942, AA-PA/ R29616.
83 Mookerjee, *Labyrinth Europa*, 138.
84 Chandra, *India's Struggle for Independence*, 464.
85 RMVP/AbtRundfunk: Memorandum dated 2 September 1942, BA/ R55/20822.
86 AA/StSzbV (Keppler) to BRAM (Megerle): Memorandum dated 5-6 August 1943, AA-PA/R27505.
87 Leg.Kabul (Quaroni) to MAE: Telegram dated 26 October 1942. MCP/IRT/ MO: Note dated 30 October 1942. ACS/JAIA/39.
88 Vyas, *Passage through a Turbulent Era*, 421-4.
89 Goebbels, Diary entry dated 22 July 1942, *Goebbels-Tagebücher* ii:5.
90 Ibid.
91 Ibid.
92 Vyas, *Passage through a Turbulent Era*, 381.
93 Gandhi, 'Suppose Germany Wins', *Harijan*, 15 February 1942; *Collected Works* 75/367.

94 AA/StSzbV (Keppler): Memorandum dated 2 July 1942, AA-PA/R60673.
95 AA/SRI (Trott) to BRAM (Schmieden): Letter dated 16 July 1942, AA-PA/ R60673.
96 BRAM (Schmieden) to AA/StSzbV (Keppler): Note dated 23 July 1942, AA-PA/R60673.
97 Chandra, *India's Struggle for Independence*, 461-3.
98 Ibid. 469-70.
99 AA/SRI (Trott) to BRAM (Megerle): Telex dated 4 August 1942, ADAP-E-III/155.
100 AA/SRI to AA/Inf (Wüster): Memorandum dated 19 August 1942, AA-PA/ R60673.
101 AIR/MS (Habib): Monitoring report dated 10 August 1942, NAI/Bose/312.
102 AIR/MS (Sharma): Monitoring report dated 17 June 1942, NAI/Bose/312.
103 AIR/MS (Khan): Monitoring report dated 19 August 1942, NAI/Bose/312.
104 Government of Punjab to GoI/HD: 'Fortnightly Report', 1 August 1942, NAI/Home-Poll/1942/18-8-42. (It may be mentioned here that the reports talk mainly about Axis broadcasts without differintiating between the German, Italian and Japanese programmes as well as the secret stations.)
105 Government of Punjab to GoI/HD: 'Fortnightly Report', 1 September 1942, NAI/Home-Poll/1942/18-9-42.
106 Government of UP to GoI/HD: 'Fortnightly Report', 2 August 1942, NAI/ Home-Poll/1942/18-8-42.
107 Government of UP to GoI/HD: 'Fortnightly Report', 2 September 1942, NAI/Home-Poll/1942/18-9-42.
108 Government of UP to GoI/HD: 'Fortnightly Report', 2 October 1942, NAI/ Home-Poll/1942/18-10-42.
109 Government of Bengal to GoI/HD: 'Fortnightly Report', 1 September 1942, NAI/Home-Poll/18-9-42.
110 Government of CP and Berar to GoI/HD: 'Fortnightly Report', 1 September 1942, NAI/Home-Poll/1942/18-8-42.
111 Government of CP and Berar to GoI/HD: 'Fortnightly Report', 1 December 1942, NAI/Home-Poll/1942/18-12-42.
112 Government of CP and Berar to GoI/HD: 'Fortnightly Report', 2 September 1942, NAI/Home-Poll/1942/18-9-42.
113 Government of Orissa to GoI/HD: 'Fortnightly Report', 1 October 1942, NAI/Home-Poll/1942/18-10-42.
114 Government of Bihar to GoI/HD: 'Fortnightly Report', 2 November 1942, NAI/Home-Poll/1942/18-11-42.
115 Government of Bihar to GoI/HD: 'Fortnightly Report', 1 September 1942, NAI/Home-Poll/1942/18-9-42.
116 AA/SRI (Trott) to BRAM (Rintelen): Memorandum dated 5 August 1942, AA-PA/R60674.
117 Orwell, Commentary dated 25 July 1942, *The War Commentaries*.
118 Banerjee to AA/StSzbV (Keppler): Letter dated 29 May 1942, AA-PA/R27504.

119 AA/StSzbV (Keppler) to RAM (Ribbentrop): Memorandum dated 12 June 1942, AA-PA/R27504.

120 AA/StSzbV (Keppler) to den Hamburger Regierenden Bürgermeister Krogmann: Letter dated 15 June 1942, AA-PA/R27504.

121 Faltis to AA (Aschmann): Letter dated 22 November 1938, AA-PA/R104777.

122 Bose to Faltis: Letter dated 26 April 1941, NAI/Bose/247.

123 Bose to Faltis: Letter dated 16 September 1941, NAI/Bose/247.

124 Bose to Faltis: Letter dated 24 June 1942, NAI/Bose/247.

125 Faltis to AA/SRI (Trott): Letter dated 4 July 1944, AA-PA/R27504.

126 Bose to AA/StSzbV (Keppler): Letter dated 1 September 1942, AA-PA/R27504.

127 'Feierliche Gründung der Deutsch-Indischen Gesellschaft in Hamburg', *Diplomatisches Bulletin*, 72, dated 15 September 1942, AA-PA/R27504.

128 Lutz, 'Jana Gana Mana', Manuscript dated 29 February 1980, BA-MA/MSg2/3070.

129 NMML (Nanda): Interview with Sarma dated 15 November 1971, NMML/OHT/325.

130 'Ansprache des Präsidenten der Deutsch-Indischen Gesellschaft, Bürgermeister Krogmann', *Mitteilungen der Deutsch-Indischen Gesellschaft*, 1, dated March 1943, 3—AA-PA/R27504.

131 'Subhas Chandra Boses Rede', *Mitteilungen der Deutsch-Indischen Gesellschaft*, 1, dated March 1943, 4—AA-PA/R27504.

132 AIR/MS (Habib): Monitoring report dated 14 September 1942, NAI/Bose/312.

133 AA/SRI (Trott) to Lorenz: Letter dated 17 September 1942, AA-PA/R60675.

134 AA/StSzbV (Keppler) to Heske: Letter dated 16 December 1942, AA-PA/R27504.

135 AA/StSzbV (Keppler) to Generalbauinspektor für die Reichshauptstadt (Speer): Letter dated 14 July 1942, AA-PA/R27504.

136 AA/SRI (Trott) to Universität München (Wüst): Letter dated July 1942, AA-PA/R27504.

137 AA/StSzbV (Keppler) to Luther: Memorandum dated 28 January 1943, AA-PA/R27504.

138 Universität München (Wüst) to AA/SRI (Trott): Letter dated 22 December 1942 *and* AA/SRI (Trott) to Universität München (Wüst): Letter dated 4 January 1943—AA-PA/R27504.

139 Günther and Rehmer, *Inder, Indien und Berlin*, 128-9.

140 AA/StSzbV (Keppler) to RAM (Ribbentrop): Memorandum dated 9 June 1942, AA-PA/R27504.

141 NMML (Nanda): Interview with Schenkl dated 11 November 1971, NMML/OHT/179.

142 BRAM (Sonnleithner) to AA/StSzbV (Keppler): Note dated 30 June 1942, AA-PA/R27504.

143 AA-PA/R27504; this file contains a number of letters documenting the

dispute between the Sonderreferat Indien and the Union Deutsche Verlansgesellschaft.

144 AA/StSzbV (Keppler) to ZFI (Nambiar): Letter dated 9 November 1943, AA-PA/R27504.

145 De Felice, 'L'India nella strategia politica di Mussolini', in *Storia contemporanea xxviii*, 1315.

146 Schedai to MAE/AT (Alessandrini): Letter dated 5 April 1941; Schedai to MAE/Gab (Lanza d'Ajeta): Letter dated 21 October 41; Schedai to MAE/Gab (Lanza d'Ajeta): Letter dated 26 December 1941—AS-MAE/Gab/408.

147 MAE/Gab (Lanza d'Ajeta) to MCP/Gab (Luciano): Letter dated 27 December 1941, AS-MAE/Gab/407.

148 MCP/Gab (Luciano) to MAE/Gab (Lanza d'Ajeta): Letter dated 16 January 1942, AS-MAE/Gab/407.

149 AA/StSzbV (Keppler) to Bot.RomQ: Telegram No. 1029 dated 7 March 1942, AA-PA/RomQ/Q164. AA/SRI (Assmann) to AA/SRI (Trott): Memorandum dated 20 February 1942, AA-PA/R60670.

150 AA/SRI (Werth) to AA/StSzbV (Keppler): Memorandum dated 14 July 1942, AA-PA/R60673.

151 Schedai to MAE/Gab (Lanza d'Ajeta): Letter dated 24 June 1942, ACS/JAIA/39.

152 MCP/IRT/MO (Lucidi) to MAE/Gab (Lanza d'Ajeta): Letter dated 30 June 1942, ACS/JAIA/39.

153 MAE/AT: Memorandum dated 21 October 1942, MAE/Gab/408.

154 Schedai to MAE/Gab (Lanza d'Ajeta): Letter dated 24 October 1942, AS-MAE/Gab/408.

155 MAE/Gab (Lanza d'Ajeta) to Leg.Kabul (Quaroni): Telegram dated 7 November 1942, ACS/JAIA/39.

156 AA/StSzbV (Keppler) to Bot.Roma: Letter dated 23 March 1943, AA-PA/RomQ/166.

157 MCP/IRT/MO (Lucidi): Memorandum dated 21 March 1942, ACS/JAIA/39.

158 Vyas, *Passage through a Turbulent Era*, 333-4.

159 SPD to Mussolini: Note dated 14 March 1942, ACS/SPD/CO/532.797.

160 AA/SRI (Werth) to AA/StSzbV (Keppler): Memorandum dated 14 July 1942, AA-PA/R60673.

161 PCM/Gab to Mussolini: Memorandum dated 21 July 1940; Mussolini: Decree undated—ACS/PCM/1940-1943/1.1.10.

162 ISMEO (Tucci) to MAE/AT: Letter dated 30 November 1942, AS-MAE/RG/80.

163 ISMEO/Consiglio di amministrazione: Protocol dated 5 June 1942, IsAIO/Verbali/2.

164 ISMEO to MAE: Report dated April 1943, AS-MAE/RG/80.

165 ISMEO (Gentile) to Mussolini: Letter dated 22 June 1943, AS-MAE/SPD/CO/519.319.

166 ISMEO/ Consiglio di amministrazione: Protocol dated 22 November 1947, IsAIO/Verbali/2.

167 Schedai to MAE/AT (Prunas): Letter dated 3 February 1942, AS-MAE/Gab/408.

168 Schedai to MAE: Letter dated 10 April 1942, AS-MAE/Gab/408.

169 MCP/IRT/MO (Lucidi): Memorandum dated 25 July 1942, ACS/JAIA/30.

170 Conti, *I prigionieri di guerra italiani*, 332-3.

171 Government of Bihar to GoI/HD: 'Fortnightly Report', 1 March 1942, NAI/Home-Poll/1942/18-3-42.

172 IO/IPI: 'The Axis Approach to India' dated August 1942, PRO/WO208/823.

173 MG/Gab (Scuero) to CS: Letter dated 24 August 1942, AUS-SME/M3/6-5.

174 Garibaldi to Cavallero: Letter dated 4 September 1942, AUS-SME/M3/6-5.

175 Garibaldi: Memorandum dated 4 September 1942, AUS-SME/M3/6-5.

176 CS to MAE: Letter dated 31 August 1942, AUS-SME/M3/6-5.

177 Ciano, Diary entry dated 10 August 1942, *Diario* ii.

178 CS/O: Memorandum dated 14 September 1942, AUS-SME/M3/6-5.

179 SMRE/SIE (Ambrosio) to CS: Letter dated 28 October 1942, AUS-SME/M3/6-5.

180 Mussolini: Protocol of the seventh conversation with General Vacca Maggiolini dated 12 February 43. *Opera Omnia* xxxi, 149-53.

181 OKW/WFSt/Amtsgruppe Ausland to OKW/WFSt/Amtsgruppe Wehrmachtspropaganda: Letter dated 4 August 1944, AUS-SME/M3/6-5.

182 CS/SMG (Cavallero) to SMRE: Letter dated 22 June 1942, AS-MAE/AP/Irak/18.

183 CS/SMG (Cavallero) to SMRE: Letter dated 22 June 1942, AS-MAE/AP/Irak/18.

184 SMRE to MG/Gab: Letter dated 2 July 1942, AUS-SME/M7/581.

185 CS/SIM: Memorandum dated 23 March 1942, AS-MAE/AP/Irak/18.

186 MAE/AT: Note dated 19 March 1942, AS-MAE/AP/Irak/18.

187 BRAM (Schmidt): Memorandum dated 30 November 1941, ADAP-D-XIII/515.

188 SMRE/PG (Gandin) to Kommando des XVII. Armeekorps: Letter dated 2 March 1942, AUS-SME/N667.

189 Rizzi, *I guanti bianchi*, 35.

190 Ibid. 63.

191 Ibid. 84.

192 Ibid. 100-1.

193 CS/SIM to SMRE: Letter dated 11 July 1942, AUS-SME/N/1400.

194 Rizzi, *I guanti bianchi*, 34.

195 War diary CMI: Entry dated 1 August 1942, AUS-SME/N/780.

196 War diary CMI: Entry dated 16 August 1942, AUS-SME/N/780.

197 War diary CMI: Entry dated 24 August 1942, AUS-SME/N/780.

198 War diary CMI: Entry dated 1 September 1942, AUS-SME/N/780.

199 War diary CMI: Entry dated 10 and 15 September 1942, AUS-SME/N/780.

200 RCM (Invrea): Order dated 23 October 1942, AUS-SME/N/780.

201 Rizzi, *I guanti bianchi*, 62.
202 Ibid. 63-4.
203 Ibid. 75-6; RCM (Invrea): Order dated 23 October 1942, AUS-SME/N/780.
204 Rizzi, *I guanti bianchi*, 75-6.
205 Ibid, 113-5.
206 Ibid. 104.
207 Ibid. 111.
208 Ibid. 134.
209 RCM (Invrea): Order dated 23 October 1942, AUS-SME/N/780.
210 Rizzi, *I guanti bianchi*, 74.
211 Ibid. 85.
212 RCI (Invrea) to SMRE/OII: Letter dated 12 November 1942, AUS-SME/N/780.
213 Rizzi, *I guanti bianchi*, 86.
214 Ibid. 84.
215 Ibid. 135.
216 RCI (Invrea) to SMRE/OII: Letter dated 12 November 1942, AUS-SME/N/780.
217 CS (Magli) to MG/Gab and SMRE: Letter dated 12 September 1942, AUS-SME/N/780.
218 RCI (Invrea) to SIM and SMRE /OII: Letter dated 15 November 1942, AUS-SME/N/780.
219 CS/SIM: Memorandum dated 12 November 1942, AUS-SME/N/1404.
220 War diary RGI: Entry dated 17 November 1942, AUS-SME/N/780; Gordon, *Brothers Against the Raj*, 487-8.
221 AUS-SME/N/780.
222 Ibid.
223 War diary RGI: Anlage 6, AUS-SME/N/780.
224 Kritter: Diary entry dated 12 February 1943, BA-MA/MSg2/3068.
225 OKW/Ausl to OKW/WFSt: Letter dated 25 February 1943, BA-MA/RH24-88/81.
226 Swiss Legation Rome (Iselin): Report dated 1 September 1943, PRO/WO224/137.
227 Mangat, *The Tiger Strikes*, 113.
228 Ibid. 123.
229 IO/IPI: War diary of the Indian Legion, English summary, dated 29 September 1946, PRO/WO208/823.
230 Mangat, *The Tiger Strikes*, 123.
231 OKH: Order dated 3 June 1942, BA-MA/RS4/1146.
232 Ganpuley, *Netaji in Germany*, 96.
233 Davis, *Badges & Insignia of the Third Reich 1933-1945*, 185 and Plate 59.
234 Davis and McGregor, *Flags of the Third Reich*, ii: *Waffen-SS*, 42 and Plate F.
235 Rudolf Hartog, Dolmetscher bei der Indischen Legion, April 1984, BA-MA/MSg2/3070.

236 Kritter: Diary entry dated 25 November 1942, BA-MA/MSg2/3068.

237 Kritter: Diary entry dated 16 June 1943, BA-MA/MSg2/3068. Also see Hartog, *Im Zeichen des Tigers*, 81. Hauner, in his book *India in Axis Strategy* (589), describes it as 'grotesque' that some Indians preferred to converse with each other in German instead of Hindustani. This judgment ignores the fact that even now many Indians prefer a European language, i.e. English, to Hindi as lingua franca for the entire country.

238 *Militärwörterbuch für den Führer und Unterführer*, i: *Deutsch-Hindustani*, edited by Oberkommando des Heeres (1943), BA-MA/MSg2/3068.

239 *Der Gruppenführer Handbuch für die Ausbildung im (Ind.) I. R. 950*, i: *Gefechtsausbildung*, 1 August 1943, BA-MA/MSg2/3068.

240 Ernst Bannerth, *Hindustani-Briefe: 15 Urdu- and 6 Hindi-Briefe mit Umschrift und Übersetzung*, Arbeitshefte für den Sprachmittler, 49 (Leipzig, 1943), BA-MA/MSg2/3068.

241 Abriß der Hindustani-Sprachlehre und deutsch-indisches Wörterverzeichnis, Bearbeitet dated Stab des (Ind.) I. R. 950, BA-MA/MSg2/3068.

242 Ernst Bannerth and Otto Spieß, *Lehrbuch der Hindustani Sprache*.

243 Copies of this publication can still be found in Freiburg in the Bundesarchiv-Militärarchiv (RS4/1143-1145).

244 CSDIC(UK): Report dated 12 January 1945, NAI/INA/242.

245 Ibid.

246 Bataillons-Befehl des I. Bataillons dated 28 May 1944, BA-MA/RS4/1142; Hartog, *Im Zeichen des Tigers*, 133-4.

247 Kritter: Diary entry dated 26 November 1942, BA-MA/MSg2/3068.

248 Kritter: Diary entry dated 10 February 1943, BA-MA/MSg2/3068.

249 Volkmann to AA/SRI (Trott): Letter dated 6 November 1942, AA-PA/R60675.

250 CSDIC(UK): Report dated 12 January 1945, NAI/INA/241.

251 Mangat, *The Tiger Strikes*, 120.

252 Kritter: Diary entry dated 18 December 1942, BA-MA/MSg2/3068.

253 Kritter: Diary entry dated 27 November 1942, BA-MA/MSg2/3068.

254 Opitz: 'Denn wir fahren gegen Engeland. Die "Indische Legion" im Zweiten Weltkrieg', BA-MA/RH37/6530.

255 Führungsgrundsätze, BA-MA/MSg2/3068.

256 Kritter: Diary entry dated 30 November 1942, BA-MA/MSg2/3068.

257 Kritter: Diary entry dated 4 December 1943, BA-MA/MSg2/3068.

258 Franzen, *Aus meinem Leben*, 103.

259 Kritter: Diary entry dated 8 March 1943, BA-MA/MSg2/3068.

260 IO/IPI: War diary of the Indian Legion, English summary, dated 29 July 1946, PRO/WO208/823.

261 Rau: Geschichte der Sonderkompanie, 1983, BA-MA/MSg2/3070.

262 Indische Legion (Krappe): Report dated 3 May 1943, BA-MA/RH24-88/81; Weidemann, 'The Mutiny of Königsbrück—1944.'

263 Hartog, *Im Zeichen des Tigers*, 85-102.

264 Kritter: Diary entry dated 12 February 1943, BA-MA/MSg2/3068.

265 IO/IPI: War diary of the Indian Legion, English summary, dated 29 July 1946, PRO/WO208/823.
266 Kritter: Diary entry dated 14 October 1942, BA-MA/MSg2/3068.
267 Franzen, *Aus meinem Leben*, 101.
268 IO/IPI: War diary of the Indian Legion, English summary, dated 29 July 1946, PRO/WO208/823.
269 Vyas, *Passage through a Turbulent Era*, 481-2.
270 Franzen, *Aus meinem Leben*, 101.
271 Hartog, *Im Zeichen des Tigers*, 115-6.
272 Bharati, *The Ochre Robe*, 61.
273 IO/IPI: War diary of the Indian Legion, English summary, dated 29 July 1946, PRO/WO208/823.
274 Kritter: Diary entry dated 15 December 1942, BA-MA/MSg2/3068.
275 Bharati, *The Ochre Robe*, 56.
276 Kritter: Diary entry dated 1 August 1943, BA-MA/MSg2/3068.
277 IO/IPI: War diary of the Indian Legion, English summary, dated 29 July 1946, PRO/WO208/823.
278 Mangat, *Indian National Army*, 99.

THE END OF INDIA-POLITICS AFTER BOSE'S DEPARTURE

1 Bot.Tokio (Stahmer) to AA: Telegram No. 1637 dated 26 May 1943, ADAP-E-VI/59.
2 Amb.Tokio (Indelli) to MAE (Mussolini): Telegram dated 25 May 1943, DDI-9-X/357.
3 Bot.Tokio (Stahmer) to AA: Telegram No. 1833 dated 12 June 1943, ADAP-E-VI/97.
4 AA/SRI (Trott): Memorandum dated 16 July 1943, BA/R9.01/60423.
5 Mussolini, Rede vor dem Direttorio nazionale der Partito nazionale fascista, *Opera Omnia* xxxi, 185-97.
6 Mussolini to Amb.Tokio: Telegram dated 6 July 1943, AS-MAE/AT/118.
7 AA/StSzbV (Keppler) to RAM (Ribbentrop): Memorandum dated 27 September 1943, ADAP-E-VI/354.
8 Goebbels, Diary entry dated 11 July 1943, *Goebbels-Tagebücher* ii:9.
9 Chandra, *India's Struggle for Independence*, 471.
10 Sareen, *Japan and the Indian National Army*, 149-50.
11 AA/StSzbV (Keppler) to RAM (Ribbentrop): Memorandum dated 10 June 1943, AA-PA/R29617.
12 Amb.Tokio (Indelli) to MAE/AT: Telegram No. 454 dated 29 June 1943, AS-MAE/AP/India/13.
13 AA/StSzbV (Keppler) to RAM (Ribbentrop): Memorandum dated 27 September 1943, ADAP-E-VI/354.
14 Government of Sindh: 'Fortnightly Report', 1 February 1943, NAI/Home-

Poll/1943/18-2-43. Also see—Government of Bombay: 'Fortnightly Report', 2 May 1943, NAI/Home-Poll/1943/18-5-43 *and* Government of Punjab: 'Fortnightly Report', 2 June 1943, NAI/Home-Poll/18-6-43.

15 Government of Bombay: 'Fortnightly Report', 1 July 1943, NAI/Home-Poll/1943/18-7-43.

16 Government of Orissa: 'Fortnightly Report', 2 July 1943, NAI/Home-Poll/1943/18-7-43.

17 Government of Bihar: 'Fortnightly Report', 1 November 1943, NAI/Home-Poll/18-11-43.

18 Government of CP and Berar: 'Fortnightly Report', 1 July 1943, NAI/Home-Poll/1943/18-7-43.

19 Gordon, *Brothers Against the Raj*, 502-3.

20 AA/UStS Pol (Hencke) to Bot.Tokio: Telegram No. 2770 dated 28 October 1943, AA-PA/R67599.

21 Mussolini to Bose: Telegram dated 1 November 1943, *Opera Omnia* xxxii, 215.

22 Goebbels, Diary entry dated 23 March 1944, *Goebbels-Tagebücher* ii: 11.

23 Sareen, *Japan and the Indian National Army*, 169-203.

24 Talwar, *Talwars of Pathan Land*, 178-9.

25 Ibid. 180.

26 Ibid. 183-6.

27 Ges.Kabul (Witzel) to AA: Telegram No. 480 dated 16 June 1943, AA-PA/R29617.

28 Talwar, *Talwars of Pathan Land*, 186.

29 Ibid. 188-90; Ges.Kabul (Witzel) to AA: Telegram No. 670 dated 16 September 1943, AA-PA/R101836.

30 FO to Emb.Moskau: Telegram dated 12 May 1943, IOR/L/P&S/12/1798.

31 FO: Memorandum dated 11 June 1943, IOR/L/P&S/12/1798.

32 Afghan Foreign Ministry to British Legation Kabul: Memorandum dated 17 July 1943, IOR/L/P&S/12/1798.

33 British Legation Kabul to FO: Telegram dated 29 July 1943, IOR/L/P&S/12/1799.

34 Ges.Kabul (Pilger) to AA/Pol VII: Telegram No. 572 dated 28 July 1943, AA-PA/R101836.

35 GoI/EAD to IO: Telegram dated 30 July 1943, IOR/L/P&S/12/1799.

36 AA (Hemmen) to Ges.Kabul: Telegram dated 30 July 43, AA-PA/R101836.

37 GoI/EAD to IO: Telegram dated 16 August 1943, IOR/L/P&S/12/1799.

38 Ges.Kabul (Pilger) to AA: Telegram No. 740 dated 11 October 1942, AA-PA/R101836.

39 Ges.Kabul (Pilger) to AA: Telegram No. 770 dated 25 October 43, AA-PA/R101836.

40 AA/Pol (Melchers) to AA/UStS Pol (Henke): Memorandum dated 26 October 1943, AA-PA/R101836.

41 IO/ED to IO/USSt: Note dated 3 November 1943.

42   British Legation Kabul (Squire) to GoI/EAD (Weightman): Letter dated 11 November 1943, IOR/L/P&S/12/1799.

43   British Legation Kabul (Squire) to FO (Eden): 'Letter Statement of the Italian Minister' dated 29 September 1943, IOR/L/P&S/12/1805.

44   Talwar, *Talwars of Pathan Land*, 195-7.

45   AA/StSbzV (Keppler) to BRAM: Memorandum dated 5 February 1944, AA-PA/R101837.

46   AA/StSbzV (Keppler) to RAM: Memorandum 24 September 1943, AA-PA/R27504.

47   Talwar, *Talwars of Pathan Land*, 197-224.

48   AA/SRI (Alsdorf): Memorandum dated 11 May 1944, ADAP-E-VII/19.

49   AA/StSzbV (Keppler): Memorandum dated 18 May 1941, BA/R9.01/60423.

50   AA/UStS Pol (Woermann) to AA/StSzbV (Keppler): Memorandum dated 11 February 42, AA-PA/R27501.

51   Bot.RomQ (Bismarck) to AA: Telegram No. 3120 dated 21 August 1942, AA-PA/R29616.

52   AA/SRI (Trott) to Bot.RomQ (Doertenbach): Telex dated 14 August 1942, AA-PA/R60675

53   AA (Ettel) to AA/StSzbV (Keppler): Memorandum dated 4 September 1942, AA-PA/R27322.

54   AA (Ettel): Memorandum dated 10 September 1942, AA-PA/R27322.

55   AA/SRI (Trott) to RAM (Ribbentrop): Memorandum dated 14 September 1942, ADAP-E-IV/50.

56   AA/StSzbV (Keppler) to BRAM (Megerle): Telex dated 21 September 1942, AA-PA/R27501.

57   AA/StSzbV (Keppler) to AA/BfI (Megerle): Memorandum dated 8 March 1943, BA/R9.01/60423.

58   AA/StSzbV (Keppler) to Bot.RomQ: Memorandum dated 3 April 1943, AA-PA/RomQ/166.

59   AA/SRI (Trott) to AA/BfI (Megerle): Memorandum dated 6 May 1943, AA-PA/R60677.

60   AA/SRI (Studnitz) to AA/StSzbV (Keppler): Memorandum dated 6 May 1943, BA/R9.01/60423.

61   AA/Pol VII (Melchers) to AA/UStS Pol (Hencke) and AA/BfI (Megerle): Memorandum dated 7 May 1943, BA/R9.01/60423.

62   AA/StSzbV (Keppler): Memorandum dated 11 May 1943, BA/R9.01/60423.

63   AA/P VIII (Baßler) to AA/StSzbV (Keppler) Memorandum dated 12 May 1943, BA/R9.01/60423.

64   AA/StSzbV (Keppler): Memorandum dated 18 May 1943, BA/R9.01/60423.

65   AA/StSzbV (Keppler): Protocol dated 22 May 1943, BA/R9.01/60423.

66   AA/SRI (Trott) to AA/P (Schmidt): Memorandum dated 29 May 1943, BA/R9.01/60423.

67   Amb.Tokio (Indelli) to MAE (Mussolini): Telegram dated 29 June 1943, DDI-9-X.

68 Unfinished manuscripts in AA-PA/R27502.

69 Trott, *Lebensbeschreibung*, 202.

70 McDonogh, *A Good German*, 205-6.

71 StSzbV (Keppler) to RAM (Ribbentrop): Report dated 5 August 1943, AA-PA/R27504.

72 Vyas, *Passage through a Turbulent Era*, 446-7.

73 Ganpuley, *Netaji in Germany*, 58.

74 Vyas, *Passage through a Turbulent Era*, 479-81.

75 Ganpuley, *Netaji in Germany*, 59.

76 Vyas, *Passage through a Turbulent Era*, 496-7.

77 MAE/AT/Ufficio India to CS/SIM: Telex dated 19 April 1943, ACS/JAIA/30.

78 MCP/IRT to MCP/Gab: Memorandum dated 7 August 1943, ACS/JAIA/30.

79 MAE/AT to MI: Telex dated 15 April 1943, AS-MAE/RSI/AT/117.

80 Ajit Singh, *Buried Alive*, 113-4.

81 MAE/Gab to MCP: Letter dated 18 July 1944, AS-MAE/RSI/Gab/36.

82 MAE/Gab to MCP (Mezzasona): Letter dated 21 January 1944 *and* MCP (Mezzasona) to MAE (Mazzolini) to MAE: Letter dated 24 January 1944—AS-MAE/RSI/Gab/26.

83 MCP (Mezzasona) to MAE (Mazzolini): Letter dated 9 March 1944, AS-MAE/RSI/Gab/26.

84 MCP to MAE/AT: Letter dated 12 March 1944, AS-MAE/RSI/Gab/26.

85 Schedai to MAE/Gab (Mellini): Letter dated 28 August 1944, AS-MAE/RSI/Gab/26. Newspaper cutting from *Corriere della Sera* dated 7 September 1944, ASMAE/RSI/AP/68.

86 Ajit Singh, *Buried Alive,* 114.

87 Chief of General Staff (Smith): 'Directive to Commander Indian Military Mission to Berlin' dated 28 March 1946, IOR/L/WS/1/737.

88 AS-MAE/RSI/AP/68. Mussolini to Bose: Telegram dated 1 November 1943, *Opera Omnia* xxxii, 215.

89 MAE to Mussolini: Note dated 14 April 1944, AS-MAE/RSI/AP/68.

90 MAE to Bot.RomQ: Note dated 14 April 1944, AS-MAE/RSI/AP/68.

91 Mussolini to Bose: Telegram dated 9 April 1944, *Opera Omnia* xliii, 125.

92 Mussolini to Bose: Telegram dated 21 October 1944, ibid. 183.

93 Amb.Tokio (Principini) to MAE: Telegram dated 29 November 1944, ASMAE/RSI/AP/68.

94 MAE to Mussolini: Note dated 9 July 1944, AS-MAE/RSI/Gab/36.

95 Amb.Berlino to MAE/Gab (Mellini): Letter dated 13 December 1944, AS-MAE/RSI/AP/68

96 Mussolini, 'L'India agli indiani', *Opera Omnia* xxxii, 329-31.

97 De Felice, *Il fascismo e l'Oriente*, 240-1.

98 CSDIC(I): 'Statement by Bannerth' dated 16 January 1945, NAI/INA/242.

99 Generalkommando LXXXVIII. Armeekorps to the Wehrmachtsbefehlshaber in the Netherlands: Report dated 11 May 1943, BA-MA/RH24-88/81.

100 Opitz: 'Denn wir fahren gegen Engeland. Die "Indische Legion" im Zweiten Weltkrieg', BA-MA/ RH37/6530.
101 CSDIC(I): 'Statement by Bannerth' dated 16 January 1945, NAI/INA/242.
102 Bose: Denkschrift, BA-MA/RH24-88/81.
103 Hartog, *Im Zeichen des Tigers,* 103-7.
104 Tödt: 'Einsatz der 9./Ind.I.R.950 to der Italien-Front im Jahre 1944', dated 26 September 1952, BA-MA/ MSg2/3069. See also Hartog, *Im Zeichen des Tigers,* 155-60.
105 Hartog, *Im Zeichen des Tigers,* 158-60. Also CSDIC(I): Report dated 20 May 1945, NAI/INA/241.
106 French partisan groups, who fought during the Second World War against German occupational forces and the government of unoccupied France, were called Maquis, and their members maquisards. Maquis is the French word for the scrub-wood forest where fugitives and robbers of yore used to hide.
107 Hartog, *Im Zeichen des Tigers,* 135-9.
108 Mangat, *Indian National Army,* 103. The ZFI had founded these decorations. Nambiar conferred them in the name of 'the president of the provisional government of free India'. Hartog in his book *Im Zeichen des Tigers* lists the following medals and decorations: Tamgha-e-Azadi (freedom medal), Tamgha-e-Bahaduri (medal for bravery, with and without swords), Vir-e-Hind (hero of India medal), and Sardar-e-Jang (supreme-commander medal). Mangat in *Indian National Army* compiles the following list: Sher-e-Hind, Sardar-e-Jang, Veer-e-Hind Shamsheerdar (with sword cross), Veer-e-Hind, Tamgha-e-Bahaduri (Sunehri Shamsheerdar), Tamgha-e-Bahaduri (Chandi Shamsheerdar), Tamgha-e-Bahaduri (Chandi).
109 Hartog, *Im Zeichen des Tigers,* 142-54; Mangat, *Indian National Army,* 104.
110 Hartog, Im Zeichen des Tigers, 163-4.
111 Mangat, *The Tiger Strikes,* 199.
112 CSDIC(UK): Report dated 12 January 1945, NAI/INA/242.
113 Hartog, *Im Zeichen des Tigers,* 144.
114 Franzen, *Aus meinem Leben,* 102.
115 Warren: Report dated 5 January 1945, PRO/WO208/802.
116 IO/IPI: Note dated 12 October 1944, PRO/WO208/831. It seems unlikely that the *Figaro* depicted the actions of enemy troops in an objective manner. However, it shows the kind of reputation the Indians had gained on their retreat march from France.
117 Mangat, *Indian National Army,* 105-6.
118 Voigt, *Indien im Zweiten Weltkrieg,* 295-6.
119 Hartog, *Im Zeichen des Tigers,* 166-71; Mangat, *Indian National Army,* 107.
120 Protocol dated 25 March 1945, *Hitlers Lagebesprechungen.*
121 Hartog, *Im Zeichen des Tigers,* 172-80; Mangat, *Indian National Army,* 108-10.
122 Mangat, *Indian National Army,* 157-8.
123 Mangat, *Indian National Army,* 162.
124 Hartog, *Im Zeichen des Tigers,* 185.

125 Lutz: 'Kriegsgerichtliches Verfahren in Bordeaux 1947-1949', MSg2/3070/73-83; Hartog, *Im Zeichen des Tigers*, 186-92.

126 WO/MI2 to Commander-in-Chief India: Telegram dated 11 May 1943, PRO/WO208/802.

127 IO/IPI to WO/MI2: Report dated 10 March 1943, PRO/WO208/802.

128 IO/IPI to WO/MI2: Memorandum dated 23 March 1943, PRO/WO208/802.

129 British Legation Bern to FO: Telegram dated 22 July 1943, PRO/WO208/823.

130 IO/IPI to WO/MI2: Report dated 23 April 1943, PRO/WO208/802.

131 General Staff (India): Memorandum dated 31 August 1943, PRO/WO208/802.

132 GHQ India: 'Weekly Intelligence Summary', dated 23 June 1943, PRO/WO208/802.

133 CSDIC(UK): Report dated 12 January 1945, NAI/INA/242.

134 Oesterheld, 'Die Indische Legion in Frankreich', 220.

135 CSDIC(UK): Report dated 12 January 1945, NAI/INA/242. It is irritating that Hauner, in his book *India in Axis Strategy* (588-9), accepts Bannerth's testimonies unquestioningly. Evidently, he did not consider the extraordinary psychological situation of the deserter, who, in order to save his skin, had to gain the enemy's confidence and therefore had to make a radical break with the other side plausible.

136 IO (Molesworth) to WO (Burnham): Letter dated 5 January 1944, IOR/L/WS/1/1363.

137 WO/MI2 (Montgomery) to IO (Reynolds): Letter dated 17 October 1944, PRO/WO208/831.

138 Ministry of Information: 'Qualified Release K170', dated 20 October 1944, PRO/WO208/831.

139 WO/MI2: Memorandum dated 17 January 1945, PRO/WO208/831.

140 WO/DMI to Commander-in-Chief India: Telegram dated 30 April 1945, PRO/WO208/831.

141 GoI/WD to IO: Telegram dated 2 May 1945, PRO/WO208/831.

142 IO/ID to GoI/WD: Telegram dated 5 May 1945, PRO/WO208/831.

143 PRO/WO208/826.

144 GoI/HD/IB: 'Notes on Suspect Civilian Indians on the Continent of Europe', July 1944, IOR/L/WS/1/1363.

145 IO/IPI: Memorandum dated 27 November 1944, PRO/WO208/802.

146 Warren: Report dated 5 January 1945, PRO/WO208/802.

147 De Gale: Report dated 26 October 1944, PRO/WO208/802.

148 IO/IPI: Memorandum dated 21 March 1945, PRO/WO208/802.

149 IO/IPI: Memorandum dated 25 March 1945, PRO/WO208/802.

150 IO/IPI: Memorandum dated 4 September 1945, PRO/WO208/823.

151 IO/IPI: Memorandum dated 27 July 1945, PRO/WO208/802.

152 Ajit Singh, *Buried Alive*, 114-20.

153 Vyas, *Passage Through a Turbulent Era*, 534-5.

154 Ibid. 538.

155 Ibid. 533.

156 Ibid. 542.

157 Ajit Singh, *Buried Alive*, 15, 125.

158 CSDIC(I): Memorandum dated 19 October 1944, IOR/L/WS/1/1516.

159 GHQ India: Order dated 18 December 1944, IOR/L/WS/1/1516.

160 Voigt, *Indien im Zweiten Weltkrieg*, 299-300.

161 Ibid. 300-2.

162 Vyas, *Passage Through a Turbulent Era*, 496.

163 Mangat, *Indian National Army*, 163; WO: Report dated March 1946, NAI/INA/435.

164 Gandhi, 'How to Canalize Hatred', *Harijan*, 24 February 1946; *Collected Works* 83/143.

165 Gandhi, 'Address to INA Officers', *Harijan*, 9 June 1946; *Collected Works* 84/236.

166 WO (Walsh): Report dated 20 February 1946, NAI/INA/416.

167 Chief of General Staff (Smith): 'Directive to Commander Indian Military Mission to Berlin', dated 28 March 1946, IOR/L/WS/1/737. The list of Indians temporarily excluded from repatriation included the following names: Nahar Govind Ganpuley, Abdul Rauf Malik, Braja Lal Mukherji, Karta Ram, Ajit Singh, Bhabesh, Chandra Bhaduri, Sukhdeo Chaudhri, Gora Chand Dey, Mohammad Iqbal, Schedai, Arathil Candeth Nambiar, Promode Ranjan Sengupta, Jogendra Kumar Bannerji, Suresh Chandra Bose and Hans Raj.

168 Indian Military Mission (Stuart) to IO/MD: Letter dated 26 April 1946, IOR/L/WS/1/737. Listed as the last inmates of the camp: Tara Chand Roy, Kartar Ram, Bannerji, Nambiar, Ganpuley, Braja Lal Mukherji, Sengupta, Suresh Chandra Bose and Ajit Singh (severely sick in the camp hospital).

169 GoI/EAD: Press release dated 28 February 1947, NAI/EAD/1947/31(8)-EUR-47.

170 Later, Fischer named himself Swami Agehananda Bharati and published his memoirs under the title, *The Ochre Robe*.

171 Vyas, *Passage Through a Turbulent Era*, 539.

172 Bharati, *The Ochre Robe*, 54.

173 Ibid. 47-66.

174 Ibid. 66-85. Pasmu: Interview with Swami Agehananda from 15 April 1951, NAI/HFM/A-10-3.

175 AA (Pappritz) to Bundespräsidialamt: Memorandum dated 25 January 1955, AA-PA/B8/981.

176 Indian Embassy Bonn to AA/Protokoll: Note dated 23 April 1955, AA-PA/B8/981.

177 Bot.Stockholm (Siegfried) to AA: Telegram No. 3 dated 17 January 1955, AA-PA/B8/981.

178 Bot.New Delhi (Meyer) to AA: Letter dated 11 January 191955, AA-PA/B8/981.

179 AA/Abteilung 3 (Maschtaler) to AA/Protokoll (Vogel): Note dated 21 April 1955, AA-PA/B8/981.
180 NMML (Nanda): Interview with Seifriz dated 28 October 1971, NMML/OHT/125.
181 De Felice, *Il fascismo el'Oriente*, 192.
182 Bhatta to Nehru: Letter undated, NAI/EAD/1947/36(36-)EUR-47.
183 GoI/EAD to Bhatta: Letter dated 1 July 1947, NAI/EAD/1947/36(36)-EUR-47.

ARCHIVAL SOURCES

1 Microfilm in ACS under JAIA/302.
2 The original of this file is in the ACS under MCP/*Gabinetto* 95.
3 Originals of the American microfilm collection, *Collection of Italian military records* (CIMR).

Bibliography

⚜

Akten der Reichskanzlei: Regierung Hitler 1933-1945, ii: *1934/35,* ed. Friedrich Hartmannsgunter (München, 1999).

Akten zur deutschen auswärtigen Politik: Aus den Archiven des Auswärtigen Amtes; series D—vii (Baden-Baden, 1956), viii (Frankfurt am Main, 1956), x (Frankfurt am Main, 1963), xii (Göttingen, 1969), xiii (Göttingen, 1970); series E—i-vi (Göttingen, 1969-79). [Quoted as ADAP-Serie-Volume/Document]

Alsdorf, Ludwig, *Deutsch-indische Geistesbeziehungen,* Indien in Einzeldarstellungen, 5 (Heidelberg, 1942).

—— *Indien* (Berlin, 1940).

—— *Indien und Ceylon* (Berlin, 1943).

Appelius, Mario, *India* (Milano, 1925).

Asiatica: Bollettino dell'Istituto italiano per il Medio ed Estremo Oriente (Roma, 1936-43).

Azad Hind: Zeitschrift für ein freies Indien, ed. Kodavooru Anantarama Bhatta (Berlin, 1942-4).

Azad, Maulana Abul Kalam, *India Wins Freedom: An Autobiographical Narrative* (Bombay, 1959).

Bannerth, Ernst, *Hindustani-Briefe: 15 Urdu- und 6 Hindi-Briefe mit Umschrift und Übersetzung,* Arbeitshefte für den Sprachmittler, 49 (Leipzig, 1943).

—— and Spieß, Otto, *Lehrbuch der Hindustani Sprache* (Leipzig and Wien, 1945).

Beythan, Hermann, *Die soziale Frage in Indien,* Indien in Einzeldarstellungen, 6 (Heidelberg, 1943).

—— *Praktische Grammatik der Tamilsprache* (Leipzig, 1943).

—— *Rassen, Klassen, Kasten, Völker, Nation in Indien* (Freiburg im Breisgau, 1944).

—— *Was ist Indien?,* Indien in Einzeldarstellungen, 1 (Heidelberg, 1942).

Bharati, Swami Agehananda [Leopold Fischer], *The Ochre Robe* (Santa Barbara, 1980).

Bhatta, Kodavooru Anantarama, *Indien im Britischen Reich,* Indien in Einzeldarstellungen, 3 (Heidelberg, 1942).

Boelcke, Willi A., *Die Macht des Radios: Weltpolitik und Auslandsrundfunk 1924-1976* (Berlin, 1977).

Bose, Mihir, *The Lost Hero: A Biography of Subhas Bose* (London, 1982).

Bose, Sisir K., 'The Great Escape', in *Netaji and India's Freedom. Proceedings of the*

International Netaji Seminar 1973, ed. Sisir K. Bose (Calcutta, 1975).

Bose, Sisir K., ed., *Netaji and India's Freedom. Proceedings of the International Netaji Seminar 1973* (Calcutta, 1975).

Bose, Subhas Chandra, *Netaji Collected Works*, vi, ed. Sisir Kumar Bose and Sugata Bose (Calcutta, 1987).

—— *Letters to Emilie Schenkl 1934-1942*, vii: *Netaji Collected Works*, ed. Sisir Kumar Bose and Sugata Bose (Calcutta and Delhi, 1994).

—— *Letters, Articles, Speeches and Statements 1933-1937*, viii: *Netaji Collected Works*, ed. Sisir Kumar Bose and Sugata Bose (Calcutta and Delhi, 1994).

—— *Congress President: Speeches, Articles and Letters January 1938-May 1939*, ix: *Netaji Collected Works*, ed. Sisir Kumar Bose and Sugata Bose (Calcutta and Delhi, 1995).

—— *The Alternative Leadership: Speeches, Articles, Statements and Letters June 1939-1941*, x: *Netaji Collected Works*, ed. Sisir Kumar Bose and Sugata Bose (Calcutta and Delhi, 1998).

—— *The Indian Struggle 1920-1940*, ii: *Netaji Collected Works*, ed. Netaji Research Bureau (Calcutta, 1981).

Casolari, Marzia, 'Nazionalismo indiano, Italia e fascismo', Dissertation, Pisa, 1997.

Chand, Uttam, *When Bose Was Ziauddin* (Delhi, 1946).

Chandra, Bipan, *India's Struggle For Independence 1857-1947* (New Delhi, 1989; 23rd edn, 1999).

Ciano, Galeazzo, *Diario*, ii: *1941-1943* (New York, 1946; 4th edn, 1947).

Conti, Flavio, *I prigionieri di guerra italiani 1940-1945* (Bologna, 1986).

Davis, Brian Leigh, *Badges & Insignia of the Third Reich 1933-1945* (London, 1992).

—— and Malcom McGregor, *Flags of the Third Reich*, ii: *Waffen-SS* (London, 1994).

De Felice, Renzo, *Il fascismo e l'Oriente: Arabi, ebrei e indiani nella politica di Mussolini* (Bologna, 1988).

—— 'L'India nella strategia politica di Mussolini', in *Storia contemporanea* xxviii (1987), 1309-63.

—— *Mussolini l'alleato: 1940-1945*, i: *L'Italia in guerra 1940-1943*, part 1: *Dalla guerra 'breve' alla guerra lunga* (Turin 1990).

Die Weizsäcker-Papiere 1933-1950, ed. Leonidas E. Hill (Frankfurt am Main, 1974).

Die Tagebücher von Joseph Goebbels: Im Auftrag des Instituts für Zeitgeschichte und mit Unterstützung des Staatlichen Archivdienstes Russlands, ed. Elke Fröhlich, ii: *Diktate 1941-1945*, pts. 3, 4, 5, 9, 11 (München 1993-1996). [Quoted as *Goebbels-Tagebücher* ii: pt. no.]

Döscher, Hans-Jürgen, *Das Auswärtige Amt im Dritten Reich: Diplomatie im Schatten der 'Endlösung'* (Berlin, 1987).

Eden, Anthony, *The Eden Memoirs*, i: *Facing the Dictators* (London, 1962).

Fay, Peter Ward, *The Forgotten Army: India's Armed Struggle for Independence 1942-1945* (Ann Arbor, 1993).

Franzen, Hans, *Aus meinem Leben und meiner Zeit* (Wiesbaden, 1981).

Furtwängler, Franz Josef, *Männer, die ich sah und kannte* (Hamburg, 1951).

Gandhi, Mohandas K., *Autobiografia*, ed. Charles F. Andrews (Milano, 1931).

—— *The Collected Works of Mahatma Gandhi*, ed. Publications Division, Ministry of Information and Broadcasting, Government of India (New Delhi, 1958-94). [Quoted as *Collected Works* Volume/Document]

Ganpuley, Nehari G., *Netaji in Germany: A Little-Known Chapter* (Bombay, 1959).

Gensicke, Klaus, *Der Mufti von Jerusalem, Amin el-Husseini, und die Nationalsozialisten*, Ethnien, Regionen, Konflikte, 1 (Frankfurt am Main, 1988).

Glasneck, Johannes and Inge Kircheisen, *Türkei und Afghanistan. Brennpunkte der Orientpolitik im Zweiten Weltkrieg* ([East] Berlin, 1968).

Gordon, Leonard A., *Brothers Against the Raj: A Biography of Indian Nationalists Sarat & Subhas Chandra Bose* (New York, 1990).

Günther, Lothar and Diethelm Weidemann, 'Das indische Infanterie-Regiment 900: Historische Realitäten und subjektive Wahrnehmungen', in Gerhard Höpp and Brigitte Reinwald, ed., *Fremdeinsätze: Afrikaner und Asiaten in europäischen Kriegen 1941-1945* (Berlin, 2000), 199-208.

Günther, Lothar and Hans-Joachim Rehmer, *Inder, Indien und Berlin: 100 Jahre Begegnung Berlin und Indien* (Berlin, 1999).

Harbich, Walter, 'A Report on the Organisation and Training of the Free India Army in Europe 1941-1942', in Walter Harbich and Alexander Werth, eds., *Netaji in Germany* (Calcutta, 1970), 47-57.

Hartog, Rudolf, *Im Zeichen des Tigers: Die Indische Legion auf deutscher Seite 1941-1945* (Herford, 1991).

Hasan, Abid, *Der Islam in Indien*, Indien in Einzeldarstellungen, 7 (Heidelberg, 1944).

—— 'A Soldier Remembers', *The Oracle*, 6/1 (1984), 24-65.

Hauner, Milan, *India in Axis Strategy: Germany, Japan, and Indian Nationalists in the Second World War* (Stuttgart, 1981).

—— 'Das nationalsozialistische Deutschland und Indien', in Manfred Funke, ed., *Hitler, Deutschland und die Mächte: Materialien zur Außenpolitik des Dritten Reiches* (Düsseldorf, 1976), 430-53.

Herde, Peter, *Der Japanflug: Planungen und Verwirklichung einer Flugverbindung zwischen den Achsenmächten und Japan 1942-1945,* Sitzungsberichte der Wissenschaftlichen Gesellschaft an der Johann-Wolfgang-Goethe-Universität Frankfurt am Main, 38/3 (Stuttgart, 2000).

Hildebrand, Klaus, *Deutsche Außenpolitik 1933-1945: Kalkül oder Dogma* (Stuttgart, 1971; 55th edn, 1990).

Hillgruber, Andreas, *Hitlers Strategie: Politik und Kriegführung 1940-1941* (München, 1965; 2nd edn, 1982).

Hitler, Adolf, *Mein Kampf*, ii (München 1927; 25th edn, 1933).

——— *Hitlers Lagebesprechungen: Die Protokollfragmente seiner militärischen Konferenzen 1942-1945*, ed. Helmut Heiber (Stuttgart, 1962).

——— *Hitlers zweites Buch: Ein Dokument aus dem Jahr 1928*, ed. Institut für Zeitgeschichte, introduced and annotated by Gerhard L. Weinberg, Quellen und Darstellungen zur Zeitgeschichte: Veröffentlichungen des Instituts für Zeitgeschichte, 7 (Stuttgart, 1961).

——— *Monologe im Führerhauptquartier 1941-1944*, recorded by Heinrich Heim, ed. Werner Jochmann (Hamburg, 1980; special edn, München, 2000). [Quoted as *Hitler-Monologe*/Document]

——— *Reden, Schriften, Anordnungen: Februar 1925 bis Januar 1933*, iv, pt. 3, ed. Christian Hartmann (München, 1997).

——— *Sämtliche Aufzeichnungen 1905-1924*, ed. Eberhard Jäckel and Axel Kuhn, Quellen und Darstellungen zur Zeitgeschichte: Veröffentlichungen des Instituts für Zeitgeschichte, 21 (Stuttgart, 1980). [Quoted as *Sämtliche Aufzeichnungen*, Document]

I Documenti Diplomatici Italiani, ed. Ministero degli Affari Esteri, commissioned by le pubblicazione dei documenti diplomatici, 1-9, v-viii (Roma, 1965-90). [Quoted as DDI-9-Volume/Document]

Il Giornale d'Italia (Roma since 1901).

Jeune Asie: Organe de la confédération des étudiants *orientaux* (Roma, 1934-5).

Katpitia, Arvinda, 'Subhas Chandra Boses Verhandlungen über eine Unabhängigkeitserklärung für Indien 1941-1943', Dissertation, Mainz, 1972.

Kershaw, Ian, *Hitler 1889-1936* (Stuttgart, 1998).

——— *Hitler 1936-1945* (Stuttgart, 2000).

Kersten, Felix, *The Kersten Memoirs 1940-1945* (London, 1956).

Kriegstagebuch des Generaloberst Halder: Herausgegeben vom Arbeitskreis für Wehrforschung, ii (Stuttgart, 1963).

Kriegstagebuch des Oberkommandos der Wehrmacht (Wehrmachtführungsstab), ed. Percy E. Schramm, i (Frankfurt am Main, 1965).

Kruse, Wilhelm, *Denkmäler indischer Kunst*, Indien in Einzeldarstellungen, 8 (Heidelberg, 1942).

Leverkuehn, Paul, *Der geheime Nachrichtendienst der deutschen Wehrmacht im Kriege* (Frankfurt am Main, 1957).

Luft, Hermann, *Die Wirtschaft Indiens*, Indien in Einzeldarstellungen, 2 (Heidelberg, 1942).

Mangat, Gurbachan Singh, *Indian National Army: Role in India's Struggle for Freedom* (Ludhiana, 1991).

——— *The Tiger Strikes: An Unwritten Chapter of Netaji's Life History* (Ludhiana, 1986).

Martin, Bernd, *Deutschland und Japan im Zweiten Weltkrieg: Vom Angriff auf Pearl Harbour bis zur deutschen Kapitulation* (Frankfurt am Main, 1969).

McDonogh, Giles, *A Good German: Adam von Trott zu Solz* (New York, 1992).

Michel-Briefmarken-Katalog Deutschland 1996/97 (München, 1996).

Misra, Bankey Bihari, *The Indian Political Parties: An Historical Analysis of Political Behaviour up to 1947* (Delhi, 1976).

Moltke, Helmuth James Graf von, *Briefe an Freya 1939-1945*, ed. Beate Ruhm von Oppen (München, 1988).

Mookerjee, Girija K., *Der Indische National-Kongress*, Indien der Gegenwart, 1, ed. the Zentrale Freies Indien (Heidelberg, 1943).

—— *Europe at War, 1938-1946: Impressions of War, Netaji and Europe* (Meerut, 1968).

—— *Labyrinth Europa* (Düsseldorf, 1956).

Mookerjee, Nanda, *Netaji Through A German Lens: A New Discovery* (Calcutta, 1970).

Mukherjee, Uma, *Two Great Indian Revolutionaries: Rash Behari Bose and Jyotindra Nath Mukherjee* (Calcutta, 1966).

Nehru, Jawaharlal, *An Autobiography* (London, 1936; 20th edn, 1955).

—— *The Discovery of India* (London, 1946; 4th edn, 1956).

Neulen, Hans-Werner, *An deutscher Seite: Internationale Freiwillige von Wehrmacht und Waffen-SS* (München, 1985; 2nd edn, 1990).

Oesterheld, Joachim , 'Die Indische Legion in Frankreich', in Gerhard Höpp and Brigitte Reinwald, eds., *Fremdeinsätze: Afrikaner und Asiaten in europäischen Kriegen 1941-1945* (Berlin, 2000), 209-26.

—— 'Zum Spektrum der indischen Präsenz in Deutschland von Beginn bis Mitte des 20. Jahrhunderts', in Gerhard Höpp, ed., *Fremde Erfahrungen: Asiaten und Afrikaner in Deutschland, Österreich und in der Schweiz bis 1945* (Berlin, 1996), 331-46.

Opera Omnia di Benito Mussolini, ed. Edoardo and Duildo Susmel (Florenz and Roma, 1951-80). [Quoted as *Opera Omnia* Volume]

Orwell, George, *The War Commentaries*, ed. William J. West (London, 1985).

—— 'War-time Diary', in *The Collected Essays, Journalism and Letters of George Orwell*, ii: *My Country Right or Left 1940-1943*, ed. Sonia Orwell and Ian Angus (New York, 1968), 339-450.

Pandit, H. N., *Netaji Subhas Chandra Bose: From Kabul to Battle of Imphal* (New Delhi, 1988).

Recker, Marie-Luise, *Die Außenpolitik des Dritten Reiches*, Enzyklopädie deutscher Geschichte, 8 (München, 1990), 28.

Rizzi, Carlo Alberto, *I guanti bianchi di Warda Ganda* (Genua, 1986).

Roon, Gerd van, *Neuordnung im Widerstand: Der Kreisauer Kreis innerhalb der deutschen Widerstandsbewegung* (München, 1967).

Rose, Eugen, *Azad Hind: Ein europäisches Indermärchen oder die 1299 Tage der Indischen Legion in Europa* (Wuppertal, 1979).

Rosenberg, Alfred, *Der Mythus des 20. Jahrhunderts: Eine Wertung der seelisch-geistigen Gestaltungskämpfe unserer Zeit* (München 1930; 5th edition, 1933).

Sareen, Tilak Raj, *Forgotten Images: Reflections and reminiscences of Subhas Chandra Bose* (Delhi, 1997).

——*Japan and the Indian National Army* (New Delhi, 1996).

—— *Subhas Chandra Bose and Nazi Germany* (New Delhi, 1996).

Schnabel, Reimund, *Tiger und Schakal: Deutsche Indienpolitik 1941-1943: Ein Dokumentarbericht* (Wien, 1968).

Selter, Gerhard, 'Zur Indienpolitik der faschistischen deutschen Regierung während des Zweiten Weltkrieges', Dissertation, Leipzig, 1965.

Singh, Sardar Ajit, *Buried Alive: Autobiography, Speeches and Writings of an Indian Revolutionary Sardar Ajit Singh*, ed. Pardaman Singh and Joginder Singh Dhanki (New Delhi, 1984).

Speer, Albert, *Erinnerungen* (Frankfurt/Main and Berlin, 1969; 1996).

Sykes, Christopher, *Adam von Trott: Eine deutsche Tragödie* (Düsseldorf, 1969).

Talwar, Bhagat Ram, 'The Great Escape: My Fifty-five Days with Netaji Subhas Chandra Bose', in Sisir K. Bose, ed., *Netaji and India's Freedom: Proceedings of the International Netaji Seminar 1973* (Calcutta, 1975).

—— *The Talwars of Pathan Land and Subhas Chandra's Great Escape* (New Delhi, 1976).

The Ghadr Directory, compiled by the Director, Intelligence Bureau, Home Department, Government of India 1934, ed. Punjabi University Patiala (Patiala, 1997).

The Transfer of Power 1943-7: Constitutional Relations Between Britain and India, ed. Nicholas Mansergh, 3 vols (London, 1970-2). [Quoted as ToP-Volume/Document]

Thierfelder, Franz, 'Deutsch-indische Begegnungen 1926-1956', in H. O. Günther, ed., *Indien und Deutschland: Ein Sammelband* (Frankfurt am Main, 1956), 146-57.

Toye, Hugh, *Subhash Chandra Bose: The Springing Tiger* (Bombay, 1962).

Trott zu Solz, Clarita von, *Adam von Trott zu Solz: Eine Lebensbeschreibung* (Berlin, 1994).

Vyas, Mukund R., *Männer und Mächte in Indien*, Indien in Einzeldarstellungen, 4 (Heidelberg, 1942).

—— *Passage Through a Turbulent Era: Historical Reminiscences of the Fateful Years 1937-1947* (Bombay, 1982).

Wassiltschikow, Marie, *Die Berliner Tagebücher der Marie 'Missie' Wassiltschikow 1940-1945* (2nd edn, München, 1996). [Quoted as *Wassiltschikow-Tagebuch*]

Weidemann, Diethelm, 'Spannungen und Interessenkämpfe unter indischen Emigranten in Deutschland während des Zweiten Weltkriegs: Erste

Anmerkungen zur Problematik', in Gerhard Höpp, ed., *Fremde Erfahrungen: Asiaten und Afrikaner in Deutschland, Österreich und in der Schweiz bis 1945* (Berlin, 1996), 239-58.

—— 'The Mutiny of Königsbrück—1944', *United Asia*, 22 (1970), 327-33.

—— 'Sources on Subhas Chandra Bose and the Freedom Struggle of India in the Central State Archives of the GDR—Some Preliminary Remarks', *Indian Archives*, 35/2 (1986), 13-28.

—— 'Subhas Chandra Bose's Passage to Germany (1941)', *Asien, Afrika, Lateinamerika*, 23 (1995), 445-59.

Weitz, John, *Hitler's Banker: Hjalmar Horace Greeley Schacht* (Boston, 1997).

Werth, Alexander, *Der Tiger Indiens: Subhas Chandra Bose: Ein Leben für die Freiheit des Subkontinents* (München, 1971).

West, William J., *Orwell: The Lost Writings* (New York, 1985).

Wirsing, Giselher, *Indien: Asiens gefährliche Jahre* (Düsseldorf, 1968).

Wolpert, Stanley, *A New History of India* (Oxford, 1977; 4th edn, 1993).

Voigt, Joachim, 'Hitler und Indien', *Vierteljahreshefte für Zeitgeschichte*, 19 (1971), 33-63.

—— 'India in the Second World War: A History with Problems', in Jürgen Rohwer and Hildegard Müller, eds., *Neue Forschungen zum Zweiten Weltkrieg: Literaturberichte aus 67 Ländern* (Koblenz, 1990), 187-201.

—— *Indien im Zweiten Weltkrieg* (Stuttgart, 1978).

Zöllner, Hans-Bernd, *Der Feind meines Feindes ist mein Freund: Subhas Chandra Bose und das zeitgenössische Deutschland unter dem Nationalsozialismus 1933-1943* (Hamburg, 2000).

General Field Marshal Erwin Rommel inspects a unit of the Indian Legion stationed at the French Atlantic coast.

*Subhas Chandra Bose shaking hands with the German dictator, Adolf Hitler.
On the left: Hitler's interpreter, Paul Schmidt.*

*Subhas Chandra Bose at a meeting with leaders of the Nazi elite organisation SS.
On the right: Heinrich Himmler, the national leader of the SS.*

Inauguration ceremony of the Free India Centre in the Hotel Kaiserhof in Berlin. Secretary of State Wilhelm Keppler conveys the greetings of the German foreign minister, Joachim von Ribbentrop.

*Upper picture: A soldier of the Indian Legion
operates a checkpoint in southern France.
Lower picutre: A German sergeant trains Indian volunteers to
handle a German rifle.*